ETHICS AS IF JESUS MATTERED

Smyth & Helwys Publishing, Inc.
6316 Peake Road
Macon, Georgia 31210-3960
1-800-747-3016
©2014 by Rick Axtell, Michelle Tooley, and Michael L. Westmoreland-White, eds.

Library of Congress Cataloging-in-Publication Data

Ethics as if Jesus mattered : essays in honor of Glen Harold Stassen /
edited by Rick Axtell, Michelle Tooley, and Michael Westmoreland-White.
pages cm
Includes bibliographical references.
ISBN 978-1-57312-695-3 (pbk. : alk. paper)
1. Christian ethics. 2. Stassen, Glen Harold, 1936- honouree.
I. Axtell, Rick, editor of compilation.
BJ1191.E84 2013
241--dc23

2013039206

ETHICS
AS IF
JESUS MATTERED

Essays in Honor of Glen Harold Stassen

Rick Axtell, Michelle Tooley, and Michael L. Westmoreland-White, eds.

Contents

Introduction

When a great rock makes a splash, the ripple effects extend to unseen shores. In the 1980s and 1990s, the three of us met at The Southern Baptist Theological Seminary, where our doctoral studies in Christian Ethics overlapped for several years. Like most theological students, we were energized by readings in Augustine and Aquinas, Calvin and Luther, Barth and Brunner, Pannenberg and Moltmann, Metz and Gutierrez, Cone and Schussler-Fiorenza. But in Glen Stassen's classes, we encountered the authors and debates that most influenced our thinking as ethicists—Reinhold and H. Richard Niebuhr, Dietrich Bonhoeffer and Beverly Harrison, Martin Luther King, Jr., and John Howard Yoder, Gene Outka and Daniel Day Williams, Gene Sharp and Walter Wink, Michael Walzer and James William McClendon. Of course, as teacher, mentor, friend, encourager, and colleague, Glen Stassen's own scholarship, teaching, and rock-solid example shaped the authors in this volume as thinkers, teachers, and engaged scholars. This rock has made quite a splash. The ripple effect continues to move a generation of scholars, activists, and church leaders who are making waves on shores Glen could not have foreseen.

It is a fitting tribute to Glen's influence that this *Festschrift* is the second volume presented in his honor. Earlier in 2013, *Perspectives in Religious Studies,* the official journal of the National Association of Baptist Professors of Religion, published a superb *Festschrift* issue for Glen Stassen, edited by our valued colleague David P. Gushee. Glen Stassen's work and influence is extensive enough for more than one *Festschrift*, and all the collaborators on this project were determined to bring it to fruition. Michelle Tooley's determination led to our contract for this work with the Baptist publisher Smyth & Helwys Publishing. We want to thank the wonderful people at Smyth & Helwys, especially Leslie Andres and Keith Gammons, for their fine work in moving this project from a collection of essays into a book. We are grateful to David Gushee for permission to reproduce material from *Kingdom Ethics.*

Kingdom Ethics, by Stassen and Gushee, was a title selected by their publisher, InterVarsity Press. Stassen's original proposal was to call that work

Christian Ethics as if Jesus Mattered. He has a long-standing frustration with the many ways that most works in Christian ethics marginalize the centrality and normativity of the concrete teachings and example of Jesus Christ as reflected in the Gospels. Stassen's entire career has been an effort to correct this misstep, to model and nurture a tradition of Christian ethics of what he has come to call "incarnational discipleship"—concrete, embodied, contextual, and faithful discipleship "as if Jesus mattered." Indeed, he has worked to live as if Jesus Christ were, as Christians from all traditions claim, central to our faith and lives and Lord over all of life, not simply of personal piety. So we gathered our contributing authors under this theme: examining aspects of Stassen's work and addressing dimensions of Christian ethics *as if Jesus mattered.*

We hope the chapters in this volume honor the life and witness of Glen Stassen, as a *Festschrift* should. But we were clear from the beginning that this was not a work of hagiography. Stassen has always been dedicated to nurturing disciples for Jesus Christ, not devotees to himself. His students, his colleagues, and his co-authors have always been encouraged to stick to their convictions when they disagree with his approach or his conclusions. Dialogue and persuasion, not coerced conformity, have been the hallmarks of Stassen's approach in the classroom, in academic societies, and in the various church bodies and peace and justice organizations he has served. So the authors of this volume were encouraged not only to celebrate and analyze dimensions of Stassen's thought, or to develop aspects further, but to state gently areas where they think his work could use its own correction or redirection. Readers will find within these pages both unifying themes and disagreements that reflect the unique ripple effects of Stassen's influence and their continuing flow into diverse tributaries.

The format of the book is first biographical and historical and then theological. Finally, it ends with concrete implications for various contemporary ethical issues. Preferring the term "historical drama," Stassen has staked out his own niche within the broad "narrative ethics" approach, alongside his friends Stanley Hauerwas, James William McClendon Jr., and John Howard Yoder. So Michael L. Westmoreland-White begins this volume with a biographical piece outlining Stassen's own "historical drama" in twentieth-century and early twenty-first-century North American Christian theology and ethics.

Stassen has long sought to return the Sermon on the Mount (Matthew 5–7), the longest section of Jesus' teaching recorded in the New Testament, to the heart of the discipline of Christian ethics, and to correct perennial misinterpretations that end up marginalizing the Sermon's concrete relevance in Christian life. So Michael Willett Newheart, in his inimitable whimsical style, examines Stassen's approach to the sermon, bringing his own perspective to bear as a professional biblical scholar, a *Neutestamentler*, into interaction with Stassen's as a Christian ethicist.

The next chapters build on this foundation. Stassen was a student of the Christian Realist Reinhold Niebuhr and wrote his doctoral dissertation on the work of Niebuhr's brother, H. Richard Niebuhr. David Fillingim examines the continuing but changing influence of the Niebuhrs on Stassen's thought. He addresses how the thought of the Niebuhrs resonates in Stassen's ethics in three areas: the relationship between the descriptive and the prescriptive in Christian ethics, the tension between realism and idealism, and the importance of concrete biblical norms.

Influenced by the work of H. Richard Niebuhr, Stassen has always identified *the mission of the Church in the world* as a "critical variable" in his method. Joon-Sik Park analyzes Stassen's ecclesiology, as shaped by Niebuhr's theology, and its impact on his work. Park discusses Stassen's understanding of the church as the authentic embodiment of transformative Trinitarian faith and explores the church's incarnational discipleship with the imagery of Pastor, Apostle, and Pioneer.

Building on the work of Yoder, McClendon, Nancey Murphy, and others, Stassen has been among those who focus on normative Christian *practices,* and Tammy R. Williams examines one central Christian practice, the Eucharistic meal, commonly called the Lord's Supper in the overlapping Baptist traditions she shares with Stassen. Her reading of the Lord's Supper as "the Meal of God's Reign," which shapes Christian engagement with the wider society, overcomes a distorting disconnect between worship and ethics in this central practice of the church. Laura Rector analyzes Stassen's central ethical norm of *delivering love*, developed in contrast to the inadequate approaches of Anders Nygren and Gene Outka, and in grateful dialogue with his teacher, the early process theologian Daniel Day Williams.

Elizabeth M. Bounds finishes this section by analyzing Stassen's approach to holistic character ethics, focusing on the development of moral character *in particular communities*. Stassen's communitarian emphasis on distinctive particularity retains a commitment to public moral engagement and employs social theory and critical reason as useful tools. Placing his thought in dialogue with that of imprisoned women who have experienced community norms more as threat than empowerment, she suggests possibilities for a more circular interaction between Stassen's dimensions of ethical deliberation.

The concluding chapters each tackle a concrete issue in social ethics that has been prominent in the work of both Stassen and the contributing author. Tina Pippin places Stassen's work in the apocalyptic context of the nuclear age. From her situated position within the "nuclear triangle" of the American Southeast, Pippin grapples with a "nuclear Jesus." Rick Axtell asks questions about economic justice "as if Jesus mattered" in the context of the growth of low-wage "day labor" among our most marginalized homeless populations. Axtell asks how the perspective "from outside the vineyard" might shape our understanding of the thicker Jesus that Stassen highlights as a resource for the work of delivering justice. Reggie L. Williams tackles the virulent, protean, and persistent threat of racism. Analyzing the narratives that support racial injustice, Williams looks for clues to combat racial injustice in North America in the narrative work of Glen Stassen and the norm of delivering justice.

Developing "just peacemaking theory" as a normative Christian response to the issues of war, violence, oppression, and injustice has been central to Stassen's work, and the volume concludes fittingly with two chapters applying just peacemaking approaches to concrete conflicts. Aldrin Peñamora applies just peacemaking to the Christian-Muslim conflict in the Philippines, showing how its practices can join forces with the Filipino Christian "theology of struggle" to repair colonial and post-colonial injustices and seek reconciliation based on repentance and justice.

Michelle Tooley applies just peacemaking to the continued structural violence of post-civil war Guatemala. Tooley demonstrates that the peace that ended thirty-six years of civil war has left many long-standing structural injustices intact. She brings the practices of just peacemaking into dialogue with the work of Paul Farmer on structural violence and inequality and looks especially at the continuing marginalization of the Mayan peoples in Guatemala and the continuing cycles of violence against Guatemalan women.

The volume concludes with a bibliography of Stassen's writings to date by Michael L. Westmoreland-White.

The editors hope this work serves several purposes: introducing Glen Stassen's work to those previously unfamiliar with it; advancing dialogue and debate in Christian ethics and more faithful discipleship; and honoring one whom all the contributors consider a mentor, even those few who were not formal students of Stassen. Glen Stassen has approached his life and work "as if Jesus mattered," and we hope the present work demonstrates that the contributors share that commitment—each in her or his own way. May this volume, in Glen Stassen's honor, add another ripple to the unending flow of the church's response to grace, toward the fulfillment of the ancient prophetic hope we share: let justice flow down like waters, and righteousness like an ever-flowing stream.

—Editors Rick Axtell, Michelle Tooley,
and Michael L. Westmoreland-White

Chapter 1

Glen Harold Stassen
Follower of a Thick Jesus

MICHAEL L. WESTMORELAND-WHITE

Family and Early Life

Glen Harold Stassen was born February 29, 1936, in St. Paul, Minnesota, to Harold E. Stassen and Esther (*neé* Glewwe) Stassen.[1] Although Franklin D. Roosevelt's New Deal had brought improvement, the country was still deep in the Great Depression, and conditions were particularly harsh in the farmlands of Minnesota. The world was a very uncertain place in 1936. Adolf Hitler, in his third year as chancellor of Germany, broke the Treaty of Versailles and sent occupying troops into the Rhineland. In Spain, the Communists and Socialists united to resist the growing power of Spanish Fascism. A military coup occurred in Japan. Jawaharlal Nehru followed Mohandas K. Gandhi as head of the Congress Party of India. Italian dictator Benito Mussolini sent troops to occupy Addis Ababa, capital of Ethiopia. Even as much of the world struggled to climb out of the Great Depression, the clouds of global war gathered as well.[2] This was the context for Glen Stassen's birth, and it came to characterize much of his life: seeking justice for those marginalized by racism and economic injustice and striving for peace and human rights in a world constantly on the brink of war. His family would ensure that he was in the midst of these issues.

Stassen's father, Harold Edward Stassen (1907–2001) was from a family of ethnic German[3] farmers in West St. Paul, the fourth of five children born to William A. and Elsie Mueller Stassen. Bright and ambitious, Harold Stassen graduated Humboldt High School in 1922 at age fourteen and had to wait a year before being old enough to enroll in the University of Minnesota. He worked his way through the university and its law school and began a successful law practice even as the nation headed toward the Great Depression. Harold Stassen gravitated toward politics in college and joined the Republican Party. This was unsurprising in a state then dominated by Republicans; Harold Stassen wanted to revive the Progressive Republican tradition of Abraham Lincoln and Teddy Roosevelt, and he founded the Minnesota Young Republican League to resist Old Guard Republicanism.[4] When Glen Stassen was only two years old, Harold Stassen was elected governor of Minnesota, the youngest governor in United States history. He won reelection in 1940 and 1942[5] before voluntarily leaving office to serve in World War II as lieutenant commander in the US Navy, serving as personal aide to Fleet Admiral William F. Halsey Jr., who commanded naval forces in the South Pacific until Stassen was released from duty with the rank of captain in 1945.

The young Glen Stassen experienced his father's early political career as the benevolent use of power to help others, as well as the voluntary surrender of power to continue to pursue the common good in the face of great evil. Although proud of his father's service, Glen Stassen shared with millions of others the foreboding of war and the worry for the safety of loved ones in the conflict. For a brief time, the Stassen family believed falsely that his father had been killed in the war. Although relieved to find this news to be false, the experience sensitized Glen to the horrors of war.[6] The other major experience of World War II for young Glen Stassen was hearing the news of the atomic bombing of Hiroshima. He relates seeing a vision in his mind of a mushroom cloud, a realization that it threatened all of humanity, and a determination to respond to this threat.[7]

Harold Stassen did return alive and uninjured from World War II. He went on to play a major role in the formation of the United Nations and was the primary author of the United Nations Charter. The elder Stassen went on to serve as "Secretary for Peace" in the Eisenhower administration, forming what became the Arms Control and Disarmament Agency. Harold Stassen ran for the presidency continually from 1964 to 1992. He sought to use these campaigns as platforms from which to communicate his vision of a renewed progressive Republicanism to the party and the nation—an effort that failed. In the 1940s and 1950s, Harold E. Stassen was a leading voice for a different kind of Republican Party: championing economic justice and civil rights at home and international cooperative leadership for democracy, peace, and human rights abroad. Although Glen Stassen changed political parties and never sought political office himself, in its broad strokes, the father's political vision became a legacy to his son, accepted with gratitude and deep conviction.

Glen Stassen is not an only child. He has a younger sister, Kathleen Esther Stassen Berger, chair of the Social Sciences Department of Bronx Community College (CUNY) and author of *The Developing Person through the Lifespan*, the definitive textbook in the field of human development.[8] Both children grew up in a loving home that valued faith in God, education, moral integrity and courage, compassion for others, and striving for excellence.

Young Glen was active in his local Baptist congregation, responding to a call for personal conversion at age eleven in 1947. Glen remembers that his pastor, John Wobig, helped him enormously by following up his public decision for Christ in meetings in his office where Glen was *not* made to memorize a catechism or confession of faith or church covenant, but instead was asked a series of probing questions about his faith and discipleship. Stassen later recalled that Wobig "helped me begin my Christian life not as a passive listener but as an active witnesser."[9]

From 1948 to 1953, Harold Stassen served as president of the University of Pennsylvania. During that time, Glen and Kathleen, who had previously attended public schools in Minnesota, attended a private high school run by the Religious Society of Friends (Quakers). This exposed Glen to spiritual disciplines such as listening prayer (a practice Stassen has continued to this day) and to a spiritual commitment to nonviolence. Stassen was especially inspired by a teacher who had been a conscientious objector during World War II. Instead of serving in the military, he participated in the scientific experiments as a human guinea pig.[10] This gave Stassen a model of personal courage that did not involve weapons or violence. Dave Ritchie of the American Friends Service Committee (AFSC), the Quaker peacemaking and service group that won the 1947 Nobel Peace Prize, led Stassen and other high school students into a lifestyle of service in urban Philadelphia and a commitment to social justice and the fight against poverty, continuing and deepening the commitments of Stassen's family and early childhood.[11] Stassen deliberately chose to go to the South when he left Philadelphia to pursue a bachelor of arts in nuclear physics at the University of Virginia.

Student Years

Stassen had been interested in science, especially physics, since early childhood, but he also recognized nuclear weapons as a threat to all humanity.[12] While at the University of Virginia, Stassen became involved in campus student efforts for civil rights. Campus minister Howard Rees's emphasis on the Sermon on the Mount shaped Stassen's peace work. American Baptist pacifist Culbert Rutenber, a member of the interfaith pacifist group the Fellowship of Reconciliation, also influenced Stassen's thinking about peace and justice.[13] By the time he finished his degree, Stassen decided that there were enough people pursuing the scientific mysteries of the atom. He felt a call to ministry, a call that definitely included working for justice and peace, especially taming the threat posed by nuclear weapons.

In 1957, Stassen married Dot Lively, and together they have raised three sons, Michael, William, and David. Dot, a nurse, committed her nursing career to work in a school for unwed, pregnant teens. Glen worked to change state and federal laws to provide more educational and support services for children with physical and mental disabilities.

After their marriage, Glen and Dot moved to Louisville, Kentucky, as Glen enrolled in The Southern Baptist Theological Seminary to prepare for his new calling. At Southern, Glen was drawn to the teaching of Christian ethicist Henlee H. Barnette[14] and theologian and Christian philosopher Eric Charles Rust,[15] a British Baptist with a background in the sciences who became an early example of evolutionary or process theology. But, in 1958, a clash between faculty and the president led to the firing of thirteen professors and the suspension of Southern's academic accreditation. It would take the school decades to rebuild both the faculty and the school's reputation.[16] Frustrated with the unwillingness of faculty, trustees, and the president to compromise, bewildered by the loss of most of those with whom he came to study, and fearful that graduation from a seminary on academic probation could undermine his future teaching ministry, Stassen finished his bachelor of divinity degree at Union Theological Seminary.

At Union, Stassen was especially influenced by the "Christian realism" of famed Protestant theological ethicist Reinhold Niebuhr; it was a force that changed shape but that continued throughout his career.[17] Others influenced Stassen at Union as well. A serious student of Scripture,[18] Stassen valued the teaching of Old Testament professor James Muilenburg, a pioneer in what came to be called rhetorical criticism,[19] and New Testament professor W. D. Davies, particularly Davies's emphasis on the Jewish background to the New Testament and his work on the Sermon on the Mount.[20] Early process theologian Daniel Day Williams contributed his view of love.[21] It was also Williams who directed Stassen's attention to the work of H. Richard Niebuhr, who was to become the subject of Stassen's doctoral dissertation.[22]

After completing his BD at Union in 1960, Stassen deliberately chose to pursue his PhD in a Southern setting so that he could simultaneously participate in the civil rights movement, which was then moving to full maturity.[23] Stassen earned his PhD at Duke University where he studied the history of theology and ethics, took extra courses in political and social the-

ory, and wrote his dissertation. He was supervised by Christian ethicist
Waldo Beach and influenced by his friend and fellow student, Lonnie
Kliever, and the Lutheran historical theologian Hans J. Hillerbrand.

Kliever was a fellow Baptist student whom Stassen had met at Union
Seminary. He was from Texas and had done his undergraduate work at
Hardin-Simmons University before becoming one of the few Southern Bap-
tists in those days to go to seminary outside Southern Baptist circles. He
and Stassen had become friends at Union, and both chose to return to the
South for doctoral work at Duke, where they participated in the civil rights
movement. Kliever shared Stassen's interest in the work of H. Richard
Niebuhr, on whom he would become an acknowledged expert.[24] Kliever left
Baptist life, became chair of the Religious Studies Department of Southern
Methodist University, and had a very different career from Stassen's. Stassen
acknowledged Kliever's strong influence on him during his days at Union
and Duke.[25]

From Lutheran historian of Christian thought Hans J. Hillerbrand,
Stassen caught a lifelong fascination with Anabaptist theology and its influence on early Baptist identity. While still a doctoral student, Stassen published his first scholarly article, which examined Anabaptist influence on
the origins of the English Particular Baptists, a revision of a paper he wrote
for Hillerbrand.[26] Over his career, Stassen would continue to write on the
Anabaptists and on questions of Baptist identity. He articulated a view of
Baptist life and faith that drew from Puritan-Separatist concern for the sovereignty of God over all of life and from the Anabaptist concern for radical
following of Jesus Christ. As David Gushee rightly notes, Stassen's perspective on Baptist identity rejects many current false alternatives (fundamentalist legalism, imperial Calvinism, or libertine individualism), instead
identifying with a Baptist heritage of discipleship, defense of religious liberty
and human rights, and pursuit of peace and justice.[27]

While at Duke University, Stassen co-founded the Christian Interracial
Witness Association, Duke's civil rights organization, which supplied many
students in the successful action to integrate Durham's public accommodations, employment policies, voting, and school policies. In 1963, Stassen
traveled to Washington, DC, to participate in the historic March on Washington for Jobs and Freedom and to hear Reverend Dr. Martin Luther King,
Jr., who became a major influence,[28] give his famous "I Have a Dream"
speech. To Stassen's surprise, he met his father, Harold, in the crowd in front
of the Lincoln Memorial. Neither father nor son knew the other was coming, but both men felt compelled to participate in this national, nonviolent

action for racial justice.[29] Stassen also began his teaching career as a PhD student, teaching undergraduate students at Duke in 1963–1964.

Academic Career

In 1964, Stassen moved back to Louisville to accept a teaching post at a small Baptist institution called Kentucky Southern College. The college was in deep financial trouble and, finding no way for it to continue as an independent school, Stassen helped it to merge with the University of Louisville in 1969. During his five years at Kentucky Southern, Stassen also continued his work for social justice; he became acting chair of the Louisville Area Council of Religion and Race and chair of the Louisville-Jefferson County Human Relations Commission. Working with the Kentucky chapter of the NAACP and the Kentucky Christian Leadership Conference (the Kentucky chapter of Martin Luther King, Jr.'s Southern Christian Leadership Conference), Stassen worked to desegregate housing locally, statewide, and nationally.[30]

With the merging of Kentucky Southern College with the University of Louisville in 1969, Stassen left Louisville and returned north, this time for a three-year post-doctoral fellowship at Harvard University. His teaching and his work for social justice had led him to realize that he had studied much in the history of theology and ethics, but he was still confused as to what factors, what "critical variables" as he came to label them, led persons to different moral choices. At Harvard, he engaged in dialogue on methodology with the work of Ralph B. Potter Jr., and he studied what worked in peacemaking and shaped foreign policy perceptions.[31]

In 1972, Stassen moved back to Kentucky to accept a teaching position at Berea College, where he became chair of the Department of Religion and Philosophy. Founded by abolitionist Christians in 1855, Berea College is a nonsectarian Christian college whose mission is the education of the poor, especially African Americans and the poor of Appalachia. Since its founding, tuition, room, and board have been free for all students at Berea College. Instead, all students are involved in work-study in the labor program, which stresses the value of work for education. Students from families whose incomes would enable them to attend elsewhere are not accepted. Stassen believes strongly in the mission of Berea College and has remained personally interested in its welfare. He has been very proud that one of his doctoral students, Michelle Tooley, contributing editor to this volume, is now teaching at Berea.

At some point during the early 1970s, Stassen read *The Politics of Jesus* by Mennonite theologian John Howard Yoder. He responded to Yoder's work at a conference hosted by Mennonites[32] and began a lifelong friendship with Yoder. Yoder became a major influence on Stassen's life and thought (and, through Stassen, on many of his students), but his interaction with Yoder also opened up contemporary Mennonite life to him. Stassen's work has been in dialogue not only with Yoder but also with such Mennonite scholars as Duane K. Friesen, Ronald J. Sider, Gayle Gerber Koontz, Theodore J. Koontz, Perry B. Yoder, Willard M. Swartley, J. Denny Weaver, John K. Stoner, Ray Gingerich, Lois Y. Barrett, and Stassen's own Mennonite students, Paul Plenge Parker, Mark Thiessen Nation, and Paulus Widjaja, to name a few. Like his fellow Baptist James William McClendon, Jr., with whom Stassen also became acquainted during this period, Stassen became increasingly an Anabaptist-leaning Baptist. Along with Martin Luther King, Jr., it is difficult to underestimate the influence of Yoder and McClendon on Stassen, influence that has only grown stronger over the years.[33]

In 1976, Stassen returned to Louisville to teach Christian ethics at The Southern Baptist Theological Seminary, which had recovered its academic strength and reputation in the years following the crisis of 1958. Stassen's teacher, Henlee H. Barnette, was retiring, and Stassen would succeed him, alongside his friend and colleague Paul D. Simmons, in the two-person Christian Ethics Department. Both men taught introductory courses, but, in both research and teaching responsibilities, Simmons concentrated on biomedical ethics, sexual ethics, professional and pastoral ethics, and the interaction of Christian ethics and philosophical ethics while Stassen concentrated on racial justice, hunger and poverty, social and economic justice, war, violence and peacemaking, and ecological ethics. Both men shared strong interest in theological ethics, emerging liberation perspectives, religious liberty and church-state separation, and the functional authority of Scripture in ethics. Doctoral students in Christian ethics took seminars with both Stassen and Simmons and learned from both.

Stassen spent twenty years teaching at Southern and never intended to leave for another institution. While at Southern, he continued his work for racial and economic justice and for peacemaking. He joined the Louisville chapter of the Fellowship of Reconciliation and became good friends with its longtime leaders Jean and George R. Edwards.[34] He helped to found the Louisville Council on Peacemaking and Religion and served as a board member for twenty years. Beginning in 1982, Stassen served on the strategy committee of the Nuclear Weapons Freeze Campaign, including serving as co-chair and developing its successful strategy for the removal of medium-range nuclear missiles from Europe. When "the Freeze" merged with the Committee for a Sane Nuclear Policy to become SANE/Freeze, Stassen remained an integral part of its work. When it reconstituted after the end of the Cold War as Peace Action in 1994, Stassen continued to serve on its board, as he does to the present day.[35] In 1984, along with his colleague, church historian E. Glenn Hinson, Stassen was part of the founding meeting of the Baptist Peace Fellowship of North America (BPFNA) at Louisville's Deer Park Baptist Church, a merger of the (American) Baptist Peace Fellowship with various peacemaking efforts by scattered groups in Southern Baptist life. He served for many years on the board of BPFNA and remains deeply involved with them.

Stassen's peacemaking work bore fruit in terms of a new paradigm for peacemaking ethics: just peacemaking theory, which complements rather than supplants the older ethics of pacifism and just war theory. David Gushee's biographical chapter on Stassen for *Twentieth Century Shapers of Baptist Social Ethics* devotes considerable space to Stassen's just peacemaking initiative and its influence on others.[36] Considerable attention is given to it as well in the special issue of the *Journal of the Society of Christian Ethics.*[37] In this volume, the chapters by Michelle Tooley and Aldrin Peñamora analyze and apply just peacemaking theory to different contexts, so no more needs to be said here. It is a major contribution to Christian ethics, and Stassen has devoted much of his personal and scholarly efforts in the development, refinement, defense, and spread of just peacemaking practices and of just peacemaking theory as an ethical paradigm with a unity and obligatory nature.[38]

The Southern Seminary years also saw Stassen's contributions to *SEEDS* magazine, published by Southern Baptists working on hunger issues, his involvement in Bread for the World, and the National Coalition for the Homeless as well as efforts to help public defenders work more effectively for sentences other than death in capital punishment cases. He became a contributing editor to *Sojourners* magazine and to the mainline journal *Christianity and Crisis,* as well as a board member of Evangelicals for Social Action founded by evangelical Mennonite Ronald J. Sider. As the 1980s drew to a close, Stassen's behind-the-scenes work with church-based grassroots peace groups in Europe, especially East Germany, bore fruit in the removal of the Euro-missiles and in the nonviolent revolutions of 1989. Stassen, on sabbatical, was eyewitness to the nonviolent "Revolution of the

Candles" in East Germany. At the same time, he published more and continued supervising PhD students.

Despite the rise of Southern Baptist fundamentalism, which grew simultaneously with the Religious Right in United States politics, with which he had numerous and severe disagreements, Stassen had no plans to leave Southern Seminary. He thought the work he was doing was too important. He tried to be a peacemaker with faculty, trustees, and the new administration ushered in with the retirement of President Roy Lee Honeycutt in 1992. Even though the first victim of the new administration's purge was his friend and colleague, Paul D. Simmons, who resigned under enormous pressure, Stassen attempted to stay and continue supervising doctoral students in the midst of the crisis. He survived until 1996, when an offer from Fuller Theological Seminary coincided with the realization of the futility of trying to continue at the post-Honeycutt Southern.

In 1996, Stassen became the first occupant of the new Lewis B. Smedes Chair of Christian Ethics at Fuller Theological Seminary, the leading seminary of progressive evangelicals in the United States and the largest theological seminary in North America. This move enabled Stassen to broaden his professional impact. He remained loyal to his Baptist identity and his long connections to mainline Protestant and Catholic scholars, but he was now able to serve students from numerous denominations and theological traditions and from many nations and cultures. The move to Fuller also helped him gain a wider hearing in the evangelical world beyond Southern Baptists. Some, including myself, wondered if this wider hearing from North American evangelicals would come at the price of influence among other longtime dialogue partners: Mennonites, mainline Protestants, progressive Catholics, the Black Church, and interfaith, especially Jewish, work. Happily, this has not been the case, or not to a large degree. Stassen's just peacemaking Initiative has involved participants from all those constituencies and more. Also, Fuller Seminary has begun major dialogues with Eastern Orthodox Christians and with Muslims. In 2013, Fuller took small steps to become more welcoming and inclusive of Lesbian, Gay, Bisexual, and Transgendered (LGBT) students, the first self-identified evangelical seminary to do so.[39]

Now in his seventies and nearing retirement, Glen Stassen continues his work for justice and peacemaking, and he is still writing in many areas of ethics. With former student David Gushee, he co-wrote a major textbook of Christian ethics, centered on the Sermon on the Mount and aimed at a broadly evangelical audience.[40] He edited some of the posthumously published writings of John Howard Yoder.[41] He assisted Assemblies of God theologian Paul Alexander in nurturing the fledgling Pentecostals and Charismatics for Peace with Justice. Along with John K. Stoner and myself, Stassen worked with Every Church a Peace Church to aid churches to recover the ethics of Jesus during the years after 9/11 when American churches seemed chained to theologies of violence, coercion, neglect for the poor, and fear of the other. In the same vein, Glen Stassen worked with Princeton Seminary's George Hunsinger in the formation of the National Religious Coalition against Torture, and with David Gushee in the evangelical-specific branch of that effort, Evangelicals for Human Rights. He participated with Rabbi Michael Lerner's efforts to grow a Network of Spiritual Progressives to counter the influence of the Religious Right, providing another alternative to the secular Left. Stassen's latest book, *A Thicker Jesus,* draws on the legacies of Bonhoeffer, King, and others to reclaim a thick understanding of Jesus for a Christian ethics of "incarnational discipleship,"[42] rather than either fundamentalist legalism or a weak liberal ethics of "thin principles."[43]

Glen Harold Stassen is still seeking to do Christian ethics "as if Jesus mattered" and to strengthen the witness of the entire Body of Christ. This *Festschrift* is a tribute to his efforts from a few of the many for whom he is a mentor and who seek, each in her or his own way, to further, strengthen, or develop that work, doing their own work "as if Jesus mattered" in their lives, too. It is a small thank you to a beloved teacher from whom we have all learned so very much.

NOTES

1. There are two main written sources for the life of Glen H. Stassen: Glen H. Stassen, "A Southern Baptist Theologian," in *Peacemakers: Christian Voices from the New Abolitionist Movement,* ed. Jim Wallis (New York: Harper & Row, 1983) 48–55; and David P. Gushee, "Glen Harold Stassen (1936–): Baptist Peacemaker in a Conflicted World," in *Twentieth-Century Shapers of Baptist Social Ethics,* ed. Larry L. McSwain and William Loyd Allen (Macon GA: Mercer University Press, 2008) 244–63. These have been supplemented by personal conversations and memories, online documents, and a recent biography of Stassen's father.

2. "Historical Events for Year 1936," *HistoryOrb.com,* http://www.historyorb.com/events/date/1936 (accessed 20 May 2013).

3. In Anne Keene's online biographical sketch, Harold Stassen's paternal ancestors are listed as Norwegian and Czech, while only his mother's ancestry is listed as German (*American National Biography Online,* http://www.anb.org/articles/07/07-00811.html [accessed 20 May 2013]). In personal conversation with Glen Stassen in 2001, he revealed learning, shortly after his father's death, that, in fact, his ancestry was entirely that of German immigrants. In response to virulent anti-German feeling in the US during and after World War I, the Stassens

had chosen to "pass" as Norwegian to avoid persecution. This was done so successfully that Harold Stassen's own children were unaware of the deception until his death, despite belonging to a denomination of German immigrants, the German Baptist Convention (later called the North American Baptist Conference).

4. Alec Kirby, David G. Dalin, and John F. Rothman, Harold E. Stassen: *The Life and Perennial Candidacy of the Progressive Republican* (Jefferson NC: McFarland & Co., 2013). Cf. Mark O. Hatfield, *Against the Grain: Reflections of a Rebel Republican, as told to Diane N. Solomon* (Ashland OR: White Cloud, 2001). Like Oregon's governor and senator Mark O. Hatfield, Harold Stassen's entire life embodied *liberal* Republicanism, a tradition all but extinct today and virtually unknown to generations of US citizens born after 1984.

5. At the time, Minnesota, like many US states, had two-year terms for governor.

6. See Stassen, "A Southern Baptist Theologian," 48.

7. Ibid., 49.

8. Kathleen Stassen Berger, *The Developing Person through the Lifespan*, 8th ed. (New York: Worth Publishers, 2011).

9. Stassen, "A Southern Baptist Theologian," 49.

10. The story of American conscientious objectors who refused to fight in World War II is told in *The Good War and Those Who Refused to Fight in It*, directed by Judith Ehrlich and Rick Tejada-Flores (2000, Arlington VA: PBS, 2002).

11. Ibid., 50. Cf. Gushee, "Glen Harold Stassen," 245–46.

12. Glen Harold Stassen, *A Thicker Jesus: Incarnational Discipleship in a Secular Age* (Louisville KY: Westminster John Knox, 2012) 83–86. A sense of his joy in scientific discovery and his participation in cutting-edge research at the Naval Research Lab is found in *A Thicker Jesus*.

13. Gushee, "Glen Harold Stassen," 246. See Culbert G. Rutenber, *The Dagger and the Cross: An Examination of Christian Pacifism* (New York: Fellowship Publications, 1950). For more on Rutenber, see David M. Scholer, ed., *Perspectives on Ethical and Social Issues: Essays in Honor of Culbert Gerow Rutenber*, NABPR *Festschrift* 11 (Waco TX: Baylor University Press, 1994), originally published as a special issue of *Perspectives in Religious Studies* 21/4 (Winter 1994): 277–380.

14. Personal conversation. For more on Barnette, see Henlee Hulix Barnette, *A Pilgrimage of Faith: My Story* (Macon GA: Mercer University Press, 2004). It was also in Barnette's class that Stassen heard a guest lecture by Clarence Jordan, a Southern Baptist minister with a PhD in New Testament who had founded an interracial community, Koinonia Farms (today, Koinonia Partners) in Southern Georgia in 1942. The influence of Jordan on Stassen's thought is shown in *A Thicker Jesus*. The chapters in this *Festschrift* by Michael Willett Newheart, Joon-Sik Park, David Fillingim, and Reggie Williams all note Jordan's important influence.

15. Bob E. Patterson, ed., *Science, Faith, and Revelation: An Approach to Christian Philosophy* (Nashville: Broadman, 1979); Bob E. Patterson, ed., *Perspectives on Science and Religion: Essays in Honor of Eric Charles Rust* (Waco TX: Baylor University Press, 1995), originally published as a special issue of Perspectives in Religious Studies 22/4 (Winter 1995).

16. One account of this crisis is found in Barnette, *A Pilgrimage*, 101–106.

17. David Fillingim's chapter in this volume does a nice job of analyzing the continued influence of Reinhold Niebuhr on the developed, mature shape of Stassen's ethics.

18. See Glen Harold Stassen, "The Fourteen Triads of the Sermon on the Mount (Matthew 5: 21-7:12)," *Journal of Biblical Literature* 122/2 (Summer 2003): 267–308. Few Christian ethicists have so mastered the disciplines of biblical scholarship that they could publish in the professional journals of biblical scholars, but Glen Stassen has done so. Stassen has noted that his biblical studies concentrate on the prophets (especially Isaiah), the Sermon on the Mount and the Sermon the Plain, Romans, and Revelation (Stassen, "A Southern Baptist Theologian," 52–53). An examination of his writings indicates that these are still the areas of Scripture he has studied the most.

19. James Muilenburg, *The Way of Israel* (New York: Harper & Row, 1961); James Muilenburg, *Hearing and Speaking the Word: Selections from the Works of James Muilenburg,* ed. Thomas F. Best (Chico CA: Scholars' Press, 1984); Bernhard W. Anderson and Walter Harrelson, eds., *Israel's Prophetic Heritage: Essays in Honor of James Muilenburg* (New York: Harper & Row, 1962); Jared J. Jackson and Martin Kessler, eds., Rhetorical Criticism: Essays in Honor of James Muilenburg (Pittsburgh: Pickwick, 1974).

20. See W. D. Davies's works: *The Setting of the Sermon on the Mount* (Cambridge, England: Cambridge University Press, 1964); *The Sermon on the Mount* (Cambridge, England: Cambridge University Press, 1966); *Paul and Rabbinic Judaism: Some Rabbinic Elements in Pauline Theology* (London: SPCK, 1948); *Christian Origins and Judaism* (Philadelphia: Westminster Press, 1962). Cf. Robert Hammerton-Kelly and Robin Scroggs, eds., *Jews, Greeks, and Christians: Religious Cultures in Late Antiquity: Essays in Honor of William David Davies* (Leiden, The Netherlands: Brill, 1976).

21. Daniel Day Williams, *The Spirit and the Forms of Love* (New York: Harper & Row, 1968); Daniel Day Williams, *God's Grace and Man's Hope* (New York: Harper & Row, 1949); Daniel Day Williams, *The Demonic and the Divine*, ed. Stacy A. Evans (Minneapolis: Fortress Press, 1990). Laura Rector's chapter in this volume, "Delivering Love," further analyzes the influence of Williams on Stassen's thought.

22. Glen Harold Stassen, "The Sovereignty of God in the Theological Ethics of H. Richard Niebuhr," PhD dissertation, Duke University, 1965.

23. Gushee, "Glen Harold Stassen," 247.

24. Lonnie D. Kliever, *H. Richard Niebuhr*, Makers of the Modern Theological Mind (Waco TX: Word Books, 1977).

25. Personal conversation.

26. Glen H. Stassen, "Anabaptist Influence in the Origin of the Particular Baptists," *Mennonite Quarterly Review* 36 (October 1962): 322–48.

27. Gushee, "Glen Harold Stassen," 261–63. The bibliography of Stassen's writings in this *Festschrift* shows his further work on Baptist identity.

28. See Glen Harold Stassen, "God and Human Dignity: The Personalism, Theology, and Ethics of Martin Luther King, Jr.," *Journal of Religion* 88/3 (July 2008): 416–18, as well as the strong interaction with King's thought in *A Thicker Jesus.*

29. Gushee, "Glen Harold Stassen," 245. Stassen has told this story of surprise and gratitude at meeting his father at the 1963 March on Washington to many a class of students. He always tears up, both at the memory of that amazing event and in gratitude to his father for an act of political courage that was rare then and is almost unthinkable today.

30. Ibid., 247; Barnette, *A Pilgrimage*, 120–21. These years also saw the assassinations of John F. Kennedy (1963), Malcolm X (1965), Martin Luther King, Jr., and Robert F.

Kennedy (both 1968). Stassen has stated in personal conversation that assassination is always the enemy of democracy, not only an act of violence against the assassinated individuals and their families but also an act of profound disrespect for the political choices of ordinary people. I am certain that the assassinations of the 1960s were foremost in his mind.

31. The results of his research were eventually published as Glen H. Stassen, "Individual Preferences vs. Role Constraints in Policy Making," *World Politics* (October 1972): 96–119; "A Social Theory Model for Religious Social Ethics," *Journal of Religious Ethics* (Spring 1977): 9–37; and "Critical Variables in Christian Social Ethics," in Paul D. Simmons, ed., *Issues in Christian Ethics* (Nashville: Broadman Press, 1980) 57–76.

32. Glen H. Stassen, "*The Politics of Jesus*—Moving Toward Social Ethics," unpublished paper presented at the Mennonite Peace Theology Colloquium, designed to respond to *The Politics of Jesus*, sponsored by the Mennonite Central Committee Peace Section, Kansas City MO, 7–9 October 1976. Stassen describes a speaking tour that he and Yoder undertook after that conference in which Stassen's work on Isaiah, Jesus' favorite prophet, reinforced Yoder's work on Jesus. They also discussed problems in the work of H. Richard Niebuhr—discussions that eventually evolved into a book co-written by Stassen, Yoder, and Diane Yeager. See Glen H. Stassen, D. M. Yeager, and John Howard Yoder, *Authentic Transformation: A New Vision of Christ and Culture* with a previously unpublished essay by H. Richard Niebuhr (Nashville: Abingdon, 1996). The speaking tour is described in Glen H. Stassen, "The Politics of Jesus in the Sermon on the Plain," in *The Wisdom of the Cross: Essays in Honor of John Howard Yoder*, ed. Stanley Hauerwas, Chris K. Huebner, Harry J. Huebner, and Mark Thiessen Nation (Grand Rapids: Eerdmans, 1999) 150–51.

33. See, e.g., Stassen, "The Politics of Jesus in the Sermon on the Plain," 150–63; Glen H. Stassen, "Narrative Justice as Reiteration," in *Theology Without Foundations: Religious Practice and the Future of Theological Truth* [a *Festschrift* for James William McClendon, Jr.], ed. Stanley Hauerwas, Nancey Murphy, and Mark Nation (Nashville: Abingdon, 1994) 201–28.

34. George R. Edwards, *Jesus and the Politics of Violence* (New York: Harper & Row, 1972); George R. Edwards, *Gay/Lesbian Liberation: A Biblical Perspective* (Cleveland: Pilgrim Press, 1984). George R. Edwards, a conscientious objector to World War II, was professor of New Testament at Louisville Presbyterian Theological Seminary, and a leader in nonviolent work for social justice, including racial and gender justice and work to end homophobia and heterosexism.

35. Glen H. Stassen and Lawrence S. Wittner, eds., *Peace Action: Past, Present, Future*, foreword by Rep. Barbara Lee (New York: Paradigm, 2007).

36. Gushee, "Glen Harold Stassen," 249–60.

37. Glen Harold Stassen, ed., "Resource Section on Just Peacemaking Theory," *Journal of the Society of Christian Ethics* 23/1 (Spring/Summer 2003): 169–284.

38. Glen Harold Stassen, "The Unity, Realism, and Obligatoriness of Just Peacemaking Theory," *Journal of the Society of Christian Ethics* 23/1 (Spring/Summer 2003): 171–94.

39. Sarah Parvini, "Fuller Theological Seminary's Acceptance of LGBT Group, 'One Table,' Creates Ripples," *Huffington Post*, 13 July 2013, http://www.huffingtonpost.com/2013/07/13/fuller-theological-seminary-lgbt-onetable_n_3593237.html (accessed 14 July 2013).

40. Stassen and Gushee, *Kingdom Ethics*.

41. John Howard Yoder, *War of the Lamb: The Ethics of Nonviolence and Peacemaking*, ed. Glen H. Stassen, Mark Thiessen Nation, and Matt Hamsher (Grand Rapids MI: Brazos Press, 2009).

42. Glen H. Stassen, Michael L. Westmoreland-White, and David P. Gushee, "Disciples of the Incarnation," *Sojourners* (May 1994): 26–30.

43. Glen H. Stassen, *A Thicker Jesus: Incarnational Discipleship in a Secular Age* (Louisville KY: Westminster John Knox, 2012).

Chapter 2

Stassen on the Mount
The Ethicist as Exegete[1]

MICHAEL WILLETT NEWHEART

In his foreword to Willard M. Swartley's *Covenant of Peace*, Glen Stassen narrates his call to peacemaking. His pastor V. Carney Hargroves was speaking about a recent trip to Moscow. Stassen was so moved that he saw a vision "of the church as truly following Jesus, making a difference for peacemaking."[2] When it was time to pursue a PhD, Stassen decided to study Christian ethics, for he knew that the New Testament was clear about peacemaking, but he wanted to "think through some of the practical implications of Jesus' teachings."[3]

Few people have "thought through" so thoroughly Jesus' teachings as found in the Sermon on the Mount (Matt 5:1–7:29). In this essay I examine Stassen's approach to the Sermon, which can easily be summarized in two words: "transforming initiatives." I list his writings on this topic, discuss his exegetical emphases, explore biblical scholars' reactions, and finally compare "transforming initiatives" with my own "hermeneutic of human dignity."

Stassen on the Mount

In twenty years, from 1992 to 2012, Stassen has published a book chapter, a major essay, and three books on the Sermon on the Mount. In these five works he functions in turn as a prophet, exegete, teacher, pastor, and theologian (though one might say he fulfills all five of these roles in all his works). First came the prophet in the 1992 book *Just Peacemaking: Transforming Initiatives for Justice and Peace*.[4] Stassen alerts us early in the book as to where he turns for these transforming initiatives. Chapter 2 is titled "Turning Toward the Sermon on the Mount." In just twenty pages, Stassen develops his perspective on the Sermon that will occupy him for the next two decades.[5]

About halfway through that time, in 2003, Stassen produced an article and a book on the Sermon. He first donned his exegete's hat in the *Journal of Biblical Literature* article "The Fourteen Triads of the Sermon on the Mount." Here he makes a careful, critical case for the transforming initiatives approach to the Sermon, which is the backbone of his chapter in *Just Peacemaking*.[6] Also in 2003, he robed himself in a teacher's gown and published a large textbook, *Kingdom Ethics: Following Jesus in Contemporary Context*, co-authored with his former student David Gushee.[7] The book represents the pair's comprehensive statement on Christian ethics. As the title suggests, it is grounded in Jesus' teaching, which they find best expressed in the Sermon on the Mount. The book's structure demonstrates how central the Sermon is for them. Section 1 discusses the kingdom of God (an important concept in the Sermon, as they point out), section 2 deals with moral authority in Christian ethics, and the rest of the book, sections 3–7, ponders issues raised or suggested by the Sermon.

Just a few years later, in 2006, Stassen came out with a more pastoral work, a little book titled *Living the Sermon on the Mount: A Practical Guide for Hope and Deliverance*, as part of the series "Enduring Questions in Christian Life," edited by David Gushee.[8] In some ways, this book is a summary for "every-person" of Stassen's other three works on the Sermon. It is well titled, for the focus is on practical guidelines for living the Sermon.

Finally (at least for the purposes of this essay), in 2012 theologian Stassen rolled out his "magnum opus," *A Thicker Jesus: Incarnational Discipleship in a Secular Age*,[9] in which the Sermon figures prominently. He first describes "incarnational discipleship" especially as it has been lived out by Bonhoeffer, King, and others, then he shows how such an approach addresses the challenges of the secular age as identified by Charles Taylor.[10] The Sermon on the Mount comes to the fore early in the book, fades into the background in the middle, and dominates at the end, in the final two chapters "Love" and "War."[11] With this book, Stassen attempts a "sophisticated, scholarly [and] . . . scientific argument for method in Christian ethics."[12] His method is Christocentric, and his Christ is the Jesus of the Sermon on the Mount.[13]

These five works on Jesus' Sermon, then, demonstrate Glen's prophetic prowess, exegetical acumen, teaching technique, pastoral power, and theological thrust. Indeed, he evidences all five qualities in all his works. But what does he say?

The Ethicist as Exegete

In his five major works about the Sermon on the Mount, Stassen has four major emphases: (1) importance for Christian ethics, (2) "realistic" approach as opposed to "idealistic," (3) grounding in the Hebrew Scriptures (esp. Isaiah), (4) centrality of the Lord's Prayer, and (5) triadic structure. In numbers 1–4, Stassen is adding his voice to others. In 5, however, Stassen makes an original contribution. Stay tuned! We will go in order, beginning with the characteristics of the Sermon on the Mount.

The Sermon's Importance for Christian Ethics

The Sermon on the Mount is Stassen's "canon within a canon."[14] Such attraction to this passage of Scripture, however, is millennia old, for he points out that in the early church the Sermon was the most often quoted section of the Gospels, and he contends that it remains the "*locus classicus* of Christian peacemaking."[15] He and Gushee write, "The way of discipleship and the commands of Jesus are most clearly taught in the Sermon. . . . [It] is a primer for kingdom ethics."[16] They continue, "Ethics as incarnational discipleship points to the incarnate Jesus, who taught the Sermon on the Mount and the Kingdom of God, in the tradition of the prophets of Israel, embodied it in his practices and called us to embody it in our practices of discipleship. This Jesus is our Lord."[17] As Stassen and Gushee address such varied ethical issues as the death penalty, creation care, and sexual ethics in *Kingdom Ethics*, they keep coming back to the Sermon on the Mount. For example, in opposing the death penalty, they write, "Jesus consistently emphasized a transforming initiative that could deliver us from the vicious cycle of violence or alienation."[18]

The Sermon's "Realistic" Approach

Stassen argues in *Just Peacemaking* that New Testament scholarship has now come to the consensus that the Sermon on the Mount is meant to be lived.[19] It sets forth "prophetic realism" over against "Platonic idealism."[20] He says that the biggest influence on this new appreciation is Martin Luther King, Jr., and the civil rights movement,[21] though his own approach has been heavily influenced by Dietrich Bonhoeffer.[22] Stassen states that the Sermon is "not about human striving toward high ideals but about God's transforming initiative to deliver us from the vicious cycles in which we get stuck."[23] Because of the transforming initiatives that God has taken, we too can take transforming initiatives. Stassen writes, "This means that the Sermon on the Mount is not a heavy guilt trip but the empowerment of delivering grace."[24]

In *Kingdom Ethics*, Stassen and Gushee present the idealistic interpretation of the beatitudes and then the "grace-based prophetic interpretation."

At the end of the discussion of each beatitude, they include a paraphrase of that beatitude. For example, they paraphrase the second beatitude, "Blessed are those [who] mourn what is wrong and unjust and repent, for God comforts those who suffer and those who truly repent."[25] Stassen does something similar in *Living the Sermon*. He begins his discussion of each beatitude with a paraphrase of that beatitude, which is a bit more literal than in *Kingdom Ethics*, although he does use "Joyful" rather than "Blessed." For example, the fourth beatitude is rendered, "Joyful are those who hunger and thirst for restorative justice, for they shall be filled."[26] Note that the traditional translation "righteousness" becomes "restorative justice."

The Sermon's Grounding in Hebrew Bible/Old Testament

Stassen and Gushee say that the grounding of the Sermon in [the] Hebrew Scriptures is "one of the guiding insights" of *Kingdom Ethics*.[27] Stassen notes in *Living the Sermon*, "One of the discoveries of this book is how often Jesus quoted Isaiah."[28] In *Just Peacemaking*, Stassen, taking his cue from his teacher W. D. Davies, argues that the beatitudes draw their imagery from Isaiah 61. Stassen also contends that the kingdom of heaven is "the fulfillment of the moral content of Old Testament expectations for a new creation."[29] He and Gushee also follow Davies in contending that Jesus' ethical teaching is grounded in the figure of Isaiah's Suffering Servant.[30] Furthermore, they build on the work of Jewish New Testament scholar Géza Vermes in arguing that Jesus related to the Scriptures the same way that the prophets did.[31]

The Centrality of the Lord's Prayer in the Sermon: God as Father

Another way in which Stassen builds on the foundation of others is by placing the Lord's Prayer—or as he calls it in *Living the Sermon*, "The Prayer of Jesus"—in the center of the Sermon on the Mount.[32] He calls the prayer the Sermon's "organizing center," and in both *Just Peacemaking* and *Living the Sermon*, Stassen demonstrates in tabular form how the prayer takes up themes developed elsewhere in the Sermon.[33]

Stassen contends that peacemaking is grounded in prayer, especially "listening (or contemplative) prayer."[34] The disciple is able to take part in "surprising, transforming initiatives" if grounded in God's own "surprising, transforming initiative" in Jesus Christ and in the community that gathers in his name.[35] Stassen even urges that prayer is important in understanding the Sermon. After telling about an experience of meditation that brushed aside an episode of momentary depression and loneliness, Stassen writes, "[T]his sense of God's presence . . . is crucial for interpreting the Sermon on the Mount rightly. The Sermon on the Mount is not first of all about what *we should do*. It is first of all about what *God has already done*. It is about God's presence, the breakthrough of God's kingdom in Jesus."[36] In *A Thicker Jesus*, Stassen recommends "a regular practice of quietly meditating in God's presence, seeking to listen for God's will in our lives." He then briefly shares his own "Spiritual Exercises," which include daily Bible reading, listening prayer, and journal writing.[37] Prayer is not only central to the Sermon but also central to Stassen. No split between the academic and the devotional exists here.

The Sermon's Triadic Structure

In these first four emphases, Stassen has furthered arguments advanced by others. His original contribution, however, is his contention that the Sermon contains fourteen triads. In *Just Peacemaking*, he calls the first element "Traditional Piety," the second the "Mechanism of Bondage," and, of course, the third "Transforming Initiative." He argues that the emphasis falls on this third aspect. Stassen also points out that no one else has argued this triadic approach.[38]

The fact that the Sermon contains fourteen triads is bolstered by Matthew's use of the number in the genealogy (1:1-17) and the transcendent use of the number among the rabbis. Stassen wryly notes, "While there being 14 triads of transforming initiatives is not essential to the arguments for the triadic triumphant initiatives, that there are fourteen does me great aesthetic, if not mystical, pleasure."[39]

He changes the terminology slightly in 2003: the first element becomes "Traditional Righteousness," and the second element becomes "Vicious Cycle and Consequences (or Judgment)." Of course, "Transforming Initiative" remains the same. Stassen and Gushee include a helpful chart of the fourteen triads in *Kingdom Ethics*.[40]

The fourteen triads of The Sermon on the Mount

Traditional Righteousness	Vicious Cycle	Transforming Initiative
1. You shall not kill.	Being angry, or saying, You fool!	*Go, be reconciled*
2. You shall not commit adultery	Looking with lust is adultery in the heart	*Remove the cause of temptation (cf. Mk 9:43-50)*
3. Whoever divorces, give a certificate	Divorcing involves you in adultery	(Be reconciled: 1 Cor 7:11)
4. You shall not swear falsely	Swearing by anything involves you in a false claim	*Let your yes be yes, and your no be no*
5. Eye for eye, tooth for tooth	Retaliating violently or revengefully, by evil means	*Turn the other cheek, give your tunic and cloak, go the second mile, give to beggar and borrower*
6. Love neighbor and hate enemy	Hating enemies is the same vicious cycle that you see in the Gentiles and tax collectors	*Love enemies, pray for your persecutors; be all-inclusive as your Father in heaven is*
7. When you give alms,	Practicing righteousness for show	*But give in secret, and your Father will reward you*
8. When you pray,	Practicing righteousness for show	*But pray in secret, and your Father will reward you*
9. When you pray,	Heaping up empty phrases	*Therefore, pray like this: Our Father . . .*
10. When you fast,	Practicing righteousness for show	*But dress with joy, and your Father will reward you*
11. *Do not pile up treasures on earth* (cf. Luke 12:16-31)	*Moth and rust destroy, and thieves enter and steal*	*But pile up treasures in heaven*
12. *No one can serve two masters*	*Serving God and wealth, worrying about food and clothes*	*But seek first God's reign and God's justice/righteousness*
13. *Do not judge, lest you be judged*	*Judging others means you'll be judged by the same measure*	*First take the log out of your own eye*
14. Do not give holy things to dogs, nor pearls to pigs	They will trample them and tear you to pieces	*Give your trust in prayer to your Father in heaven*

In *Living the Sermon*, Stassen includes a diagram for each triad. Below is the diagram for the first triad that appears in *Kingdom Ethics*.[41]

Traditional Righteousness	Vicious Cycle	Transforming Initiative
Matthew 5:21: You have heard that it was said to those of ancient times, "You shall not kill; and whoever kills shall be liable to judgment." (In Greek, "shall not" and "shall be" are not imperatives, but futures; as translations of the Hebrew in the Ten Commandments, they do of course imply a command.)	Matthew 5:22: But I say to you that every one being angry with his brother will be liable to judgment; whoever insults his brother will be liable to the council, and whoever says, "You fool!" will be liable to the hell of fire. (No imperatives in the Greek.)	Matthew 5:23-26: So if you are offering your gift at the altar, and you remember that your brother or sister has something against you, *leave* your gift there . . . and *go*; first *be reconciled* to your brother, and then coming, *offer* your gift. *Make friends* quickly with your accuser. (Italics mark the Greek imperatives.)

Stassen begins with Matthew 5:21-48, which has typically been known as the "antitheses." Building on the work of Davies, who called this section "exegeses" rather than "antitheses," Stassen demonstrates that the discussions are not structured in dyads: "You have heard it said . . . But I say to you . . . ," but rather in triads, in which the emphasis falls on this third element. In the first discussion (5:21-26), Jesus sets forth the "Traditional Righteousness": "You have heard that it was said to those of ancient times: 'You shall not murder'" (5:21). Then the Vicious Cycle: "But I say to you that if you are angry with a brother or sister, you will be liable to judgment," to the council, to hell (5:22). The emphasis, however, falls on the Transforming Initiative, in which the hearer reconciles with the brother or sister and comes to terms with the accuser (5:23-26).

Stassen argues that this threefold pattern persists not just through this first major section of the Sermon but throughout its body, through 7:12, as Jesus discusses almsgiving, prayer, fasting, investing in earthly treasures, serving two masters, judging, and giving holy things to the dogs. It is in this final triad, 7:6-12, that Stassen offers a solution to a problem that has vexed interpreters for millennia. The saying in 7:6, about giving holy things to the dogs and casting pearls before swine, has proven elusive because it seems disconnected from its context. Stassen, however, shows that it is actually the first term, the Traditional Righteousness, of the fourteenth triad. Building on the work of Warren Carter in his *Matthew and the Margins*, Stassen argues that the dogs and swine in 7:6 refer to the Romans. Disciples are not to give their loyalty to Rome ("Traditional Righteousness"), which leads to self-destruction ("Vicious Cycle"); rather, they are to ask, seek, and knock at the door of the heavenly Father, who "gives good things to those who ask" ("Transforming Initiative"). With God setting the example, disciples are to follow "the golden rule" (7:12). Stassen summarizes, "[A]s God gives good gifts of love to those who ask, therefore you should give good gifts of love to others, rather than following the ethics of giving gifts to those who might advance your prestige and wealth as those who put their trust in the Roman power structure do."[42]

These are Stassen's exegetical emphases: the Sermon's importance for ethics, the realistic approach, the Sermon's grounding in Hebrew Scripture, the centrality of the Lord's Prayer, and the fourteen triads. How do other exegetes appraise his findings, especially the triadic approach?

The Ethicist and the Exegetes

In *Living the Sermon*, Stassen makes a curious statement: "The most respected scholarly journal for biblical studies, *The Journal of Biblical Literature (JBL)*, published my technical evidence for this interpretation of the Sermon on the Mount as the longest article I have ever seen in the journal. It means many scholars are saying yes to these discoveries."[43] The first sentence is correct,[44] but the second sentence does not follow. Publication in *JBL*, no matter what the length of the article, does not indicate that "many scholars" agree. It simply means that the *JBL*'s panel of reviewers, which probably consists of "few" rather than "many," determines that an article contributes to biblical scholarship. Stassen's article undoubtedly contributes to the field, and its length indicates that it contributes significantly. Whether or not scholars say "yes to these discoveries" is another matter.

In much the same vein, Stassen writes near the end of *A Thicker Jesus*, "The transforming initiatives interpretation pattern of the Sermon on the Mount is receiving good corroboration from New Testament scholars." As evidence, he notes that in the Matthew section of the 2006 annual meeting of the Society of Biblical Literature, in which the focus was the Sermon, the moderator announced that the group had reached the consensus that "the Sermon on the Mount is transforming initiatives."[45] Stassen's paper for the panel can be found on the society's website, as can two papers delivered that year in a session titled "Reading Matthew in a Time of War."[46] Both refer to the Sermon, but neither refers to Stassen or transforming initiatives. One wonders about this "consensus" of which Stassen and the moderator speak.[47]

Willard Swartley holds fast to it. He calls Stassen's *JBL* study "insightful" and dubs his treatment of 7:6 "a breakthrough."[48] Nobody else, however, is quite as enthusiastic, at least in print. Most scholars simply ignore this work. Since Stassen's 2003 *JBL* article, eleven scholarly works (eight articles and three books) on the Sermon have appeared in English, and eight commentaries on Matthew, also in English, have been published. Of the nineteen, only four (two articles and two commentaries) refer to Stassen's article, all in footnotes, two appreciative and two dismissive. First, on the positive side, Dale C. Allison, Jr., whose work on the Sermon Stassen critiques, agrees that 5:43-48 are "climactic transformative initiatives." He continues that this approach "works remarkably well for much of the Sermon on the Mount and is a contribution to interpretation, but it does not work well for all of it."[49] Also on the positive side, Grant R. Osborne finds the "triadic" approach to the so-called antitheses "interesting."[50] On the negative side, Craig R. Blomberg writes, "Not all [of the fourteen triads] are equally convincing, esp[ecially] not 7.6 as foil to 7.7-11."[51] R. T. France is also unpersuaded by this perspective on 7:6-12.[52]

Of nineteen recent English works on the Sermon, then, only four refer to the *JBL* article. Of the remainder, four do refer to other of Stassen's writings. *Kingdom Ethics* is cited appreciatively twice. James R. Wicker summarizes the fourteen-triad approach and seems to accept it, though he abandons the language of "transforming initiative" with his discussion of 5:26.[53] Charles Quarles commends the "excellent treatment" of Matthew 5:28 in *Kingdom Ethics*.[54] Furthermore, Stassen's *Just Peacemaking* and his *Review and Expositor* article are listed in John Nolland's bibliographies.[55] Finally, Stassen's *Living the Sermon* is reviewed positively by John Yieh in *Interpretation*.[56] He calls the book "delightful," and he considers "[m]ost innovative" Stassen's three-stage analysis of traditional righteousness, vicious cycle, and transforming initiative. He states that this analysis explains well Matthew 5:21–6:18, but not so well the rest of the Sermon (Matt 6:19–7:27).[57]

It may be an exaggeration, therefore, to say that "many scholars are saying yes" to the Sermon's transforming initiatives. The moderator who announced a "consensus" was apparently speaking about discussion in that particular session. Stassen writes on the Just Peacemaking website, "[T]he transforming initiatives structure . . . has been accepted by all the New Testament scholars I have heard from, and I know of no dissent."[58] Unfortunately, most New Testament scholars writing on the Sermon are not saying anything about Stassen's work. Eleven of nineteen recent works do not mention it at all. Of the eight that do cite him, only two do so in the body of their articles, and one of those is a book review.

A particularly interesting case is that of Charles H. Talbert, who wrote a book on the Sermon in 2004 and a commentary on Matthew in 2010. In neither of these works does he refer to Stassen, although the two have published in the same journals, such as *JBL* and *Review and Expositor*, and both have been active in the National Association of Baptist Professors of Religion. Talbert does not refer to Stassen, and Stassen does not refer to Talbert.

Why is this? Why are most biblical scholars ignoring Stassen's work? Is it because he's not a member of "the club," even though he has published a *JBL* article? Biblical scholars only refer to other biblical scholars, who carry some such professional position and publish exclusively on biblical subjects. Much is made these days of interdisciplinary work, and biblical scholars have been enriched by dialogue with colleagues in literature and in the social sciences. But what about colleagues in theology and ethics and history and ministry? Is there something, though, about Stassen as an ethicist? ("My gosh, if I actually take this guy's arguments seriously, I may have to do something about this Sermon on the Mount instead of just studying it.")

Our scholarship tends to take on the quality of texts we are studying. The Sermon on the Mount, like the New Testament in general, has much to say about "insiders and outsiders," and we recreate this division in our exegesis. It appears in "insider" publications, written and read by biblical scholars, but not "outsiders," scholars in religious studies other than biblical studies, and those in other disciplines such as literature and social sciences. Certainly on the outside are those in non-academic settings, no matter their interest in or passion for this collection of texts. For most scholars writing on the Sermon on the Mount, Stassen is an outsider, perhaps because his specialty is Christian ethics rather than New Testament.

The Sermon on the Mount, though, is about turning outsiders into insiders through "transforming initiatives," in Stassen's words. Is there some transforming initiative that can be done so that exegetes and ethicists, prophets and pastors, scholars and students can sit down at the table of brotherhood and sisterhood and talk about texts? What can we do to be reconciled to our brother or sister colleague (Matt 5:24)? How can we remove the log from our own eye and then take the speck out of the colleague's eye (7:5)? How can we together seek first the kingdom (6:33)? How can we pray together for that kingdom to come and God's will to be done (6:10)? How can we help create the beloved community where there are no outsiders, only insiders—where everyone's voice is heard?

The Ethicist and *This* Exegete

But maybe you need to hear my voice now. What can I say? I say, "Dignity."

I said it quite often in another recent *Festschrift* essay where I crafted a "hermeneutic of human dignity."[59] I interpret Scripture in order to affirm the dignity of all inhabitants of planet Earth. My research assistant Juliana Holm noted how much overlap she saw between Stassen's "transforming initiative" approach to the Sermon and my own "dignitarian hermeneutic." She e-mailed me these thoughts about Stassen: "I am very struck by the attention to dignity that he finds in the words of Jesus and the Sermon on the Mount, particularly when talking about turning the other cheek, walking the extra mile, giving your cloak, and addressing justice. . . . When your hermeneutic of dignity is juxtaposed with Stassen's approach to the Sermon, both are illuminated by the other."[60] Let's shine the light, then.

Staying with Stassen

I leaf through my essay and spotlight many points of contact with Stassen, especially in the areas of "biblical activism," writing style, and prayer. I begin at the end. Compare the concluding sentence of Stassen's *A Thicker Jesus* with that of my essay:

> Now the one remaining question: Will you join in the apostolic witness to a thicker Jesus—in the tradition of incarnational discipleship?[61]

> The message, then, is this: Let us read the Bible (and ourselves and our world) with dignity. (Can I get a witness?)[62]

I can hear the hymn "Just As I Am" playing in the background. (The buses will wait!) Both Stassen and I are at heart Baptist preachers, always extending the invitation, always opening the doors of the church (exit doors, that is), always calling believers to "put feet to their faith" in pursuing peace and justice.[63] And both of us proclaim Jesus, that babbling, baffling, biblical blessed of peacemakers (Matt 5:9).

In Stassen's work and in mine, each of us makes the case for "biblical activism," though neither of us actually uses that term. "Biblical" here refers to the written source that is foundational to the call for activism for peace and justice.[64] If I were to be more specific, I might say "Jesus activism,"[65] since both Stassen and I are primarily interested in the Jesus material as found in the New Testament Gospels. Stassen stresses the Sermon on the

Mount, while I magnify the miracles ("the powers," *dummies*, to use more Gospel language, see Mark 6:2 etc.).[66]

Of course, Stassen's call to activism is the core of his "thicker Jesus," which, Stassen emphasizes, is *historically embodied.*[67] In my article, I refer to the biblical text in this way:

> Maybe, though, the text is not really a window or mirror, but rather a *swinging glass door* that opens both to the inside and the outside. Yes, you can see yourself and what's outside, but you can also go through it; indeed, you must go through it, for it is the only way you can uphold your dignity . . . and that of others.[68]

Both Stassen and I ground our activism in the writing and work of two Baptist activists, Martin Luther King, Jr., and Clarence Jordan. References to both are scattered throughout *A Thicker Jesus*, but especially early in the book where Stassen devotes a section to the ways that King and Jordan lived out incarnational discipleship.[69] I refer to King and dignity in my essay, and I follow the spirit of Clarence Jordan's Cotton Patch Gospels in setting forth my "NEV" (Newheart Earthy Version) of Mark's first feeding (6:30-44), the text on which I demonstrate my hermeneutic.[70]

Just as we share great admiration for King and Jordan, we also share great appreciation for prayer. For Stassen, the Lord's Prayer is central to the Sermon, and prayer is central to Stassen. In addition to his daily practice, Stassen also speaks of his "pausing to marvel," and he invites the reader to "pause to marvel at the truly remarkable and awe-inspiring wonders of this universe."[71] Similarly, I discuss the importance of mindfulness in my hermeneutic of human dignity. I emphasize four "P's": persons, play, place, and presence. I write, "As persons of dignity, we have a place to play, but we must be *present* to it. . . . That means being mindful, centered, in touch with the body NOW."[72]

One way that Stassen is present to his readers is by communicating clearly. "I write in plain English, aiming my books to be readable by ordinary people."[73] He says that his students often tell him how understandable his books are. The readability is due in part to two things: first, fondness for figures and formulae. *A Thicker Jesus* is a "six-figure book." It contains six figures (diagrams, not digits of dollars). Most contain triads, such as the triad of incarnational discipleship and the triads of the Sermon. My essay includes no figures but a formula—the "magic formula" in fact: "HHD = (4 x P) + (M + W). "HHD" stands for "Hermeneutic of Human Dignity."

"(4 x P)" represents the four P's that I emphasize in my hermeneutic: Persons (readers and hearers, and characters in the text), Play (humor), Place (Earth!), and Presence (mindfulness). "(M + W)" is "Mirror and Window"; in the biblical text, I see myself *and* the world around me.[74]

In addition to figures and formulas, another reason for readability is that we both include autobiographical material in our works. For example, Stassen dedicates *A Thicker Jesus* to his father, Harold E. Stassen. Stassen recounts a number of episodes involving his father, the first time he has done so in print. Particularly poignant is the story of hearing that his father's ship in World War II had been torpedoed, and that his father had died. The family learned later that he had in fact survived. When he returned home from the war, he told his son, "Glen, war is so horrible that we have to do all we can to prevent World War III and atomic war."[75] In my essay, which concludes with a "dignitarian reading" of the feeding of the 5000, I recount a story about my mother Eleanor Hall Willett, who turned back from death's door and shared conversation and meals with me before finally succumbing a few weeks later.[76]

A final factor in our "plain-folks" writing is that we're both Midwesterners. Stassen hails from Minnesota, and I from Missouri. I was born in Independence and raised at Liberty. Like most Midwesterners, neither of us likes to "put on airs."[77]

Stassen and I, then, share a commitment to biblical activism, a debt to King and Jordan, a persistent pursuit of the presence, and an accessible writing style. I can hardly say that we each developed these ideas independently. As I write this essay, I am aware of the tremendous debt I owe him.

Straying from Stassen

Just as I see many convergences with Stassen, though, I also find a few divergences, particularly involving hermeneutics. What was that "magic formula" again? Oh yeah, HHD = (4 x P) + (M + W). And the 4 P's are what? They're Persons, Play, Place, and Presence. Let's play! In my "Earthly Exegetical Dignity Dig" of Mark 6:30-44, I write, "Jesus disembarks and sees this GREAT CROWD, and he feels compassion (*esplanchnisthe*) from his guts or bowels (*splanchna*). Jesus has a 'gut feeling,' a 'bowel movement.'"[78] Later I say, "Let's admit it: Jesus is a loafer, first for 5000 and then for 4000, and on the third sea crossing he indicates that his loafing is the key to understanding him (8:14-22)."[79] And concerning the disciples, who misunderstand here and throughout Mark, I write, "Forgetful? Faithless? Foolish? And am I disrespecting the disciples' dignity by discussing their ditziness? Or is it Mark who is defacing them by making them a foil for Jesus' fantastic feats?" And when the Gospel writer "marks" attendance at the feeding, I say, "Mark gives the count: '5000 men.' Does he mean 5000 people, or 5000 men plus women and children? Either way, for Mark, women and children don't count. They're either counted as men, or they're invisible. No women are mentioned in this story at all. Indignity!"[80]

What? You suggest I climb up the Mount and play with the Sermon? Okay, if you insist. Certain Sermonic sections summon sarcasm and skepticism. What else can you do with Jesus' commands to "tear your right eye out" and "cut your right hand off" (Matt 5:29-30)? And that whole "log and speck" thing (6:3-5)—what a hoot! And how about a session on "Sex and the Single Sermon"! The Sermon is the Sermon on the MAN's Mount; it is a man's masterpiece.[81] It speaks about looking at a woman with lust (5:28) and divorcing a wife (5:31-32). (The Mount is a Heterosexual Man's Mount . . . and I intend NO double entendre here.) And on this Mount we speak to God Man to Man, Son to Father (5:45, 48; 6:4, 6, 9, 14-15, 18, 26, 32; 7:11, 21). And this Mount(ain) Man motivates men primarily through reward and punishment. Mount(ain) men are to secretly (shh!) give alms, pray, and fast, so that "the secretly seeing Father" will reward them (6:3-4, 6, 18). When persecuted, they will be greatly heavenly rewarded (5:11-12), but when angrily insulting, "Fool," they're liable to conciliar judgment: "Gehenna!" (5:22), the destination of sinning, non-mutilating men (5:29-30). Furthermore, Father forgives forgivers but not non-forgivers (6:14-15), and his Son turns away from the heavenly kingdom "evildoers" who don't do the Father's will (7:21-23). Yes, of course, the Father, the Main Man, has a "kingdom" (5:3, 10, 19-20; 6:10, 33; 7:21), a concept that seems to us thoroughly modern men (and women) so far away and foreign and feudalistic.

Enough play today, one of the four P's in my "magic formula." There are also "M" and "W." I look at the biblical text as both mirror and window, but I see slight nuances in these images that vary from the way they are usually described. Historical critics are said to view the biblical text as a window, and literary critics as a mirror. These images seem to "distort" reality. I write (exaggerating perhaps a little bit for the sake of emphasis):

> One looks through a window to see what's on the other side. Historical critics, on the other hand, don't see what's really there; they simply make up what they guess might have been there. It's fascinating and enlightening and sometimes even halfway convincing, especially when they make analo-

gies to contemporary situations. (These analogies, though, are often strained and distort both the past and the present.) Still, however, a historical critic's work is imaginative and speculative; it has little to do with "what's really there," or even what might have been there.[82]

I have similar complaints about the mirror image, but I retain both window and mirror. I describe simply their function differently:

> The "dignitarian exegete" . . . can use both a window and a mirror to speak in a more exact sense about the biblical text. It is a window, allowing one to look at the world as it is, with all its evil and good and everything in between, with crucifixions and floods and sea-partings and healings and other (extra)ordinary stuff. And it's a mirror, allowing one to see oneself as one is: evil and good and everything in between, with messiahs and monarchs and murderers and messengers and middle-of-the-road folk.[83]

This approach diverges from Stassen's "analogical contextualization." Stassen wants "careful study of the meaning in the original context, and critical study of the present social context, so that the analogy is not only imaginative but also analogous in social meaning."[84] Stassen pursues his program in *A Thicker Jesus'* final chapter, "War," which he's "fighting" on two fronts, ancient and contemporary. (Who is the enemy in this "War"? Idealism?) Stassen finds a text's meaning in "its original context," and that meaning is "applied" to our contemporary context. The ancient warfront, then, is primary. (That's why Stassen's *JBL* article is so central for him.)

But is it really? When Stassen correlates the Sermon (or sections of the Sermon) with just peacemaking, the "meaning" of the Sermon sounds awfully—how can I say it?—contemporary. Stassen includes another helpful chart that correlates the Sermon on the Mount with the practices of just peacemaking.[85]

For example, Matthew 5:38-48[86] supports six of ten peacemaking practices, including "nonviolent direct action" and "cooperative international networks." But does that Sermonic section really carry all that meaning "in its original context" or even in its current literary context? Jesus sounds awfully foresighted.

Stassen extracts "principles" from these passages and shows how just peacemaking exemplifies these principles. His exegesis, then, becomes the servant of his ethics. It's that way for all of us. Stassen's hermeneutic is transformative initiatives, and mine is human dignity. Our ethic shapes our exegesis. Sometimes we pretend that it's the other way around: our exegesis shapes our ethic. It goes both ways, moving in the famed "hermeneutic circle." It's sometimes vicious, sometimes gentle. But it's always a dance.

I want a "thinner Jesus" who's light on his feet, who can dance. This "thicker Jesus" is a bit bloated. He's "a glutton and a wine-bibber" (Matt 11:19; Luke 7:34 KJV). He's been porking out at peacemaker potlucks and wine-and-cheese jubilees. That's okay; let him eat up. I'll call him when it's time to dance.

Conclusion

Prophet/Professor/Pastor/PREACHER Glen Stassen mounts the pulpit to preach the sermon, titled "Transforming Initiatives." It's a great sermon. I love it! Hey, biblical scholars, are you listening? Not really. Well, I am. I find Stassen's sermon so scintillating, so stimulating, that I wrote this poem a couple of years ago.

The Beat Attitudes (for Glen Stassen)
Blessed
(ly joyful) are
the exegetes
the "X"-e-GEE-ts
who "X" out (that is, make the sign of the cross on)
violent
and unjust interpretations
of the word. (GEE!)

Joyful
(ly blest) are
the theologians
thee-oh-low-gians
OH, how LOW canst THEE go?
Down to the scum,
the earth.

Blessed (and highly favored)
are the ethicists
the ETH-i-CYSTS
who de
anESTHitize us 2

the CYSTS (lesions, legions—of demons)
on our faith.

Blest 2
are all the rest of us
but there is no rest
All are
theologians
speaking God word
exegetes
interpreting texts
ethicists
living out the gospel

Blessed (joyful) are
all all.

NOTES

1. Two prefatory notes: (1) I am pleased to contribute this essay in honor of my friend and mentor Glen Harold Stassen. I was with him in Louisville, Kentucky, in the late 1970s to mid-1980s, both at The Southern Baptist Theological Seminary (SBTS) and in the World Peacemakers group at Crescent Hill Baptist Church. In both contexts, he helped shape my worldview as a scholar and as a believer. (2) In preparing this essay, the research assistance of Juliana Holm was invaluable, and I express my thanks to her.

2. Glen H. Stassen, foreword to Willard M. Swartley, *Covenant of Peace: The Missing Peace in New Testament Theology and Ethics* (Grand Rapids MI: Eerdmans, 2006) ix.

3. Stassen, foreword, x.

4. Louisville: Westminster/John Knox, 1992.

5. Stassen, *Just Peacemaking: Transforming Initiatives*, 33–52. See also his "Grace and Deliverance in the Sermon on the Mount," *Review and Expositor* 89 (1992): 229–44, and "Recovering the Way of Jesus in the Sermon on the Mount," *Journal of the European Pentecostal Theological Association* 22 (2002): 103–26.

6. Glen H. Stassen, "The Fourteen Triads of the Sermon on the Mount," *Journal of Biblical Literature* 122 (2003): 267–308.

7. Glen H. Stassen and David P. Gushee, *Kingdom Ethics: Following Jesus in Contemporary Context* (Downers Grove IL: InterVarsity, 2003). It was awarded "Best Book of the Year" in the Theology/Ethics category by *Christianity Today* in 2004.

8. Glen H. Stassen, *Living the Sermon on the Mount: A Practical Guide for Hope and Deliverance* (San Francisco: Jossey-Bass 2006).

9. Glen Harold Stassen, *A Thicker Jesus: Incarnational Discipleship in a Secular Age* (Louisville KY: Westminster John Knox, 2012). "Magnum opus" is the term Larry Rasmussen uses to describe the book in an endorsement on the very first page.

10. Charles Taylor, *A Secular Age* (Cambridge MA: Harvard University Press, 2007).

11. The full titles of the final chapters are instructive: Chapter 10, "Love: The Sermon on the Mount as Realistic Deliverance," and Chapter 11, "War: Jesus' Transformative Initiatives and Just Peacemaking's Initiatives."

12. Stassen, *A Thicker Jesus*, x.

13. In his chapter on the cross in *A Thicker Jesus*, Stassen includes an extended treatment of the Gospel of Mark as an example of an incarnational view of the cross, such as seen in the theology of Dietrich Bonhoeffer. See *A Thicker Jesus*, 153–63, esp., 153, where he writes, "*Mark shows how Jesus' enacted teaching leads to the cross*" (emphasis original). One might say that Stassen's Jesus is "thicker" in the book because he is informed not only by chapters 5–7 of Matthew but also by the entire Gospel of Mark. Yet when Stassen enters the final, key chapters of the book, the preeminence of the Sermon on the Mount is maintained, and the Gospel of Mark has left no mark at all.

14. Stassen and Gushee, *Kingdom*, xiii.

15. Stassen, *Just Peacemaking: Transforming Initiatives*, 37.

16. Stassen and Gushee, *Kingdom*, 30.

17. Ibid., 58–59.

18. Ibid., 213.

19. Stassen, *Just Peacemaking: Transforming Initiatives*, 34.

20. Stassen, *A Thicker Jesus*, 185–86.

21. Stassen, *Just Peacemaking: Transforming Initiatives*, 36. I would like to read more from Stassen about this interesting point.

22. Stassen, *A Thicker Jesus*, 21–24, 44–46, 176–85.

23. Stassen, *Just Peacemaking: Transforming Initiatives*, 37.

24. Ibid., 42

25. Stassen and Gushee, *Kingdom Ethics*, 40.

26. Stassen, *Living the Sermon*, 51.

27. Stassen and Gushee, *Kingdom Ethics*, xiii.

28. Stassen, *Living the Sermon*, xvi.

29. Stassen, *Just Peacemaking: Transforming Initiatives*, 40. Also Stassen, *A Thicker Jesus*, 185, where he notes Robert Guelich's "realization" that the beatitudes are patterned after Isa 61.

30. Stassen and Gushee, *Kingdom*, 22–23.

31. Ibid., 91–92.

32. Stassen, *Living the Sermon*, 106.

33. Stassen, *Just Peacemaking: Transforming Initiatives*, 51; *Living*, 110.

34. Stassen, *Just Peacemaking: Transforming Initiatives*, 201–203; Stassen and Gushee, *Kingdom Ethics*, 449–75; Stassen, *Living the Sermon*, 7–8, 124; Stassen, *A Thicker Jesus*, 84, 122.

35. John Dominic Crossan recently wrote a book titled *The Greatest Prayer: Rediscovering the Revolutionary Message of the Lord's Prayer* (San Francisco: HarperOne, 2010). He says that the prayer is "revolutionary" because "it presumes and proclaims the radical vision of justice that is the core of Israel's biblical tradition" (p. 2). Alas, Crossan does not refer to Stassen, though Crossan is not alone among biblical scholars in ignoring Stassen's work. See below.

36. Stassen, *Living the Sermon*, 8 (emphasis original).

37. Stassen, *A Thicker Jesus*, 122.

38. Stassen, *Just Peacemaking: Transforming Initiatives*, 46. Stassen is fond of triads. In *Thicker*, 17, he has a triadic figure of "Incarnational Discipleship," which consists of "Thicker Jesus," "Lordship of Christ," and "Holy Spirit."

39. Stassen, *Just Peacemaking: Transforming Initiatives*, 47.

40. Stassen and Gushee, *Kingdom Ethics*, 142 (used by permission of author David Gushee).

41. Ibid., 135 (used by permission of author David Gushee).

42. Stassen, "Fourteen," 294. In my book *"My Name Is Legion": The Story and Soul of the Gerasene Demoniac* (Collegeville MN: Liturgical, 2004), 82–84, 96–97, I use Warren Carter, as well as Paul Hollenbach and Richard Horsley, in interpreting Mark 5:1-20, in which Jesus puts a "legion of demons" into a herd of pigs. They then drown in the sea, thus fulfilling the fantasy of what the Mediterranean people wished for the Romans. Perhaps Stassen could delve more into the work of Carter and others in order to develop the idea of how the entire Sermon, not just 7:6, might be understood as anti-imperial polemic.

43. Stassen, *Living the Sermon*, xvi.

44. In a glance through *JBL* issues 1987–2003, I did not see an article over thirty pages, much less forty, as Stassen's is.

45. Stassen, *A Thicker Jesus*, 225.

46. Glen Stassen, "Transforming Initiatives of Just Peacemaking Based on the Triadic Structure of the Sermon on the Mount"; Lidija Novakovic, "Turning the Other Cheek to a Perpetrator: Denunciation or Upholding of Justice?"; Barbara Reid, "Matthean Perspectives on Bloodshed, Obedience, and Bearing Arms," Society of Biblical Literature Annual Meeting Seminar Papers and Websites, http://www.sbl-site.org/Meetings/AMseminarpapers.aspx (accessed 15 July 2013).

47. It seems unclear whether Stassen delivered his paper in the session on reading Matthew in wartime or the session on the Sermon. Novakovic and Reid both note that they are writing for the "wartime" session. Stassen notes that the leaders of the Matthew group had invited him to discuss the connections between the Sermon's fourteen triads and just peacemaking.

48. Swartley, *Covenant*, 65–66.

49. Dale C. Allison, Jr., *Studies in Matthew: Interpretation Past and Present* (Grand Rapids MI: Baker Academic, 2008) 183 n. 24, 193 n. 41. Stassen, *A Thicker Jesus*, 252 n. 51, quotes Allison as evidence that NT scholars affirm the Sermon's pattern of transforming

initiatives. Stassen, however, omits the last clause of Allison's comment, that the pattern does not work for all the Sermon.

50. Grant R. Osborne, *Matthew* (Zondervan Exegetical Commentary on the New Testament; Grand Rapids MI: Zondervan, 2010) 187 n. 6.

51. Craig L. Blomberg, "The Most Often Abused Verses in the Sermon on the Mount: And How to Treat Them Right," *SWJT* 46 (2004): 10 n. 44.

52. R. T. France, *The Gospel of Matthew* (New International Commentary on the New Testament; Grand Rapids MI: Eerdmans, 2007) 278 n. 15; 279 n. 4.

53. James R. Wicker, "Preaching through the Sermon on the Mount," *Southwestern Journal of Theology* 46 (2004): 73–89; also in this issue, J. Daryl Charles, "Do Not Suppose that I Have Come": The Ethic of the Sermon on the Mount Reconsidered," *Southwestern Journal of Theology* 46 (2004): 47–70, surprisingly makes no reference at all to Stassen's work. Other articles that do not refer to Stassen include Francois P. Viljoen, "Jesus' Teaching on the Torah in the Sermon on the Mount," *Neotestamentica* 40 (2006): 135–55; Elian Cuvillier, "Torah Observance and Radicalization in the First Gospel: Matthew and First-century Judaism: A Contribution to the Debate," *New Testament Studies* 55 (2009): 144–59; Johan Carl Thom, "Justice in the Sermon on the Mount: An Aristotelian Reading," *Novum Testamentum* 51 (2009): 314–38.

54. Charles L Quarles, *Sermon on the Mount: Restoring Christ's Message to the Modern Church* (Nashville: B&H Academic, 2011) 117 n. 94, referring to Stassen and Gushee, *Kingdom Ethics*, 295–98. Two books on the Sermon that do not refer to Stassen are Charles H. Talbert, *Reading the Sermon on the Mount: Character and Moral Decision-Making in Matthew 5–7* (Grand Rapids MI: Baker Academic, 2004), and Bonnie B. Thurston, *Religious Vows, the Sermon on the Mount, and Christian Living* (Collegeville MN: Liturgical, 2006).

55. John Nolland, *The Gospel of Matthew: A Commentary on the Greek Text* (New International Greek Testament Commentary; Grand Rapids MI: Eerdmans, 2005) xcii, 189. Recent commentaries on Matthew that do not refer to Stassen include Russell Pregeant, *Matthew* (Chalice Commentaries for Today; St. Louis: Chalice, 2004); Barbara E. Reid, *The Gospel According to Matthew* (New Collegeville Bible Commentary: New Testament; Collegeville MN: Liturgical, 2005); David L. Turner, *Matthew Baker Exegetical Commentary on the New Testament* (Grand Rapids MI: Baker Academic, 2008); Charles H. Talbert, *Matthew* (Paideia: Commentaries on the New Testament; Grand Rapids MI: Baker Academic, 2010); Craig A. Evans, *Matthew* (New Cambridge Bible Commentary; New York: Cambridge University Press, 2012).

56. John Y. H. Yieh, review of *Living the Sermon on the Mount* by Glen H. Stassen, *Interpretation* 62 (2008): 108–109. This is Allison's point. See above, 14.

57. Yieh, review, 109.

58. Glen Stassen, "Holistic Hermeneutical Method for Just Peacemaking Practices," Just Peacemaking Initiative, http://justpeacemaking.org/the-holistic-hermeneutical-method (accessed 15 July 2013).

59. Michael Willett Newheart, "A Hermeneutic of Human Dignity: The Future of Psychological Biblical Interpretation?" in *Psychological Hermeneutics for Biblical Themes and Texts; New Directions in Biblical Studies: A Festschrift in Honor of Wayne G. Rollins* (ed. J. Harold Ellens; New York: T&T Clark, 2012) 121–39. It can also be found at http://howard.academia.edu/MichaelNewheart/Papers/1086396/A_Hermeneutic_of_Human_Dignity_The_Future_of_Psychological_Biblical_Interpretation.

60. Juliana Holm, e-mail communication, 29 September 2011.

61. Stassen, *Thicker*, 221.

62. Newheart, "Hermeneutic," 136.

63. Although I am now a member of the Religious Society of Friends (Quakers), I still maintain my ordination as a Baptist minister at the request of the D.C. Baptist Convention. My participation in World Peacemakers with Stassen helped pave the way for me to join this "peace church."

64. I hesitate to use the adjective "biblical" because it has been co-opted by folks who use the term to validate their own (usually extremely conservative, though occasionally, but rarely, liberal) views, so that we hear much these days of the "biblical view of marriage," which means "one man, one woman," which means that the state should not legislate same-sex marriage. There is even a "Biblical Marriage" website, http://abiblicalmarriage.com. For a critique of the idea of "biblical marriage," see the article by one of Stassen's former students, Miguel de la Torre, "Biblical Marriage Unmasked," *The Huffington Post*, http://www.abp-news.com/opinion/commentaries/item/8209-%E2%80%98biblical%E2%80%99-marriage-unmasked#.UekjUVN07eY (accessed 19 July 2013).

65. The label "Jesus activism," however, gets into the whole question about WWJD? ("What Would Jesus Do?"). Rita Nakashma Brock, *Journeys by Heart* (New York: Crossroad, 1988) xiv, writes, "Such a question leads the focus of feeling and action away from self-awareness, . . . because we are not compelled to ask, 'How do I feel right now, how are others feeling, and what can I do to lessen all our pain and suffering in this context?'"

66. I was pleased to see Stassen's extended treatment of Mark in *A Thicker Jesus* (pp. 153–63), where he gives attention to Jesus' "power," such as healing a leper and a woman with a hemorrhage and raising a girl from the dead. He writes, "All these encounters made Jesus ritually unclean" (p. 159). Amy-Jill Levine, *The Misunderstood Jew* (San Francisco: HarperOne, 2006) 172–77, refutes this popular interpretation that Stassen has adopted. She contends that Jesus broke no laws in touching a corpse or a hemorrhaging woman (or allowing her to touch him).

67. Stassen, *Thicker*, 16.

68. Newheart, "Hermeneutic," 131.

69. Stassen, *Thicker*, 31–34.

70. Newheart, "Hermeneutic," 122, 132. Clarence Jordan earned a doctorate in New Testament at The Southern Baptist Theological Seminary in 1939 before going back to Georgia to form an interracial farming experiment and translate the New Testament. I hold that same degree from the same institution, and Stassen and I were together there.

71. Stassen, *A Thicker Jesus*, 84.

72. Newheart, "Hermeneutic," 130, also see p. 128.

73. Stassen, *A Thicker Jesus*, x.

74. Newheart, "Hermeneutic," 129–31.

75. Stassen, *A Thicker Jesus*, 200.

76. Newheart, "Hermeneutic," 135–36.

77. Ibid., ix.

78. Ibid., 133.

79. Ibid.

80. Ibid.

81. See Carolyn Osiek, "When You Pray . . . ," *Catholic Biblical Quarterly* 71 (2009): 737.

82. Newheart, "Hermeneutic," 130–31.

83. Ibid., 131.

84. Stassen, *A Thicker Jesus*, 204.

85. Ibid, 188.

86. Four times Stassen says 5:38-43 (pp. 188, 205) and once 5:38-48 (p. 206). The "turn the other cheek" section is 5:38-42, and "love your enemies" 5:43-48. I assume that Stassen is referring to both sections in all these references.

Chapter 3

And Who Is My Niebuhr?
Resonances of Reinhold Niebuhr and H. Richard Niebuhr in the Thought of Glen Stassen

DAVID FILLINGIM

The question "And who is my neighbor?" (Luke 10:29) plays a prominent role in the formation of Glen Stassen's approach to Christian ethics because it is the question that prompts Jesus' telling of the parable of the compassionate Samaritan—the parable from which Stassen develops his understanding of "delivering love," the core imperative in Christian ethics.[1] The centrality of the neighbor question in Stassen's ethics lends itself to a nice pun whereby we can ask, "And who is my Niebuhr?" To say that Stassen's thought is influenced by the thought of the Niebuhr brothers, Reinhold and H. Richard, is merely to state the obvious. The Niebuhrs cast a long shadow over American theology in the middle of the twentieth century, influencing every theologian and/or Christian ethicist in Stassen's generation. But some consideration of how the thought of the Niebuhr brothers resonates in the thought of Glen Stassen is called for. One of the PhD seminars Stassen taught regularly at The Southern Baptist Theological Seminary was "The Christian Social Ethics of Reinhold and H. Richard Niebuhr." Stassen co-authored a book engaging H. Richard Niebuhr's *Christ and Culture*.[2] And Reinhold Niebuhr stands as the preeminent representative of the dichotomy between love and justice that Stassen seeks to overcome with his concept of delivering love. Reinhold Niebuhr defines love as self-sacrifice and declares it an impossible ideal, leaving justice rather than love to stand as the regulative principle by which ethical calculations are to be made, while Stassen aims for the integration of love and justice.

In this essay I examine how the thought of the Niebuhrs resonates in Stassen's ethics in three areas: the relationship between the descriptive and the prescriptive in Christian ethics, the tension between realism and idealism in Christian ethics, and the importance of concrete biblical norms in Christian ethics. I will argue that although Stassen's ethics engages H. Richard Niebuhr's ethics more directly, it embodies Reinhold Niebuhr's ethics more accurately—an irony that Reinhold would appreciate and that Glen, I hope, will at least find amusing.

The Descriptive and the Prescriptive in Christian Ethics

H. Richard Niebuhr's best-known work, *Christ and Culture*, is a description of five typical Christian approaches to the question of how Christian faith relates to secular culture. In *Christ and Culture*, Niebuhr asserts his intention to present an objective typology—merely "to define typical partial answers that recur so often in different eras and societies that they seem to be less the product of historical conditioning than of the nature of the problem itself and the meaning of its terms"[3]—rather than to advocate a single answer to the question of the relationship between Christ and culture. The resulting typology, then, should be descriptive rather than prescriptive. Yet prescriptive advocacy is evident even in the names given to the five types. "Transforming" culture is self-evidently preferable to being "of" or "against" it, and surely preferable to being "above" it or "in paradox" with it as well. Criticism of Niebuhr's use of an ostensibly objective typology to achieve an underhanded prescriptive advocacy echoes throughout the relevant literature.[4]

Stassen is apparently unfazed by Niebuhr's fainthearted if disingenuous avowal of objectivity; he takes for granted that transformation is the normative approach and seeks to develop a theory of transformation adequate for contemporary Christian ethics, drawing on H. Richard Niebuhr's thought along with other sources. Stassen's willingness to overlook H. Richard Niebuhr's problematic blending of the descriptive and prescriptive is ironic because a similar blending occurs in reverse in Stassen's work. In his essay, "Critical Variables in Christian Social Ethics,"[5] Stassen introduces a schema for discussing the various elements, or "variables," of a theory of Christian social ethics, and he repeats and revises the schema in later works. The variables are divided into four broad categories: perception, reasoning, loyalties, and convictions. The four broad categories of variables are laid out in a chart with arrows indicating the flow of ideas among the four boxes and between the boxes and the world in which ethics is applied and lived.[6]

The Four Dimensions of Character

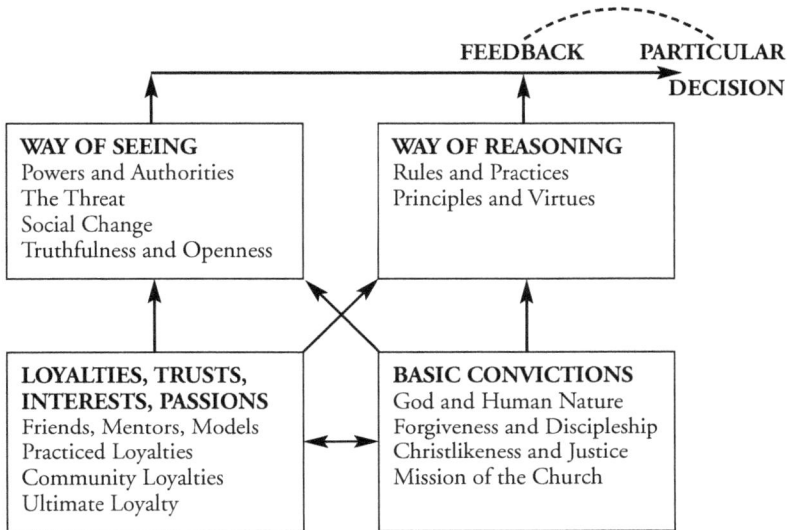

FEEDBACK   PARTICULAR
DECISION

WAY OF SEEING
Powers and Authorities
The Threat
Social Change
Truthfulness and Openness

WAY OF REASONING
Rules and Practices
Principles and Virtues

**LOYALTIES, TRUSTS,
INTERESTS, PASSIONS**
Friends, Mentors, Models
Practiced Loyalties
Community Loyalties
Ultimate Loyalty

BASIC CONVICTIONS
God and Human Nature
Forgiveness and Discipleship
Christlikeness and Justice
Mission of the Church

Stassen attempts to apply his variables model prescriptively by indicating which orientation with respect to each of the variables is most consistent with the model's overall dynamic of "continuous repentance" (or "continuous conversion"[7]). Ultimately, however, the variables schema proves more useful as a descriptive heuristic than a prescriptive tool. Looking at the boxes in the chart, one can see that any theory of Christian ethics—or even any pre-critical, non-theoretical approach to Christian ethics—can be analyzed and classified according to the variables listed simply by describing how the perspective under consideration expresses each of the variables in the chart.

For example, consider Jerry Falwell's approach to Christian ethics in his leadership of the Moral Majority.[8] Beginning in the "Perception" box in the chart on p. 47, we would note first that Falwell's activism is indeed a response to a perceived threat. The degree of the threat is very grave. The nature of the threat is primarily that God might remove "his" blessing from America because of the nation's tolerance of the sins of abortion and homosexuality. The progressive moral decline of America threatens the special place the nation is to play in God's plan for redeeming all the nations. The Bible is posited as the only fully reliable source of authority for ethics (as interpreted by fundamentalist Christianity, though Falwell would perhaps be reluctant to admit that his beliefs were an interpretation rather than the plain sense of Scripture). On some issues, appeals to natural law can also be seen in Falwell's rhetoric. Falwell's move into political activism suggests that he viewed the state as the main agent of social change and that governmental processes such as legislation and judicial decisions upholding traditional values are the primary means of social change.[9] Alliances with other (i.e., non-evangelical) groups concerned about conservative values are also effective.

In the "Reasoning" box, Falwell and his constituents can be seen as reasoning primarily at the rules level and relying on absolutist rules as their main type of moral norm, but some effort to translate biblical rules into broader principles—such as the "sanctity of life" or "right to life," or the "sanctity of marriage"—is also present.

In the "Loyalties" box, Falwell's advocacy is largely altruistic and reflects transgenerational loyalty: the Moral Majority's aim not to promote their own self-interest but to preserve what they see as America's true heritage for future generations. Loyalty is to America as a nation blessed by God, and to the God whose continued blessing is seen as being contingent upon the nation's continued faithfulness (a covenantal loyalty, in other words).

In the "Convictions" box, Falwell's views are closely aligned with evangelical theology. God is seen as merciful in providing salvation and other blessings and in tolerating America's shortcomings up to the present, but the current situation is seen as potentially incurring the judgment of God, who can only tolerate sin for so long. Human nature is seen as inherently sinful (the Calvinist notion of total depravity is relevant); yet positive social action based on biblical values remains part of human potential. Traditional evangelical emphases on conversion over discipleship and doctrine over praxis are retained to some extent, but the need for sustained action in the form of voting and political pressure is also asserted. The mission of the church is seen as both saving souls and influencing the nation to adhere to principles of righteousness.

In fact, Stassen's variables schema is easily adapted for the analysis of any approach to ethics—Christian or not, theoretical or not, explicit or implicit. Below is a version of Stassen's chart that I have adapted for use in analyzing the ethical messages implicit in popular culture texts.

Perception	Reasoning Mode/Method

Threat: nature, degree, linkage
 	
Authority:
locus: central vs. diffused
legitimacy
limits
 	
Social Change (if applicable):
agent: Who?
means: How?
allies: cooperation vs. suspicion
timing: incremental vs. decisive
 	
Information Integrity:
openness vs. closedness
truthfulness vs. manipulativeness
	Level:
	gut reaction
	rules orientation
	principled reasoning
	basic conviction level
	
	Types of Rules:
	legalist/absolutist vs.
	    situationalist/contextual
	
	Types of Principles:
	Theological (consequentialist) vs.
	    Deontological (absolutist)

Loyalties/Interests/Passions	**Grounding**
Group loyalties: family, church, town, state, nation, race/ethnicity, etc. (may be conscious or unconscious) Practiced loyalties: commitments, self- interest Ultimate loyalty: transcendent value, meaning, purpose?	Relativist or absolutist? God, nature, society, or none of the above? Human Nature: optimism vs. pessimism (or sin vs. potential) virtues and vices Purpose of life: individual vs. community future vs. present

Using this chart to analyze the ethical messages in the television series *Xena: Warrior Princess*,[10] we note first that Xena is always on threat alert, but that the threat is amorphous and different in every episode. Xena's primary source of moral authority is her own intuition, awakened by a moral conversion experience she had in the first episode of the series, and informed by her sympathies toward those who are suffering. Xena generally is not engaged in a campaign for social change; entrenched powers remain entrenched and are resisted only in piecemeal fashion. But Xena does show a tendency to encourage people to abandon their dependence on gods and unjust rulers and act independently. Xena trusts the integrity of information only if she has verified it through her own investigation, or if it comes from a trusted friend. Her level of moral reasoning is basically the gut level, relying on her moral intuition. Rules and principles, to the extent that they are used, are always situational; the end of resolving this week's crisis or helping this week's victim justifies any means. Xena is loyal to her sidekick Gabrielle, to her family, to certain friends, and to those who need her help. Her only practiced commitment and ultimate loyalty is to use her skills to right wrongs and redeem herself from the sins of her past. The ultimate grounding of Xena's moral convictions is her sympathy toward those who are suffering at the hands of cruel and capricious powers, whether those powers be gods or warlords. She is pessimistic about human nature and tentative about ascribing any ultimate purpose or meaning to life.

Both Stassen and H. Richard Niebuhr, then, develop schemes for blending the descriptive and the prescriptive in Christian ethics. Niebuhr's implicit prescriptiveness, despite his critics' complaints, should probably be seen more as a product of the style of academic writing deemed appropriate in mid-twentieth-century theology than as a disingenuous effort to manipulate readers. After all, his own preferences are barely hidden; the transformationist type has the most appealing label and is the only type for which no weaknesses are listed alongside the strengths. Stassen's effort to be explicitly prescriptive when developing a basically descriptive framework is a product of both intellectual honesty and Stassen's constructive method. In terms of intellectual honesty, the effort to be upfront about one's prescriptive views reflects the awareness that there is no objectivity—that one always reasons from one's own perspective. Moreover, Stassen's constructive method in Christian ethics is to draw from many sources and seek places where a confluence between diverse sources supports and informs one's core convictions and/or principles.

Idealism and Realism in Christian Ethics

Reinhold Niebuhr, as is well known, is the progenitor of a school of thought known as "Christian Realism." He saw most approaches to Christian ethics—especially the Christian pacifism he himself had once embraced—as idealistic and thus irresponsible. Jesus' command to love the neighbor, which Reinhold Niebuhr interpreted as a command to love self-sacrificially, is an impossible ideal—an option available only to "mothers, mystics, and martyrs."[11] Persons who wish to deal with the ongoing realities of life in this world, especially if they intend to venture into the realms of politics and social structures addressed by Christian social ethics, need more realistic norms, such as justice. Niebuhr's realism further asserts that collective entities such as nations (or churches) are even less able to act morally than individuals, thus heightening the need to abandon ideals such as sacrificial love in favor of more concrete and practical norms such as justice. Appeals to ideals such as love may have some direct relevance in close interpersonal relationships like family or friendship, but social ethics requires more realistic norms. Social change, to the extent that it is possible, can occur through one of two means. Either it will result from faltering and incremental progress, or, more often, it will require coercive use of force in a battle of entrenched powers.

Among those whom Reinhold Niebuhr accused of unrealistic idealism was his brother, H. Richard. In a series of articles in 1932 in *The Christian Century*, the Niebuhr brothers debated whether and how the United States should respond to Japan's invasion of Manchuria.[12] In the opening salvo in what he would eventually label a "fraternal war between my brother and me,"[13] H. Richard Niebuhr suggests that the United States lacks moral standing to act because of its own imperialist sins and calls American Christians to "divorc[e] themselves from the program of nationalism and capitalism, [and] unite in a higher loyalty which transcends national and class lines of division."[14] Reinhold views such a stance as just the kind of irresponsible idealism that his own realism is intended to counter. As a persecuted sect on the fringes of first-century society, Jesus and the first Christians could adopt an unrealistic and apocalyptic moral idealism because they had no hope of influencing political and socioeconomic forces. But in the modern world, where Christians reside close to (and sometimes in) the seats of political and economic power, such a stance represents a shirking of responsibility, for "as long as the world of man remains a place where nature and God, the real and the ideal, meet, human progress will depend upon the judicious use of the forces of nature in the service of the ideal."[15]

In essence, Reinhold accuses his brother of adopting the stance that H. Richard Niebuhr would later describe in *Christ and Culture* as the "Christ against culture" type—the sectarian position of viewing the alternative community of the church as the sole location where the moral teachings of Christ can be implemented. The wider society, in this view, operates according to lesser values and cannot be an arena for the implementation of Christian norms. The "Christ against culture" type, then, is seen as escapist. In turn, H. Richard Niebuhr accuses Reinhold of embodying what *Christ and Culture* will depict as the dualist "Christ and culture in paradox" type, in which distinctively Christian norms are practiced only within the intimate confines of church or family but are displaced in the public realm by the allegedly more realistic values of the political and economic status quo. If Christian ethics is to be in any meaningful way "Christian," H. Richard Niebuhr suggests, then distinctively Christian ideals must be retained. Reinhold's surrender of Christian distinctiveness for the sake of secular relevance is the real "irresponsible religion"—one that "thinks of itself as responsible to society for God rather than to God for society": "Instead of, 'What doth the Lord require?' the question in the mind of the church which has fallen into this temptation is, 'What does the nation or the civilization require?'"[16]

The Niebuhr brothers' views on the philosophy of history and on the role of Christian norms in social ethics are actually not as far apart as this debate and most subsequent characterizations of their respective theologies would suggest. Both emphasize a tension between the demands of Christian ethics and the realities of human social existence that results in a sense of tragedy. Both advocate an ethic of continuing responsibility to attend to the dynamic tension between the way things are and the way things ought to be. H. Richard Niebuhr traces the ways that Christian ideals such as "radical monotheism" and the kingdom of God have already shaped modern society and helped to create the social conditions in which God is acting in all actions upon the believer and in which the believer must discern the fitting response to God's actions in the social and historical circumstances in which we find ourselves. Reinhold Niebuhr sees the ideal of sacrificial love not as completely irrelevant to social ethics, but as continually standing in judgment over our current provisional arrangements of justice and calling us always to a more perfect justice.

This continual tension between the actual and the possible in Christian social ethics is seen also in Glen Stassen's call for continuing repentance. A sort of hermeneutical circle emerges in which each action becomes part of the ongoing context for continued ethical reflection and action. To the extent that the Niebuhr brothers represent opposite poles on the realism/ idealism continuum, Stassen seeks to preserve both. Stassen's insistence on concrete biblical norms, to be discussed below, echoes H. Richard Niebuhr's insistence that Christian distinctiveness not be lost in the quest for sociopolitical relevance. But Stassen also insists on a realist understanding of Christian ethics. The ethical teachings of Jesus, for example, are not to be understood—as Reinhold Niebuhr suggests—as unrealistic ideals whose relevance is limited to the needs of a first-century apocalyptic sectarian movement, but as realistic teachings that believers in all generations are called to practice.[17] Through careful exegesis of the Sermon on the Mount,[18] Stassen discerns that Jesus teaches the practice of "transforming initiatives"— surprising and creative responses to difficult situations that can transform the situation from one of gridlocked conflict to one of renewed possibility. Such initiatives would have been useful to Jesus' original listeners for extricating themselves from situations of hopeless oppression caused by the injustices and inequalities of the debt system and of imperial rule without resorting to violence. Transforming initiatives also work in other social ethics contexts, such as nuclear disarmament negotiations among modern nations and the movement to end communism in Eastern Europe.[19]

Stassen's close attention to biblical texts ensures that the Christian distinctiveness of Christian social ethics is retained. Yet his discovery there of norms and practices such as transforming initiatives conforms to Reinhold Niebuhr's concern that Christian social ethics be infused with realism. Transforming initiatives represent not only a practical means of social change whose effectiveness is empirically verifiable across a wide range of social contexts but also a third way between Reinhold Niebuhr's limited options of faltering incrementalism and coercive use of force. Moreover, Stassen's insistence on the need for continuous repentance is consistent with Reinhold Niebuhr's realist rediscovery of the omnipresent relevance of human sinfulness.

Concrete Biblical Norms in Christian Ethics

Stassen's ethical methodology is centered on concrete biblical norms. Throughout his writing, detailed exegesis of biblical texts is found. Often, Stassen takes great pains to show links between the ethical teachings of different biblical texts, such as the link between the Sermon of the Mount and the book of Romans[20] or the similarities between Jesus' and Isaiah's vision of the reign of God.[21] Stassen's Anabaptist-inspired hermeneutical method is to take the life and teaching of Jesus, especially the Sermon on the Mount, as a lens through which to read Scripture as a whole. He frequently surveys the Bible to find reiterations of the teachings of Jesus with the goal of compiling a manageable but adequately comprehensive list of the central biblical norms and practices of Christian ethics.[22]

The Niebuhr brothers, on the other hand, are seldom accused of emphasizing the importance of concrete biblical norms for Christian social ethics. Both are cited by John Howard Yoder as paradigmatic of the theological effort to assert the ethical irrelevance of the teachings of Jesus.[23] Reinhold Niebuhr draws on Scripture for broad ethical themes such as love or justice, but he infuses them with concrete meaning primarily through a combination of philosophical analysis and phenomenology of modern experience rather than detailed exegesis. Though Stassen argues that H. Richard Niebuhr asserted the importance of concrete biblical and christological norms, he is alone among Niebuhr interpreters in making such a claim. Most interpreters criticize Niebuhr's Christology as too vague,[24] and William Joseph Werpehowski specifically criticizes Niebuhr's "apparent rejection of Christocentric concreteness."[25] The two best-known trajectories of H. Richard Niebuhr's thought in Christian ethics are James Gustafson's post-Christian theocentric ethics, in which Scripture plays little or no role, and Stanley Hauerwas's vaguely biblical narrative-shaped hypothetical Christian community. Even Stassen has to add the actual concrete biblical norms from other sources to his reconstruction of Niebuhr's model.[26]

For H. Richard Niebuhr, the Bible is primarily a source of symbols and "dramas" (what would later be known as narratives) that shape Christians' perceptions of the world and our discernment of God's action in it. Symbols such as the cross also become models for Christian action, but are more suggestive than concretely prescriptive. The specific content of cruciform response to any situation is known only through discernment of God's action within the situation and reflection on how to respond to the situation by responding to God.[27] What appears to happen here is that H. Richard Niebuhr's existentialism trumps his concern for Christian distinctiveness: prescribing specific norms or even dispositions in advance would negate the existentialist demand for authentic discernment of the fitting response in the situation into which one is thrown.

Reinhold Niebuhr's existentialism, on the other hand, is somewhat mitigated by his realism. His theory of justice offers concrete norms in the form of dynamically interrelated "regulative principles" such as equality, freedom, and need.[28] Such norms are only vaguely biblical and are not as concrete as the sets of biblical norms and practices that Stassen develops, but they are at least as biblical as and more concrete than any specific norms offered by H. Richard Niebuhr. Just as Reinhold Niebuhr's development of concrete regulative principles of justice is prompted by his realism, Stassen's focus on concrete biblical norms is driven in part by his own concern for realism. Unlike Hauerwas and Yoder, who assert that the biblical practices and virtues they advocate are obligatory despite their ineffectiveness in influencing or "transforming" society, Stassen argues that the concrete biblical practices he advocates are indeed effective in creating positive social change and that their effectiveness has been demonstrated empirically. Partly by default, then, and partly out of concern for effectiveness, Stassen's focus on concrete biblical norms is closer to Reinhold Niebuhr than to H. Richard, despite Stassen's explicit effort to link concrete biblical norms to H. Richard Niebuhr's thought.

Conclusion

Like every theologian who came of age in the middle of the twentieth century, Glen Stassen has been influenced by the thought of the Niebuhr brothers. It would be misleading to imply, however, that the Niebuhrs were the most important influences. Among theologians and ethicists, Bonhoeffer, Yoder, Daniel Day Williams, and Henlee Barnette are more central in Stassen's early development, while his contemporaries Larry Rasmussen and James William McClendon are more frequently cited in his later work— and of course the thought of Jesus of Nazareth and the apostle Paul are more central still. His father, Harold Stassen, probably affected Glen's orientation toward political and ethical realism more than Reinhold Niebuhr did. As a thinker whose intellectual generosity matches his generosity of spirit, Stassen has continued to allow his thought to grow and acquire new influences throughout his career. He absorbs and incorporates new developments in theology, biblical studies, and the social sciences, and he regularly seeks collaboration with colleagues, often respecting their views and methodologies to a fault. Glen Stassen will leave no stone unturned in his ongoing project of constructing an approach to Christian discipleship that is biblically normative, accessible, and adequate to address the ethical challenges facing Christians in the twenty-first century.

NOTES

1. See Glen H. Stassen and David P. Gushee, *Kingdom Ethics: Following Christ in Contemporary Society* (Downers Grove IL: InterVarsity, 2003) 333–42.

2. Glen Stassen, Diana M. Yeager, and John Howard Yoder, *Authentic Transformation: A New Vision of Christ and Culture* (Nashville: Abingdon, 1995).

3. H. Richard Niebuhr, *Christ and Culture* (New York: Harper & Row, 1951) 40.

4. See Yoder, "How H. Richard Niebuhr Reasoned: A Critique of *Christ and Culture*," in *Authentic Transformation*, 41–43; Stanley Hauerwas and William H. Willimon, *Resident Aliens* (Nashville: Abingdon, 1989) 39–42; and Peter R. Gathje, "A Contested Classic: Critics Ask: Whose Christ? Which Culture?" *Christian Century* 119/13 (19–26 June 2002): 28–32.

5. In Paul D. Simmons, ed., *Issues in Christian Ethics* (Nashville: Broadman, 1980) 57–76.

6. Chart reprinted with permission from authors, Stassen and Gushee, *Kingdom Ethics*, 59.

7. Glen Stassen, "A Computer-Ethical Call to Continuous Conversion," *Review & Expositor* 87 (Spring 1990): 195–211.

8. My brief "analysis" here is intended only as an introductory sketch or outline of how one might proceed in applying Stassen's model. Any thorough analysis of Falwell's ethics would require an entire monograph.

9. The move by Falwell and other leaders into more overt political activism in 1980 represents a move beyond what had been the main evangelical view, represented for example by Billy Graham, that individual conversion was the main force behind social change. Falwell, of course, continued to promote individual conversion, but he clearly came to see the apparatus of the state as a necessary ingredient in the preservation of traditional values.

10. See David Fillingim, "By the Gods—or Not: Religious Plurality in *Xena Warrior Princess," Journal of Religion and Popular Culture* 21/3 (Fall 2009), http://www.usask.ca/relst/jrpc/articles21(3).html.

11. Reinhold Niebuhr, "Some Things I Have Learned," *The Saturday Review* 48 (6 November 1965): 22.

12. H. Richard Niebuhr, "The Grace of Doing Nothing," *Christian Century* 49 (23 March 1932): 378–80; H. R. Niebuhr, "A Communication: The Only Way into the Kingdom of God," *Christian Century* 49 (6 April 1932): 447; and Reinhold Niebuhr, "Must We Do Nothing?" *Christian Century* 49 (30 March 1932): 415–17. For an analysis of the debate, see John D. Barbour, "Niebuhr Versus Niebuhr: The Tragic Nature of History," *Christian Century* 101 (21 November 1984):1096–99.

13. H. Richard Niebuhr, "A Communication," 447.

14. H. Richard Niebuhr, "The Grace of Doing Nothing," 379.

15. Reinhold Niebuhr, "Must We Do Nothing?" 416.

16. H. Richard Niebuhr, "The Responsibility of the Church for Society," in *The Gospel, the World and the Church* (ed. Kenneth Scott Latourette; New York: Harper Brothers, 1946), reprinted at www.religion-online.org.

17. *Kingdom Ethics*, 125–45; Glen H. Stassen, *Just Peacemaking: Transforming Initiatives for Justice and Peace* (Louisville: Westminster John Knox, 1992) 33–52.

18. Ibid. See also Glen H. Stassen, "The Fourteen Triads of the Sermon on the Mount (Matthew 5:21–7:12)," *Journal of Biblical Literature* 122/2 (Summer 2003): 267–308.

19. Stassen, *Just Peacemaking: Transforming Initiatives*, 13–31, 114–36.

20. See Stassen, *Journey into Peacemaking* (Nashville: Brotherhood Commission of the SBC, 1987) and *Just Peacemaking: Transforming Initiatives*, 53–88.

21. *Kingdom Ethics*, 19–31.

22. See especially "Concrete Christological Norms for Transformation," in *Authentic Transformation*, 162–70; also see *Kingdom Ethics*, 19–31 and "The Ethical Demands of Sound Theology," *Church Training* (April 1981): 24–25.

23. John Howard Yoder, *The Politics of Jesus* (Grand Rapids MI: Eerdmans, 1972) 16–18.

24. See for example Gathje, "A Contested Classic."

25. William Werpehowski, "Practical Wisdom and the Integrity of the Christian Life," *Journal of the Society of Christian Ethics* 27/2 (Fall/Winter 2007): 71.

26. Stassen, "Concrete Christological Norms for Transformation," in *Authentic Transformation*, 162–70.

27. Richard B. Miller, "H. Richard Niebuhr's War Articles: A Transvaluation of Value," *The Journal of Religion* 68/2 (April 1988): 247, 251–53.

28. For a brief summary of Reinhold Niebuhr's theory of justice, see my dissertation, *A Christian Ethical Analysis of the Family as a System of Power, Justice, and Love* (Louisville: The Southern Baptist Theological Seminary, 1996) 112–16. For a more accessible account, see Karen Lebacqz, *Six Theories of Justice* (Minneapolis: Augsburg, 1986) 83–99, or Merle Longwood, "Niebuhr and a Theory of Justice," *Dialog* 14 (1975): 253–62.

Chapter 4

The Church as Embodiment of Transformative Trinitarian Faith

Joon-Sik Park

Introduction

Glen Harold Stassen is an ethicist for whom the reformation of the church has been central in his theological reflection and writing. In his preface to *A Thicker Jesus*, Stassen writes, "I deeply believe churches need renewal . . . and I write hoping for church renewal."[1] Examining a social theory model for Christian ethics in a foundational essay, Stassen introduces four dimensions of ethical reasoning based on the work of Ralph Potter: mode of moral reasoning, perception of data, loyalties and interests, and ground-of-meaning beliefs. Each dimension embraces crucial presuppositions or variables that shape the outcome of moral arguments. He identifies the concept of "the mission of the church" as one of the variables in the basic-conviction (ground-of-meaning beliefs) dimension that profoundly undergirds and affects one's moral reasoning.[2] The understanding of the mission of the church is to be grounded in the perception of what God is doing in the world through creation, the revelation in Jesus Christ, and the witness of the Holy Spirit. Stassen stresses that "how we understand the mission of the church shapes our ethics strongly."[3]

Stassen's understanding of the nature and purpose of the church is spread over most of his writings and often indirectly shared. Yet, without doubt, the church has been a constant companion in his theological journey as both the subject and the locus. In this essay I reflect on Stassen's ecclesiology and show how he has sympathetically, as well as critically, engaged and integrated the work of H. Richard Niebuhr in constructing his own view of the church as the authentic embodiment of transformative Trinitarian faith. I then interpret the mission of the embodied transforming church as Pastor, Apostle, and Pioneer.

Transformative Faith in the Sovereignty of God

One of the key themes that runs through most of Stassen's writings is "history as the laboratory" in which our faith and theology is tested and validated.[4] Stassen strongly argues that Christian ethics not avoid historical particularity: "The importance of historically situated, historically particular, concrete ethical norms disclosed in the particular history of Jesus Christ" should not be ignored.[5] A particular ethic is to be assessed in light of how it has worked out in history, that is, by its historical fruits. Undergirding this is the conviction that God is faithful in "working patiently and sometimes surprisingly through history to bring deliverance and community."[6] The biblical prophets best illustrate realistic historical testing—paying attention to actual historical data to discern the faithfulness or unfaithfulness of specific human actions in response to God's will for justice and peace.

Stassen's profound conviction of the need to test kinds of ethics by their faithfulness in the crucible of history can be traced to his own study of H. Richard Niebuhr. The work of Stassen, a sympathetic critic of Niebuhr, in a way reflects a serious, integrative attempt to complete the trajectory suggested and implied in Niebuhr's life and work. When Niebuhr is read in the context of his life's path and his lifetime reflections on the church and the world, it is possible "to notice obstacles that blocked him from proceeding as he intended, and to notice ways he developed for proceeding around those obstacles."[7] Reflecting on the actual life testimony of H. Richard Niebuhr, Stassen seeks to show that God's concrete self-disclosure in Christ is integral to Niebuhr's Trinitarian understanding of God's sovereignty.

In the 1920s, Niebuhr's frustration over the divided condition of the church in America led him to undertake a study that resulted in the publication of *The Social Sources of Denominationalism* (1929). Throughout the book, Niebuhr cast harsh criticisms upon denominationalism, considering it an ethical failure of the church. Denominationalism reflected compliance with divisive social forces—like economics, nationalism, and race—rather than theological differences. It was doubly evil, since its ethical failure was unacknowledged and gave in to false pride and hypocrisy.

Troubled and dismayed by the denominationalism in America, Niebuhr came to look for an ideal church that could "transcend the divisions of the world" and commit itself "not to the local interests and needs of classes, races, or nations but to the common interests of [hu]mankind and to the constitution of the unrealized kingdom of God."[8] Yet, in describing the ideal church, Niebuhr remained ambiguous and inexplicit. He failed to provide a pivotal clue that would connect his critical description of the condition of the church and his hope for the ideal church.

Discontented with the external sociological approach in his previous book, in *The Kingdom of God in America* (1937) Niebuhr turned to probe the internal dynamics of the church in those periods of history when the church had the vitality to transform culture. He began to perceive the church as a movement that has its center in faith in the kingdom of God. He also came to understand this movement, first, as "dialectic" with its direction both toward God and toward the world and, second, as "continuous" in the sense that "no one time, but only all times together, can set forth the full meaning of the movement toward the eternal and its created image."[9]

Niebuhr's thought shifted significantly in this period. Directing his attention more toward God the sovereign, he came to see the church more as an instrument for the service of God's purposes than as an end in itself, and to trust in the sovereignty of God as the center of faith. According to Stassen, three essential themes were included in Niebuhr's understanding of and faith in the sovereignty of God: "the universal rule of God" who is the source and judge of all life; "the independence of the living God" who is dynamic and personal, and thus cannot be possessed by or identified with any doctrine, church, ideology, or institution; and "the manifestation of God within our history" whose character is disclosed in fullest clarity in Jesus Christ. "Niebuhr's life-changing discovery was," writes Stassen, "that in each prophetic period, faith with authentic transformative power was marked by these three essential characteristics."[10]

Stassen believes that these three Trinitarian norms, centered on the sovereignty of God, provide us with "powerful grounding for authentic transformation." He points to the Christ-centeredness of those churches that have demonstrated a transformative, prophetic faith. They believed in and had a personal loyalty to God as revealed in Jesus Christ, "who teaches and embodies concrete [content and] criteria" for authentically transformative faith and discipleship.[11] Thus, Stassen strongly argues that an ethic that has the power to transform requires clear, concrete norms revealed in Christ:

> A vague stance for conversion without standing for anything specific is unlikely to have strong impact. More likely it will degenerate into cheap grace and accommodationism, a mere symbol without concrete biblical and theocentric content, or a cover for hidden, idolatrous assumptions.

In order to be authentically transformationist in our relation to culture, we need ethical norms, a prophetic plumbline, with which to measure the rightness or wrongness of different parts of culture.[12]

Niebuhr's ethics, however, has been criticized for being abstract and lacking concrete action-guiding moral principles and values. Critics question whether it provides Christians and communities of faith with specific and substantive guidance for discerning what God is doing and for forming their fitting responses to it. Stassen sees that there is a point to the charge: "There was another side to Niebuhr, a side that became dominant in the 1950s when Niebuhr rebelled against what he called Karl Barth's Christomonism. This other side made his ethics more abstract and relativist . . . ."[13] He identifies the issue, however, as the "temporary de-emphasis," during the 1950s, on "the Christological element, the knowable disclosure of the character of the sovereign in Jesus Christ."[14] Clearly inherent in Niebuhr's Trinitarian understanding of the sovereignty of God were elements that had promise for an authentically transformative faith.

Stassen argues that "Niebuhr's logic calls for concrete disclosure of God's character in Israel's history and in Jesus Christ as normative for Christian ethics."[15] Niebuhr understands God as the social, responsible self we meet in history—a God who is in faithful covenant relationship and who is known within the drama of historical interaction. God's self and the faithfulness of God's own character are revealed in God's own act of disclosure, which is not without recognizable pattern. For Niebuhr, the revelation in Jesus Christ is "the intelligible event" or "the revelatory moment," which brings unity and significance to all human history. The life and death of Jesus provides us with "a parable and an analogy" through which we can discern, though dimly, some meaning and pattern in our present situation full of confusion. His cross revealed "the great divine, dominating purpose" for history.[16] What is noteworthy is that, for Niebuhr, revelation embraces not only the presence of God but also the content of God's will.

Reflecting on Niebuhr's understanding of the sovereignty of God, Stassen is convinced that Niebuhr "had a basis for concrete, theocentric norms that can give backbone to the authentic transformation he sought."[17] He calls attention, in particular, to the third theme of Niebuhr's belief in the sovereignty of God—the concrete disclosure of God in the incarnate Jesus Christ, the Rosetta stone. Niebuhr's central affirmation of the sovereignty of God requires the disclosure of God's character and redemptive action in Christ within our real historical experience. Then, "the sovereignty of God needs to be defined in terms of the character of God as disclosed in Christ."[18]

Stassen himself is deeply committed to embodying the transformative power of the sovereignty of God in his ethics. He seeks to construct an ethics that is unreservedly Christocentric in the context of an integral Trinitarian understanding of God. He believes in the necessity of concrete norms in Christian ethics, grounded in the triune God whose sovereign grace is disclosed in history, and most clearly and fully in Jesus Christ. For Stassen, the embodiment of authentic transformation is to take shape concretely in the church, at the level of the local congregation.

The Church as Embodiment of Transformative Trinitarian Faith

Revisiting *Christ and Culture* (1951) on the occasion of the one hundredth anniversary of the birth of H. Richard Niebuhr, Stassen notes that "the farther the book goes, the less specific it gets about the ethics of the New Testament Jesus." It reflects early signs of "another side" of Niebuhr that would become dominant in the 1950s. Even in the chapter on "Christ the Transformer of Culture," Niebuhr remains general and abstract without referring to Jesus' concrete ethics and practices, although he clearly asserts the importance of the Lordship of Christ and of the norms revealed in Christ for transformative faith. The danger is that "readers may be convinced to call themselves transformationists without committing themselves to any specific ethics."[19] Niebuhr also neglects to suggest which ecclesiastical forms the conversionist type would require. His ecclesiology remains vague in terms of "how his ideal types would be embodied in actual congregations."[20] Consequently, Niebuhr's readers could go away thinking they are transformationists, yet with no interest in discovering a type of church that would transformatively engage culture. They then may succumb to dualism or accommodationism, sanctioning the status-quo norms of the society.

As Ernst Troeltsch clearly showed, however, the very structure of the church itself reflects its own understanding and interpretation of church teachings. The church communicates its own identity and beliefs more by its life and practices than by its official declarations and proclamations.[21] Hence, "disembodied ideas and official church teachings have little historical impact; first they need to be embodied in church practices, procedures, policies, and structures."[22] Stassen fully agrees with John Howard Yoder that "the primary social structure through which the gospel works to change other structures is that of the Christian community."[23]

If, as Niebuhr believed, history is the laboratory in which Christian faith is tested, then the church is to be historically situated and to embody authentic transformation in history. The crucial question to be asked, then, is what kind of church embodies authentic transformation in history. When authentic transformation remains "ideas without embodiment in the structures and practices of churches," it becomes "cheap transformation" or gnostic. Thus, Stassen explores "what shape, what form, what structure, what practices, what actual visible embodiment authentic transformation is likely to take in a local congregation."[24]

As described above, Stassen's understanding of authentic faith, based on that of Niebuhr, affirms and includes these three themes: God's rule over all; the independence of the dynamic, living God who cannot be possessed by our systems; and the concrete disclosure of God's character in Christ within human history and experience. Such transformative faith is to be formed and manifested in the community of faith that both nurtures and corrects the faith of its members. Stassen believes that these three dimensions of God's sovereignty correspond to Niebuhr's own understanding of the church's responsibility as Pastor, Apostle, and Pioneer.[25]

The Church as Pastor/Servant

For Stassen, the pastoral and servant role of the church originates in the sovereign rule of God over all:

> All are included in God's rule and God's love, all of society, including members of the church and outcasts, friends and enemies, the powerless and the powerful, the orphans and the powers and authorities. . . . The response for God's universal mercy is universal caring. The church's response to God's universal, gracious sovereignty is to be embodied in its structures and practices of caring. Through an act of faithful caring for all persons, the church participates in God's universal, gracious sovereignty.[26]

In Niebuhr's thought, the interrelations of God, church, and world are so intertwined that none can be loved without the others. He stresses that devotion to God should be expressed in service to and in the world. He is convinced that the church exists for witness and service and not for itself. Seeking to help the church keep a proper perspective on its relations to both God and the world, Niebuhr aptly distinguishes the church's being "responsible to" from its being "responsible for": "To be responsible is to be able and required to give account *to* someone *for* something. . . . The question about the one *to* whom account must be rendered is of equal importance with the question about the what *for* which one must answer."[27] The church responsibly responds to God when it becomes responsible for the world. On the one hand, since the church renders its account to God-in-Christ, the universal in the particular, its responsibility is universal. "All beings existent in the world are the creatures of this creator and the concern of this redeemer," and thus also the concern of the church. The church is to respond, on the other hand, to Christ-in-God, that is, "the redemptive principle in the world," whose content is always mercy; therefore, "the Church is not responsible for the judgment or destruction of any beings in the world of God, but for the conservation, reformation, redemption and transfiguration."[28]

Stassen calls attention, in particular, to both the inclusive and the preferential nature of God's caring. First, since God's rule is over all the world, everyone in it is the object of God's concern. As Niebuhr argued, faith should be radically monotheistic in that it is expressed in loyalty to the One's cause as well as trust in the One. God's cause is universal, and thus one with true faith should be loyal to all who exist or to whatever is. Since God's caring grace is radically inclusive, in response to such grace, the practice of the church is to be boundary-crossing; an intentional and genuine effort to cross significant racial, ethnic, and socioeconomic boundaries should be an essential and integral part of the church's mission. The church is to be the agent of service and liberation for all without distinction.

Second, as clearly revealed in Jesus' ministry, God is concerned for the lost, the outcast, and the needy. The pastoral mission of the church is carried out "*directly by itself giving aid, and indirectly by prodding other institutions to do justice to the needy.*"[29] Charity and advocacy are both needed for and essential to the church's faithful response to God's gracious care for the poor and marginalized.

At the synagogue in Nazareth, Jesus read from Isaiah 61: "The Spirit of the Lord is upon me, because he has anointed me to bring good news to the poor. He has sent me to proclaim release to the captives and recovery of sight to the blind, to let the oppressed go free, to proclaim the year of the Lord's favor" (Luke 4:18-19). Most New Testament scholars agree that in the brief phrase "to bring good news to the poor," we find Jesus' own statement of his primary mission. The question then is, "Who are the poor?" The phrase "the poor" should not be deprived of metaphorical meaning; it should not be limited either to the spiritually poor or to the economically poor. As Robert Tannehill points out, however, it first of all refers to those economically oppressed and poor.[30] Joel Green extends the meaning of "the poor" to embrace not simply the economically oppressed but also "the excluded, and disadvantaged," all who are on the margins of society and devalued by the community.[31]

One of the contributions of liberation theology is the rediscovery of "the poor" as a hermeneutical focus, which leads to a new understanding of the Christian gospel and to a legitimate attention to the priority of "the poor" in mission and evangelism. The emphasis of liberation theology on "the preferential option for the poor" does not imply that God is only interested in the salvation of the poor, but that "the poor are the first, though not the only ones, on which God's attention focuses and that, therefore, the church has no choice but to demonstrate solidarity with the poor."[32] It cannot be denied that Jesus particularly demonstrated his solidarity with the poor and made them the principal recipients of the good news.

The rediscovery of the poor in theology has had significant implications for the mission of the church as pastor/servant. Considering solidarity with the poor "a central and crucial priority in Christian mission," David Bosch argues that "once we recognize the identification of Jesus with the poor, we cannot any longer consider our own relation to the poor as a social ethics question; it is a gospel question."[33] When the church seeks to be faithful to its pastoral and servant role, it should pay careful attention to the kinds of people with whom Jesus associated throughout his ministry. When the church fails to be on the side of the poor and marginalized and remains silent in the face of injustices, it loses the credibility of the gospel it preaches and inevitably becomes culturally captive. Orlando Costas thus demands that mission and evangelism "be undertaken from below . . . from the depth of human suffering, where we find both sinners and victims of sin."[34] As Stassen well puts it, "To respond to the love of God revealed in Christ means to respond to need by entering into the situation and participating in the way of deliverance."[35]

The Church as Apostle/Prophet

The church is above all, according to Niebuhr, "by nature and commitment an apostolic community which exists for the sake of announcing the Gospel to all nations and of making them disciples of Christ."[36] The apostolic/prophetic mission of the church is "the logical implication of the historic-revelation dimension of the sovereignty of God—the presently experienced shape of God's redemptive action in Christ, disclosing the normative pattern of God's faithfulness."[37]

In sharing the gospel, the church proclaims and teaches faith, repentance, and discipleship "not only as a doctrine, but as a present experience." The proclamation of the church is a call for "commitment to the particular way of God incarnated in Jesus." Stassen writes, "It calls for fundamental *metanoia*—i.e., transformation of mind, repentance, conversion, and commitment. It wants people to experience God's grace; God's faithful, merciful, redemptive action in Christ; love for enemies; justice for all persons; faith; repentance; and discipleship."[38]

One of the most comprehensive and integral definitions of evangelism, which would well correspond to Stassen's understanding of the church's responsibility as apostle/prophet, comes from David Bosch. Bosch understands evangelism as

> that dimension and activity of the church's mission which, by word and deed and in the light of particular conditions and a particular context, offers every person and community, everywhere, a valid opportunity to be directly challenged to a radical reorientation of their lives, a reorientation which involves such things as deliverance from slavery to the world and its powers; embracing Christ as Savior and Lord; becoming a living member of his community, the church; being enlisted into his service of reconciliation, peace, and justice on earth; and being committed to God's purpose of placing all things under the rule of Christ.[39]

It is noteworthy, first, that for Bosch evangelism involves witnessing to what God has done, is doing, and will do. Evangelism is "not a call to put something into effect, as if God's reign would be inaugurated by our response or thwarted by the absence of such a response"; it is rather "a response to what God has already put into effect."[40] Evangelism is thus essentially grace-based, as Stassen would argue; it is based on what God has redemptively done in human history in and through the person and ministry of Jesus—incarnate, crucified, and risen.

Second, evangelism invites people to a radical orientation of their lives that leads to service. The gospel enlists people "for the reign of God, liberating them from themselves, their sins, and their entanglements, so that they will be free for God and neighbor."[41] It issues a call to a life of commitment, sacrifice, wholeness, and love—a life of allegiance to God's purposes and priorities. Thus, the cardinal responsibility of the church as apostle/prophet is to make the demands, as well as the promise, of the gospel clear.

Lesslie Newbigin raises a question about the ethical content of conversion, which has a serious implication for Christian faith and discipleship. "Is there any knowledge of God," asks Newbigin, "that is not *at the same time* the doing of God's will?" Genuine discipleship includes radical obedience to the teachings of Jesus; there cannot be a separation between faith and obedience. Newbigin defines conversion as "a total change of direction, which includes both the inner reorientation of the heart and mind and the outward reorientation of conduct in all areas of life."[42] Such a view of conversion certainly resonates with that of Stassen, who understands it as a fundamental "reorientation . . . toward *discipleship, faithful following of the demonstration of God's way in Christ.*"[43] The gospel-sharing in the New Testament was always a call to repentance, belief in the present reality of God's reign, and commitment to follow Jesus and his way. Conversion, when it is authentic, always leads to "a new way of behaving and therefore a new decision on the ethical and political issues of this time and place."[44]

Stassen urges churches "to be far more concrete in communicating the meaning of Christ's teachings for our life-context."[45] He is deeply concerned about the abstract vagueness of Christian discipleship, and instead calls for "incarnational discipleship" based on the way of "a thicker Jesus." Incarnational discipleship fully embraces and integrates the three key dimensions of God's sovereignty. In particular, it reflects "a *thick, historically-embodied, realistic understanding of Jesus Christ* as revealing God's character and thus providing norms for guiding our lives."[46] Or, to put it differently, incarnational discipleship "does not split God's character from Jesus' love," since "[God's] grace is not formless, but christomorphic."[47] Stassen accordingly is deeply committed to recovering the Sermon on the Mount and interpreting it not as high and impossible ideals but as concrete and realistic guidance.[48] To illustrate his understanding of incarnational discipleship, Stassen points to witnesses who were proved faithful in historical times of testing, including Dietrich Bonhoeffer, André Trocmé, Martin Luther King, Jr., Clarence Jordan, and Dorothy Day. For Stassen, incarnational discipleship can pass the test in the crucible of actual history, and the thicker Jesus "can give guidance for the Lordship of Christ in all of life, including the political struggle."[49]

The apostolic/prophetic mission of the church also includes "correct[ing] idolatry by speaking of God and justice concretely, in order to guard against idolatrous accommodation of God to cultural corruptions of greed and injustice."[50] Furthermore, the church is to preach to the Powers, which according to Yoder were part of the good creation of God, yet have rebelled and now are fallen. They have now enslaved humanity and history.[51] The prophetic message of the church is that God is still in charge and rules, and that Christ is Lord even over these Powers and redeeming them. The "victory over the Powers constitutes the work of Christ," and "it must be also a message for the church to proclaim."[52] In fact, "the very existence of the church," the embodiment of transformative Trinitarian faith, "is itself a proclamation, a sign, a token to the Powers that their unbroken dominion has come to an end."[53]

The Church as Pioneer/Distinctive Community

The church serves as pioneer as it responds to God in repentance, faith, and obedience, and as it seeks to model the kind of community that God wills for the whole of humanity. The pioneering mission of the church is the logical implication of God as independent Spirit who is living and dynamic, and thus cannot be possessed by any ideology or institution. According to Stassen, "to respond to God is always to pioneer because God's will is always ahead of where society is,"[54] and because the Holy Spirit is ever doing new things. The purpose of the living God cannot be reduced to or identified with the way things are; the response of the church always includes repentance and transformative initiatives.

For Niebuhr, the church as pioneer denotes its representative responsibility for and on behalf of the world:

> the Church is that part of human society, and that element in each particular society, which moves toward God, which as the priest acting for all men [and women] worships Him, which believes and trusts in Him on behalf of all, which is first to obey Him when it becomes aware of a new aspect of His will. . . . In ethics it is the first to repent for the sins of a society and it repents on behalf of all. . . . It does this *not as the holy community separate from the world but as the pioneer and representative.*[55]

In all the church does as pioneer, its ontological and moral solidarity with the world is not to be ignored or forgotten. Thus, according to Stassen, "the church can hardly be pioneer without leading in the act of repentance."[56] The church itself is a sinful community, and thus "keeping [its own] particular judgments, rules, principles and basic convictions in continuous conversation, continuous reformation, continuous repentance, while always remaining accountable above all to God in Christ, in the power of the Holy Spirit, should be the church's experience."[57]

The church's role as pioneer is also inseparably interrelated with its call to be an alternative community, since a major way the church transforms society is by being a distinctive community. Believing that the church is to create a radical alternative to the dominant structures of the world, Stassen shares Yoder's deep commitment to the church as an exemplary community. The distinctive life-together of the Christian community is, for Yoder, a vital part of the gospel:

> Pragmatically it is . . . clear that there can be no evangelistic call addressed to a person inviting him to enter a new kind of fellowship and learning if there is not such a body of persons . . . distinct from the totality of society. . . . But this congruence between the free visible existence of the believers' church and the possibility of valid missionary proclamation is not a merely pragmatic or instrumental one. It is founded deeply in the nature of the gospel itself. If it is not the case that there are in a given place people of various characters and origins who have been brought together in Jesus Christ, then there is not in that place the new humanity and in that place the gospel is not true.[58]

Yoder understands mission as the church's witness to its distinctiveness; mission is meaningful only when there is a community that reflects authentic differences from the rest of the world.

Yoder is convinced that the church as a minority constitutes a new kind of social reality: "The alternative community discharges a modeling mission. The church is called to be now what the world is called to be ultimately."[59] The alternative community is not a form of withdrawal but a structure of transformation that poses a direct challenge to the powers and authorities. Yoder thus contends that the church itself is "a deep social change" and "if it lives faithfully . . . the most powerful tool of social change."[60]

It is then crucial for the church as the pioneering and alternative community to pay keen attention to its own moral and spiritual formation through shared practices. Practices may be defined as "*things Christians do together over time in response to and in the light of God's active presence for the life of the world* [in Jesus Christ]."[61] Stassen lists these practices as essential for moral formation and development: the Lord's Supper and baptism, delivering processes of forgiveness, inclusion, and delivering justice.

Stassen also considers prayer essential to the life and ministry of the church as pioneer. The significance of prayer is highlighted in his *The Journey into Peacemaking*—a small group study-and-action guide with an emphasis on both the journey inward and the journey outward, based on the vision and practices of the Church of the Saviour in Washington, DC. Prayer is to be the source of all the actions of the church for service and justice, as well as for its life-together. "Christian obedience on the *outward journey* of peacemaking action," writes Stassen, "and Christian gratitude on the *inward journey* of peacemaking prayer are tightly related."[62] The pioneering mission of the church requires the convergence between prayer and justice.

The church as visible alternative community is above all to counter the prevailing patterns of homogeneous human relationships in society, crossing racial, ethnic, and other boundaries. Yet there is always a danger for the church to pursue "culturally exclusive forms of Christian witness and church formation" that could result in "the pollution of Christian witness with racism, classism, and ethnocentrism."[63]

There are, however, churches across the nation that seek to build relationships across racial, cultural, and socioeconomic differences. In *We Are the Church Together*, Foster and Brelsford carefully examine the life and ministry of three multicultural congregations in the Atlanta area. Among their distinctive characteristics as a multicultural congregation, I find two particularly important.

First, there is a new emerging ecclesiology different from the one prevailing among homogeneous congregations. The three congregations have endeavored to embrace racial and cultural diversity as integral to their identity as a community of faith, and to draw from it as a resource for their life and mission. In other words, the "differences have come to be viewed not so much as problems to be overcome but as gifts to be accepted, explored, and affirmed."[64]

Second, they bear a sign of the cross. In their living against the persistent and dominant practice of cultural and racial homogeneity both in congregational life and in society, they cannot avoid facing difficulties. They constantly live in ambiguity and uncertainty. The sense of loss is inevitable, since not everyone understands their vision, and since some long-time members have left in search of a more comfortable and familiar congregational setting. What they possess is "a particular sort of faith . . . a faith without the certainty of uniformity and sameness. It is a faith that does not rely on what is, but lives instead with multiple possibilities and imagines what might be. This is not an easy faith."[65] These three congregations demonstrate a life of vibrancy in the midst of fragility.

One of the pastors often refers to an eschatological vision from Revelation 7:9–10:

> There was a great multitude that no one could count, from every nation, from all tribes and peoples and languages, standing before the throne and before the Lamb, robed in white, with palm branches in their hands. They cried out in a loud voice, saying, "Salvation belongs to our God who is seated on the throne, and to the Lamb!"

This vision is a constant reminder to the congregation that the church is to bear faithfully the multicultural nature of the kingdom of God. The church as pioneer is to live out the future in the present in the power of the Holy Spirit.

Conclusion

A major contribution of Glen Stassen to Christian ethics is his consistent and constructive argument for faith in the sovereign God as the foundation and criterion for authentic transformation—God who is universal ruler, who is independent judge, and who is concretely revealed. The concrete historical revelation in Christ is central for the sovereignty of God, and thus for authentic transformation. The church has been called to be the embodiment of transformative Trinitarian faith—in its life in, and its witness to, the redemptive reality of the incarnation of God in Jesus Christ. As Pastor, Prophet, and Pioneer, the church continues to participate in what God is doing now in history, guided by the life and teaching of the incarnate Jesus and empowered by the Holy Spirit.

Yet Stassen rightly warns the church, as did Niebuhr, of the danger of its evasive tendencies, the most prevalent form of unfaithfulness and disloyalty. Throughout their history, churches often have evaded full faithfulness to God. Since the time of the New Testament, sinful fallibility has been a reality for the church; however, the presence of God in the life and ministry of the church still remains. Newbigin offers a profound insight into the tension between the fallibility and missional call of the church:

> If the church is the bearer of the presence of the kingdom through history, it is surely not as the community of the righteous in a sinful world. . . . It is a sinful community. It is, during most of its history, a weak, divided, and unsuccessful community. . . . [Yet] the reign of God is present in the midst of this sinful, weak, and divided community, not through any power

or goodness of its own, but because God has called and chosen this company of people to be the bearers of his gift on behalf of all people.[66]

For Stassen, the call for the church to embody authentic, transformative faith does not rely on human effort but on participation in God's gracious initiatives—what God has done and is actively doing for the restoration of the whole of creation. Thus, the keynote here is not a heavy sense of obligation but "the joy of participation in deliverance."[67] To be a community embodying transformative faith in Sovereign God is a grateful response to and joyful participation in the gift of God's delivering grace, the grace of authentic transformation.

NOTES

1. Glen Harold Stassen, *A Thicker Jesus: Incarnational Discipleship in a Secular Age* (Louisville KY: Westminster John Knox, 2012) x.

2. Glen H. Stassen, "A Social Theory Model for Religious Social Ethics," *Journal of Religious Ethics* 5 (Spring 1977): 18–22.

3. Glen H. Stassen and David P. Gushee, *Kingdom Ethics: Following Jesus in Contemporary Context* (Downers Grove IL: InterVarsity, 2003) 61.

4. See, for instance, Stassen, "Who Stands the Test of History?" in *A Thicker Jesus*, 3–15.

5. Glen H. Stassen, in Stassen, D. M. Yeager, and John Howard Yoder, *Authentic Transformation: A New Vision of Christ and Culture* (Nashville: Abingdon, 1996) 128.

6. Stassen, *A Thicker Jesus*, 9.

7. Stassen, *Authentic Transformation*, 129.

8. H. Richard Niebuhr, *The Social Sources of Denominationalism* (New York: Henry Holt, 1929) 280.

9. H. Richard Niebuhr, *The Kingdom of God in America* (New York: Harper & Row, 1937) xiv–xv.

10. Stassen, *Authentic Transformation*, 131–34.

11. Ibid., 131, 135.

12. Ibid., 143.

13. Ibid., 142.

14. Glen H. Stassen, "The Sovereignty of God in the Theological Ethics of H. Richard Niebuhr," PhD diss., Duke University, 1967, 244.

15. Ibid., 151.

16. H. Richard Niebuhr, *The Meaning of Revelation* (New York: Macmillan, 1941) 124, quoted in Stassen, *Authentic Transformation*, 153.

17. Stassen, *Authentic Transformation*, 161–62.

18. Ibid., 193.

19. Ibid., 143.

20. Ibid., 222.

21. Ernst Troeltsch, *The Social Teachings of the Christian Churches*, trans. Olive Wyon (New York: Macmillan, 1931).

22. Stassen, *Authentic Transformation*, 169.

23. John Howard Yoder, "Christ and Power," in *The Politics of Jesus: Vicit Agnus Noster*, 2d ed. (Grand Rapids MI; Carlisle UK: Eerdmans and Paternoster, 1994) 157.

24. Stassen, *Authentic Transformation*, 223.

25. H. Richard Niebuhr, "The Responsibility of the Church for Society," in *The Gospel, the Church and the World*, ed. K. S. Latourette (New York: Harper & Brothers, 1946) 111–33.

26. Stassen, *Authentic Transformation*, 243–44.

27. Niebuhr, "Responsibility of the Church for Society," 114–15 (emphasis original).

28. Ibid., 119–20.

29. Stassen, *Authentic Transformation*, 243 (emphasis original).

30. Robert C. Tannehill, *The Narrative Unity of Luke-Acts: A Literary Interpretation*, vol. 1 (Minneapolis: Fortress, 1986) 64. This section on liberation theology and the one below on the multicultural nature of the church draw from my article, "Hospitality as Context for Evangelism," *Missiology: An International Review* 30/3 (2002): 385–95.

31. Joel B. Green, *The Theology of the Gospel of Luke* (Cambridge UK: Cambridge University, 1995) 84.

32. David Bosch, *Transforming Mission: Paradigm Shifts in Theology of Mission* (Maryknoll NY: Orbis, 1991) 436. Gustavo Gutierrez also writes, "The very word 'preference' denies all exclusiveness and seeks rather to call attention to those who are the first—though not the only ones—with whom we should be in solidarity") *A Theology of Liberation*, 15th anniversary ed. [Maryknoll NY: Orbis, 1988] xxv–xxvi).

33. Bosch, *Transforming Mission*, 437.

34. Orlando E. Costas, *Liberating News: A Theology of Contextual Evangelization* (Grand Rapids MI: Eerdmans, 1989) 31.

35. Glen Stassen, *The Journey into Peacemaking*, 2d ed. (Memphis: Brotherhood Commission, SBC, 1987) 8.

36. Niebuhr, "Responsibility of the Church for Society," 126.

37. Stassen, *Authentic Transformation*, 226.

38. Ibid.

39. Bosch, *Transforming Mission*, 420.

40. Ibid., 412.

41. Ibid., 418.

42. Lesslie Newbigin, *The Open Secret: An Introduction to the Theology of Mission*, rev. ed. (Grand Rapids MI: Eerdmans, 1995) 135.

43. Stassen, *Authentic Transformation*, 226 (emphasis original).

44. Newbigin, *Open Secret*, 136.

45. Stassen, *Authentic Transformation*, 230.

46. Stassen, *A Thicker Jesus*, 16 (emphasis original).

47. Ibid., 148, 151.

48. See Glen H. Stassen, *Living the Sermon on the Mount: Practical Hope for Grace and Deliverance* (San Francisco: Jossey-Bass, 2006).

49. Stassen, *A Thicker Jesus*, 195.

50. Stassen, *Authentic Transformation*, 185.

51. Yoder, "Christ and Power," 141–42.

52. Ibid., 147.

53. Ibid., 147–48, citing Hendrik Berkhof, *Christ and the Powers*, trans. John Howard Yoder (Scottdale PA: Herald, 1962) 51.

54. Stassen, *Authentic Transformation*, 233.

55. Niebuhr, "Responsibility of the Church for Society," 131 (emphasis mine).

56. Stassen, *Authentic Transformation*, 233.

57. Stassen and Gushee, *Kingdom Ethics*, 118.

58. John Howard Yoder, "A People in the World: Theological Interpretation," in *The Concept of the Believer's Church*, ed. James Leo Garrett, Jr. (Scottdale PA: Herald, 1969) 259.

59. John Howard Yoder, "The Kingdom as Social Ethic," in *The Priestly Kingdom: Social Ethics as Gospel* (Notre Dame: University of Notre Dame, 1984) 92.

60. John Howard Yoder, "The Original Revolution," in *The Original Revolution* (Scottdale PA: Herald, 1971) 31.

61. Craig Dykstra and Dorothy C. Bass, "Times of Yearning, Practices of Faith," in *Practicing Our Faith: A Way of Life for a Searching People*, ed. Dorothy C. Bass (San Francisco: Jossey-Bass, 1997) 5 (emphasis original), quoted in Benjamin T. Conner, *Practicing Witness: A Missional Vision of Christian Practices* (Grand Rapids MI: Eerdmans, 2011) 55.

62. Stassen, "Transforming Prayer," in *Journey into Peacemaking*, 32 (emphasis original).

63. Darrell L. Guder, *The Incarnation and the Church's Witness* (Harrisburg PA: Trinity Press International, 1999) 48.

64. Charles R. Foster and Theodore Brelsford, *We Are the Church Together: Cultural Diversity in Congregational Life* (Valley Forge PA: Trinity Press International, 1996) 109. Glen Stassen and his wife Dot have consciously sought to participate actively in ethnic minority and multicultural communities of faith. See, for instance, Stassen, *Authentic Transformation*, 202–205, for his transformative experience through his involvement in Canaan Baptist Church of Christ, an African-American congregation in Harlem, in the mid-1990s.

65. Ibid., 159.

66. Newbigin, *Open Secret*, 53–54.

67. Stassen, *Authentic Transformation*, 255.

Chapter 5

The Lord's Supper as the Meal of God's Reign

Tammy R. Williams

The Work of Glen Stassen[1]

In their highly acclaimed *Kingdom Ethics: Following Jesus in Contemporary Context*,[2] Glen Stassen and David Gushee speak of Christian ethics as encompassing an entire way of life. Refusing to confine ethics to moral decision-making, Stassen and Gushee insist that putting into practice the teachings of Jesus is indispensable to pursuing a total way of life as Christian disciples. In fact, the test of discipleship or "following Jesus" faithfully is whether we *act* on his teachings.

Yet, sadly, many Christians fail to embody the words and practices of Jesus. Fine teacher that he is, Stassen identifies and rectifies the interpretive and theological obstacles that permit us to evade the words of Jesus and to avoid walking in the way of Jesus. In this regard, he showcases the Sermon on the Mount as one of the most cited biblical passages, yet one of the most neglected New Testament texts for doing Christian ethics. In seeking to remedy the split between the Sermon and ethics that circumvents discipleship, Stassen offers a corrective in which the heart of the Sermon—Jesus' provision of transforming initiatives, accessible practices that offer deliverance from embroiling cycles of sin—supersedes traditional readings that characterize Jesus' teachings as admirable yet unrealistic moral standards.

The revised reading of the Sermon highlights participative grace as God's gracious delivering activity on our behalf that conforms us to the image of Christ and enables us to participate in God's ongoing work in the world. It also remedies other ethical splits, such as those that pit attitudes against action as in the case of love and justice. Far too many Christians reduce love to a heart-felt emotion that is severed from action. Our passion enables us to believe, however falsely, that we can fervently love the poor in our hearts without ever pursuing justice for the poor. For Stassen and

Gushee, such sentiment "allows Christians to dismiss the significance of how we actually live our lives in favor of an illusory sense of attitudinal moral goodness."[3] Moreover, when left unchallenged, such dualisms have the capacity to confine the scope of Jesus' teachings to the inner life of the individual believer and render them irrelevant in the public sphere. Therefore, by repairing the ruptures that constrain authentic Christian engagement with the wider society, Stassen offers a path that facilitates the church's following of Jesus in all areas of life.

The Meaning of the Lord's Supper

This article addresses the split that Stassen identifies, viewed from a different angle. It examines the disconnect between worship and ethics in the Lord's Supper[4] and reflects on the Lord's Supper as the Meal of God's Reign, a designation that transcends denominational boundaries.[5] In this act of worship, the church gives thanks for what God through the life, death, and resurrection of Christ has accomplished for our salvation and the renewal of all creation. Memorial (*anamnesis*) and the Lord's death are essential theological categories for understanding the Supper's significance. In this Christ-appointed covenant meal (1 Cor 11:25), the church ritually reenacts the Last Supper, proclaims the Lord's death (1 Cor 11:26), and communes with Christ who is graciously present as host, guest, and life-nurturing food.[6] By communing with Christ, believers commune with one another. As the Meal of the Reign of God, which was, and is, and is to come, the Lord's Supper manifests the already/not yet character of God's reign. Therefore, at the Lord's Table, the church recalls God's delivering activity throughout history, encounters Christ in the present, and through eating and drinking in God's presence begins not only to anticipate but also to experience *in part* the unceasing fellowship that will mark the heavenly banquet. In this manner, the Lord's Supper is "*the reality-filled promise* to be eaten in *hope* of the final kingdom."[7]

The paradigmatic significance of the Lord's Supper in shaping Christian engagement with the wider society is this essay's point of departure. This dimension of the Supper is underscored in light of the ecumenical conviction that the Lord's Supper "embraces all aspects of life."[8] This corollary follows from the church's proclamation of the Lord's death during the Meal. As God's scandalous intervention to transform the world that presages an end to the old aeon while ushering in a new creation, Christ's death transforms all of life.[9] As an act of self-giving love for the benefit of others, Christ's death is an act of unbounded grace on behalf of creation. It follows, then, that the event that commemorates Christ's all-encompassing and cosmic work of deliverance, the Lord's Supper, impinges upon all spheres of life. Yet, all too often, the social compass of the church's celebration is circumscribed to the degree that the Supper is experienced primarily as a spiritual act of worship centered in a symbolic meal that ritualizes Christ's redemptive death and lends itself to attitudinal responses of gratitude for the gift of soul salvation.

The Split between Worship and Ethics

Not unlike the disconnect that Stassen observes between reading the teachings of Jesus in the Sermon on the Mount and his emphasis on implementing the words of Jesus in everyday life, an ethical split between liturgy and life accounts for a truncated celebration of the Lord's Supper, which can be stated as follows: As a ritualized meal of words and actions that bears witness to the all-embracing scope of Christ's gracious act of self-giving on the cross for the benefit of all creation, the Lord's Supper calls Christians as recipients of God's grace to be agents of this grace[10] and to actively participate in God's ongoing work in the world through words and concrete actions that reflect the character of Christ and the power of the cross. *By confining the sphere of participation in the Lord's Supper to the ritualized worship event, the church fails to enact the socioethical obligations that are rooted in the meaning of Christ's death and inscribed in the Supper.*[11] Moreover, the neglect of social responsibilities calls into question the integrity of the liturgical performance of the meal as a faithful proclamation of the Lord's death and an authentic celebration of the Lord's Supper. In sum, the church fails to fully embody in its practice of everyday life what it ceremonially proclaims in its celebration of the Lord's Supper.[12]

In order to better illustrate and address the split between worship and ethics at the Lord's Table, 1 Corinthians 11:17-34 is instructive. In this account, the meal is eaten in a context of socioeconomic divisions, class privilege, and hunger, a setting not unlike our own. During the meal Paul, the founder of the Corinthian community, hearkens back to the words and deeds of Jesus at the Last Supper in order that the community might renounce self-centeredness and repair divisions. Although the meaning of Paul's instructions regarding dining practices at the chapter's end continues to be debated, this essay features a reinterpretation that takes seriously divine self-giving as a pattern for transforming the community's practices. It ends by highlighting the paradigmatic significance of the Lord's Supper as a means by which the neglect of enactment in daily life can be countered.

The Lord's Supper as the Meal of God's Reign

In his landmark study, *Eucharist and Eschatology*, Geoffrey Wainwright argues that our remembrance of Christ's passion during the Lord's Supper should be situated in a broader commemoration of Christ himself.[13] After all, "Jesus said: 'Do this in memory of *me*.'"[14] This more expansive commemoration remembers Christ's death in conjunction with his life, ministry, resurrection, and return, while retaining the redemptive singularity of his death. Wainwright's point regarding the need for a more robust remembrance also has relevance for understanding how the Lord's Supper as the Meal of God's Reign stands in relationship with other meals through which God encountered God's people.[15] The Lord's Supper not only commemorates the Last Supper but also connects with the broader meal ministry of Jesus, for the final meal of Jesus' earthly ministry is the last of a long series of suppers that Jesus shares with others.[16] At the same time, the meal ministry of Jesus incorporates the post-resurrection meals through which he revealed himself to his disciples. These meals are continued through the Lord's Supper,[17] a sign of God's reign that discloses that "God has acted to deliver humanity and now reigns over all of life, and is present to and with us, and will be in the future."[18] As the hopeful sign that heralds the consummated reign, the Lord's Supper is an anticipation and foretaste of the Marriage Supper of the Lamb (Rev 19:9). Through Jesus' practices of eating and feeding, he enacts the nearness of God's reign.[19]

Robert J. Karris underscores the centrality of meals in the mission of Jesus, particularly those in Luke's Gospel, by noting that in the Third Gospel "Jesus is either going to a meal, at a meal, or coming from a meal."[20] He observes that in feeding the crowds (9:10-17), Jesus pursues God's justice, for "Jesus' fulfillment of God's promises of giving food to his needy creation is linked to his preaching of the kingdom of God. A hungry creation mocks God's kingly justice. Jesus' kingly justice . . . embraces those who in their hunger cry out for God's justice."[21]

Jesus' table fellowship with outcasts also discloses the imminence of God's kingdom. By eating with tax collectors and sinners, Jesus extends God's reign to them, offers God's love, and puts into practice his own teaching on forgiveness. In these meals, Jesus shares not only food but his very life with those who are deprived of love and recognition.[22] Indeed, the very act of Jesus' eating with outcasts constitutes an offer of the salvation that God's reign embodies and an invitation to repentance.[23] As a result of his table interaction with sinners, criticism of the religious leaders' exclusive table fellowship, and objections to purity codes, Jesus comes into conflict with the authorities.[24] Refusing to minimize the consequential nature of Jesus' dining practices, Karris concludes that "Jesus got himself crucified because of the way he ate."[25] The religious establishment could not tolerate the "glutton and drunkard" who proclaimed the reign of a God who feeds the hungry, rectifies injustices, and rejoices to eat with sinners.[26]

In an attempt to recover the meal as a theological category for interpreting and participating in the Lord's Supper, Wainwright observes that, although the Lord's Supper was instituted during a meal and entails food and drink, its nature as a meal has not been self-evident to Christians throughout church history.[27] Indeed, particularly for traditions in which people drink from individual cups in place of a common chalice, or churches that make use of a pre-packaged cup and wafer combo, too many congregants experience the Supper as a single-serving appetizer for individual consumption in contrast to "the common Supper of the whole churchly people of God in the last days."[28] Accordingly, many communicants perceive the Lord's Supper as a token meal, a meal that purports to be a meal but in reality is not. In turn, this token meal is further downsized when it is viewed as fundamentally different from the "real" meals that Christians indulge in after church.

What is at stake theologically is considerable if we gnosticize the food character of the Lord's Supper. Beyond a failure to link the Supper with both the meal ministry of Jesus and the eschatological banquet, and the ways that God has related to humanity through food throughout history, we may never perceive the connection between eating and drinking in the Lord's Supper and eating and drinking in everyday life in a manner that brings glory to God.

> [A]s long as the communion bread bears little or no resemblance to the staff of life served at ordinary human meals, and as long as the cups holding the fruit of the vine look like props from the movie "Honey, I Shrunk the Kids"—the theological relationship between the Eucharist and the phenomenon of a human meal will . . . rarely [be] experienced.[25]

Apart from encountering the Lord's Supper as a meal, participants may fail to experience the profound fellowship, recognition, mutual sharing, and identity-formation that are part and parcel of eating with others. In fact, it is precisely the element of *koinonia* or communal sharing in the Lord's Supper that Paul stresses in his correspondence with the Corinthians (1 Cor 10:16, 17; 11:17-22).[26] Finally, acknowledging the importance of the meal character of the Lord's Supper does not denigrate the indispensable spiritual dimension of Christ's communion with believers. Indeed, it allows for a deepening of an encounter with Christ, inasmuch as many who speak of empowering experiences of communing with Christ invariably use meal language.[27]

As the Meal of God's Reign, the Lord's Supper is a sign that not only points toward God's reign but also enables us as partakers of God's grace to have a share in what is signified: God's salvation and deliverance, righteousness, justice and peace, joy, and God's presence as a result of what God through Christ has done for us.[28] Through the bread and wine of this Meal, the material gifts of God's creation, we are graciously fed by Christ who communes with us by offering his very self as sustenance. As we feed upon him, he sustains true life within us. At the same time, we commune with one another through eating and drinking and experience no conflict between our physicality and spirituality, for the God who created bodily and spiritual appetites satisfies both until we hunger no more.[29] Through our own eating, we remember Jesus' feeding of others as an act of justice against deprivation and as a material form of spiritual nourishment. Our response to God's provision is to extend God's offer of life in abundance to a profoundly hungry world, as we anticipate the fulfillment of the promise that, in God's reign, the hungry shall be filled (Luke 6:21).

The Lord's Supper at Corinth

Baptism, Eucharist and Ministry, the widely transmitted ecumenical document adopted by the World Council of Churches' Commission on Faith and Order in 1982, identifies the Lord's Supper or Eucharist, its preferred term that means thanksgiving, as the Meal of the Kingdom, particularly with reference to the coming kingdom. Under the rubric Communion of the Faithful, the document underlines aspects of the celebration that bear upon the church's unity and universality as the body of Christ. It notes,

> The eucharist embraces all aspects of life. It is a representative act of thanksgiving and offering on behalf of the whole world. *The eucharistic celebration demands reconciliation and sharing among all those regarded as brothers and sisters in the one family of God.* . . . All kinds of injustice, racism, separation and lack of freedom are radically challenged when we share in the body and blood of Christ.[30]

The linking of reconciliation and sharing with the Lord's Supper, whether one understands both as a requirement for or as a result of participation in the Meal, is particularly poignant when read in tandem with the account of the first-century celebration of the Lord's Supper recorded in 1 Corinthians 11:17-34.

The problem of an ethical disconnect in the church's practice of the Lord's Supper is not solely a contemporary issue. Paul confronted a similar breach in practice in the first-century Corinthian congregation that he founded. Unlike the contentious medieval and Reformation eucharistic debates that often centered on the sacramental nature of the Lord's Supper, the dissension surrounding the Lord's Table at Corinth was social: the conflict was between members of the upper classes, whose few members made up the dominating minority, and the many members of the lower classes who formed the majority of the Corinthian community.[31] Or one might say, less precisely but more incisively, that the conflict was between rich and poor Christians.

Archaeological findings of first-century edifices and studies of Greco-Roman dining practices have led biblical scholars to reconstruct the Corinthian conflict along lines that take seriously the constraints of physical space on church-based hospitality and the dining practices of the dominant culture in Paul's day. With respect to the site of the Lord's Supper, members gathered together in a private home or house church.[32] Research on mid-first-century Roman villas reveals that the dining room in a typical villa could accommodate nine guests in contrast to the courtyard hallway or overflow room that had the capacity for nearly fifty persons.[33] If one assumes that social standing served as the criterion for seating assignments, then the host's tendency to reinforce existing social codes more than likely resulted in preferential seating for the well-to-do members who feasted in the dining room as honored guests, while lower-status members were relegated to the courtyard.[34] In adducing the effects of spatial limitations on social conduct, Jerome Murphy-O'Connor notes that the difficulty of gathering the entire church together regularly in the same room "goes a long way towards explaining the theological divisions within the Corinthian community . . . ."[35]

With respect to dining practices, it is important to bear in mind the particular shape of the Lord's Supper ritual in the first century. The Corinthian Lord's Supper consisted of an actual meal of nourishment.[36] The ceremonial sharing of the bread and cup of the Lord's Supper bracketed this full meal, which the members themselves provided or which wealthier members provided for the entire group.[37] Not unlike the preferential seating that

was offered to socially advantaged classes in the wider society, dining privileges that included the provision of finer food and larger portions were
bequeathed to wealthier members of Greco-Roman society during private
banquets.[38] Richard B. Hays likens these customs of class-based hospitality
to the contemporary practice of first-class airline passengers receiving better
food and service.[39] In light of its prevalence in the wider culture, it appears
that class-specific hospitality was imported into the dining practices of some
members of the Corinthian church. What is more, it is unlikely that wealthier members felt remorse for their exercise of class privilege; indeed, it is far
more likely that they thought of themselves as generous patrons who were
supporting poorer members of the community.[40]

The Problem of Social Inequality: The Lack of Sharing of Food

Now in the following instructions I do not commend you, because when
you come together it is not for the better but for the worse. For, to begin
with, when you come together as a church, I hear that there are divisions
among you: and to some extent I believe it. Indeed, there have to be fac-
tions among you, for only so will it become clear who among you are genuine. When you come together, it is not really to eat the Lord's supper.
For when the time comes to eat, each of you goes ahead with your own
supper, and one goes hungry and another becomes drunk. What! Do you
not have homes to eat and drink in? Or do you show contempt for the
church of God and humiliate those who have nothing? What should I say
to you? Should I commend you? In this matter I do not commend you!
(1 Cor 11:17-22, NRSV)

Inevitably, preferential dining prerogatives influence the actual sharing
or, more accurately, lack of sharing of the Supper. Although the actual reconstruction of events continues to be debated,[41] one view is that conflict
arises during the common meal when wealthier members consume or even
"devour" more plentiful quantities of food as their own private supper (*idion
deipnon*) without sharing with socially disadvantaged believers, whose mea-
ger portions allow them to go hungry.[42] Injustice and social inequality, therefore, are at the root of the divisions.[43]

What is beyond conjecture is the result of the community's meal practice: "One remains hungry, another gets drunk" (v. 21).[44] The reprehensible
conduct of upper-status members, which has effectively divided the church
into two mutually exclusive groups, the haves and have nots, has also caused
humiliation.[45] What is more, the humiliation of the have nots by privileged

members is tantamount to "despising the church of God" (v. 22). Therefore, although the Corinthians partake of the Lord's Supper, their self-centered, albeit socially acceptable conduct nullifies the very meaning of the ritual: Christ's self-giving death for others. The meal has become the occasion for showcasing social status rather than the cruciform event that "subverts and cuts across all human distinctions of race, class, gender and status to make room for divine grace alone as sheer unconditional gift."[46]

After confronting the well-to-do members of the church with their abusive conduct toward poorer brothers and sisters, Paul appeals to another commemorative meal. He cites the words of institution, the words and actions of Christ during the Last Supper, his final meal with his disciples prior to his death through which he establishes the church's ongoing meal of commemoration, the Lord's Supper (vv. 23-25). The Last Supper tradition, through its use of word-acts over the bread and the cup, gestures toward Christ's self-giving action that results in a new covenant that binds God to God's people and God's people to one another.[47] Paul's use of this tradition serves as a theological corrective to the problem of divisions.[48] By drawing attention to Christ's self-offering as an act that stands in sharp contrast to the selfishness of privileged Corinthians, Paul says, in so many words, "Now compare this meal to your meal!"[49] As the Meal of God's Reign, the Lord's Supper is a meal of justice that challenges exclusive forms of table fellowship, just as Jesus challenged the dining practices of the scribes and Pharisees.

Paul's Closing Directives as a Practical Corrective of Divisions

> What! Do you not have homes (*oikia*) to eat and drink in? . . . So then, my brothers and sisters, when you come together to eat, wait for one another. If you are hungry, eat at home (*oikos*), so that when you come together, it will not be for your condemnation. (1 Cor 11:22, 33-34, NRSV)

Paul ends his discussion of the Lord's Supper by issuing directives that function as a practical corrective to the community's divisive table fellowship (vv. 33-34). Paul's closing instructions in verses 33 and 34, however, when read in many major translations, seem to *validate* the very social mores that give rise to congregational divisions.

The problem that the traditional reading[50] presents is that it assumes that Paul refers to the private residences of the privileged when he makes mention of homes and home in verses 22 and 34 respectively.[51] Carrying these assumptions to their logical conclusion, Paul's final instruction would permit members of higher status to exercise discriminatory dining conventions in their private homes; once present in Christian community, however, the wealthy would be obligated to wait for fellow Christians and to share the common meal.[52] If we frame Paul's instructions in the same manner that we represented the relationship between worship and ethics, we could say that Paul's attempt to concretely resolve the gap between ritual celebration and enactment in the Lord's Supper, in order that the humiliated hungry poor are welcomed and fed during the church's common meal, gives rise to another split—that of engaging in one form of conduct in one's private residence and a divergent form of conduct in public worship. One scholar crystallizes Paul's seeming concession in the following manner: "It is difficult to understand Paul's conclusion at 11:33-34 if such inequities were actually present. For Paul does not correct the inequities; he merely says not to bring them into the assembly. Thus his instruction at 11:34, would have the same effect as if he were to say, 'let them eat cake.'"[53]

A recent proposal by New Testament scholar Suzanne Watts Henderson challenges the dual assumptions of the traditional reading by honing in on the self-giving character of Christ's death in the church's tradition, for this feature of the cross has the capacity to transform the community's practices.[54] As evidence of the community's call to imitate the cruciform logic of self-giving, Henderson draws attention to Christ's command to "do this in memory of me," a command that traditionally has been understood to pertain to the four-fold action of blessing, breaking, distributing, and eating in the ritual meal.[55] By drawing a rhetorical connection between Christ's bestowal ("*this* is my body") and the concomitant command ("do *this* in memory of me"), however, Henderson broadens the scope of the command beyond ritual proclamation to quotidian life: "Do *this*, that is, give yourselves (and your resources) up for others, just as I am doing for you . . . ."[56]

This same logic of self-giving gets played out in Henderson's translation:

> For is it not that you (pl.) have houses [precisely] for [the community's] eating and drinking? Or do you show scorn for the church of God [by not having all eat and drink] and shame those who don't have [houses of their own for eating and drinking]? . . . Therefore, my brothers [and sisters], when you gather to eat, welcome one another. If someone hungers, let that one eat in the house, lest it is for judgment that you gather.[57] (1 Cor 11:22, 33-34, Henderson's translation)

She argues by way of a careful lexical study that Paul has the hungry have
nots in mind when he makes reference to "houses" in his reprimand and
"house" in his instructions, for both residences refer to the meeting places
of the church.[58] If selfish meal practices are the cause of divisions, then Paul's
pragmatic solution, or transforming initiative that breaks sinful patterns of
acquisitiveness and consumption, is the sharing of food with the *hungry*. "if
someone hungers, let that one eat in the house[church]."[59] Indeed, by
shifting the exegetical center of gravity from the sated to the deprived, Henderson demonstrates how the rift between worship and enactment in the
Lord's Supper can be healed when the self-giving character of the community's worship proclamation—"this is my body . . . do this"—is brought to
bear on the social problem of hunger. Her alternative reading in which
houses serve as the structures for the gathering and upbuilding of community[60] enables her to refute the "let them eat cake" accusation leveled against
Paul, whereby the split between private and public never materializes.
Furthermore, her proposal permits her to gesture toward the paradigmatic
capacity of the Lord's Supper to function as a pattern for everyday life. Called
to embody Christ's self-giving love that is inscribed in the Meal, the
Corinthians are "to live every facet of their lives in the way of the cross:
'Therefore, whether you eat or drink or whatever you do, do everything for
the glory of God' (10:31)."[61]

Overcoming the Invisibility of Social Inequality

Honestly, if *Take This Bread* had been written when I was a doctoral student,
I never would have bothered to write a dissertation on the Lord's Supper,
for few individuals could narrate the kind of church-rooted, Table-centered
embodied theology that integrates worship and social ethics as Sara Miles
does.[62] In this stunning spiritual memoir, Miles tells the story of her radical
conversion. It is the story of how she as a white, middle-class atheist who
lived in San Francisco walked into an Episcopal church that had a policy of
open Communion, and, although she had no knowledge of Communion,
she partook of bread and wine with the rest of the congregation. Then, in
her own words, "Jesus happened to me."[63] Miles was forever changed by
this Damascus Road moment.

After a year of actively participating in church and receiving Communion, she asked herself, "Now that you've taken the bread, what are you going
to do?"[64] What she did was pioneer a food pantry in her church despite
objections in a divided congregation.[65] Having been radically welcomed by
Christ into God's reign and lavishly fed at Christ's table, Miles fed others as

an act of profound gratitude. The pantry was not a social service but an extension of the worship service. Her communion with God placed her in communion with others: extended Latino families, old Moldavian ladies, black grandmothers, homeless crackheads, widows, children, and the physically disabled—people who had been invisible to the church.[66] She notes, "We knew that they were there, but we couldn't see them."[67] Forming relationships with those who wait in line for the pantry allowed her to see them "like Jesus . . . as God, made flesh and blood."[68]

Over time, she incubated multiple food pantries throughout the city, in schools, housing projects, and churches, as an act of justice in a city where it "seemed easier to buy drugs than to find a fresh tomato" in certain neighborhoods and food deserts.[69] Communion is not a mystical means to accomplish a social end but the event in which God's people participate in a greater end. In the very act of sharing food at Christ's Table, the church is brought into "the ongoing work of making creation whole."[70]

Throughout Miles's story, Communion functions as the compass that helps her navigate her journey. It enables her to evaluate her actions (the need to welcome people "who didn't belong") and her relationships (because she can't be a Christian by herself).[71] It is the lens through which she views the whole of life, which is to be lived eucharistically—in thanksgiving and service.

Before turning to the paradigmatic role of the Lord's Supper in shaping Christian social engagement, so compellingly exemplified in Miles's life, I want to point to the visionary capacity of the Meal by extending Miles's observation about the invisibility of the hungry poor. The revelatory prowess of the Supper lies in its power to reverse our opacity and foster our ability to view the world from God's perspective. Seeing the hungry is no small matter. In his work on the Eucharist, William Cavanaugh writes persuasively about the power of market forces to obscure our vision and prevent us from recognizing the marginalized in our society.[72] I suspect that a number of factors facilitate our overlooking of the hungry, one of which is the hyper-visibility of food in popular culture.

The unappealing realities regarding market-based food systems[73] are often obscured when food is dished up as an endless form of entertainment, as evidenced by celebrity chefs who make front-page headlines, food columns that analyze the ubiquity of bacon, travelogues that map exotic safaris in search of the quintessential meal, cooking shows dedicated to niche desserts such as the *Cupcake Wars*, over-indulgent talk about barbeque as an addiction for which few seek help, and celebrity cook-offs on steroids that parallel contact sports. One would never know from this deceptive, yet tantalizing, cultural production of food that 50 million people in this country struggle with hunger.[74] By offering us a radically different story about eating and drinking that is rooted in divine provision (rather than the one ladled out by *The Food Network*), the church can help us to account for and hold us accountable to the hungry poor.

The Lord's Supper is one means through which the church can see the world from God's standpoint, and this brings us back to the Corinthians passage. What is particularly salient about the Pauline account of the Meal is Paul's refusal to tell the story of God's costly covenant love that is expressed supremely through Christ without beginning with the table scraps of the hungry poor. Could it be that by beginning in the middle of the story with the betrayal of Jesus (v. 23), as most of us do, then ending in the middle where Paul identifies the Supper as a form of proclamation (v. 26), that we betray both Jesus and the poor by telling a story about salvation that bypasses the socially stratified contexts in which Christians live out their faith? What accounts, in part, for the church's incommensurate celebration of the Lord's Supper is our omission of the opening segment of the Lord's Supper text where Paul excoriates the Corinthians for disgracing the poor. The neglect of the passage has not only enabled the widening of the gap between ritual proclamation of the Lord's Supper and corresponding engagement in God's mission to the wider world but, more important, has also obscured the fact that such a disconnect exists.

Engaging the text in its entirety alerts us to the reality that the conduct of the Corinthians is consequential.[75] Reading to the end shows us too that Paul not only reprimands members of the community but also instructs them to engage in the inter-relational practices of self-examination and discernment, in addition to food sharing (vv. 28-29). Self-examination is a community-oriented practice. Far from an introspective exercise in spiritual navel-gazing that reinforces the believer's sense of "unworthiness," the purpose of self-examination is to consider how our actions affect others in the body of Christ.[76] Therefore, we examine ourselves in relation to others who can help us to see ourselves more truthfully. In a related fashion, discernment begins with our acknowledgment of the community of believers as the body of Christ.[77] It then requires that we "identify truthfully where the body is not whole, where divisions exist."[78] Beyond identifying actual fractures in the community, discernment involves overcoming those divisions, "blurring the lines between 'them' and 'us.'"[79] For only by facing up to the ways that we marginalize some by privileging others can we rectify injustices and their resulting ruptures.

The Paradigmatic Significance of the Lord's Supper

In its celebration of the Lord's Supper, the church continues Jesus' unbounded welcome of sinners and boundary-crossing table fellowship with outcasts that demonstrates the imminence of God's reign. As the sign of God's reign, the Lord's Supper enables the church to recognize the shape of God's reign in the world by first perceiving its inbreaking among the community of believers:

> The Eucharistic table is the one place where at least this much of God's kingdom is perceived, this much of Christ's real presence is felt: where suffering has meaning, where all are welcomed, where those who are elsewhere excluded, despised, oppressed, and left to starve are invited up to the head table. This is the way God intends the world to look, not just in the church, but always.[80]

The Lord's Supper trains us to see as God sees. From the angle of the Table where we are gathered, a Table that alters our perspective, the Meal privileges us to see the world as the object of God's love and the beneficiary of God's active presence.

The Meal offers us this glimpse of divine compassion for creation because worship "is not a doorway out of the world, or a path deeper into the self, but a way into the world *through an alternative vision.* The instruments of sacramental worship are the worldly things of everyday life: bread, wine, water, touch, gesture, movement."[81] The Meal leads us out into the world where we can discern the world's divisions and brokenness, and then envision our role in everyday life in God's restorative work of creation.

The ability of the Lord's Supper to address us in ways that speak to our conduct and character in everyday life points to the paradigmatic meaning of the Meal—its role as a model for ordinary eating and its capacity to cultivate alternative practices of acquiring and consuming. Yet, as a model, the Lord's Supper is neither myopic nor limited in scope to "eating and drinking" or "life at the table." At this particular set-apart meal, we learn ways of being and acting in the world in relation to others and for the benefit of others that have as much relevance for the negotiating table as for our dining room tables. At the Lord's Table, we remember that God through Christ has acted decisively for the life of the world. In gratitude, we, too, act. We give ourselves up to God by making God's work in the world our ongoing labor of love. By enabling us to act in light of God's purposes for the world, the Lord's Supper directs us to extend God's reign in all areas of life.

NOTES

1. Glen Stassen does not mention the Lord's Supper often in *Kingdom Ethics*. But this is no evasion. He incorporates a theology of grace and gratitude throughout its pages and embodies this theology in everyday life. As one who has been blessed by his teaching and his friendship, it is fitting in an article on the Eucharist that I express my gratitude.

2. Glen H. Stassen and David P. Gushee, *Kingdom Ethics: Following Jesus in Contemporary Context* (Downers Grove IL: InterVarsity, 2003).

3. Ibid., 94.

4. See L. Edward Phillips, "Liturgy and Ethics" in *Liturgy in Dialogue* (London: SPCK, 1993) 86–99, for a helpful template of the relationship between worship and ethics.

5. My purpose is not to present a full-blown confessional theology of the Lord's Supper but to outline broad ecumenical themes rooted in Scripture, such as those that are highlighted in the Faith and Order "Lima Document." See the "Eucharist" document in *Baptism, Eucharist and Ministry*, Faith and Order Paper 111 (Geneva: World Council of Churches, 1982). In view of those traditions for which Scripture is the primary source for understanding the shape and meaning of the event, such as my own Baptist tradition, I use the term "Lord's Supper" and point to the efficacy of "the Lord's death" in light of their place in the Lord's Supper narrative recorded in 1 Cor 11:17-34.

6. Geoffrey Wainwright, *Eucharist and Eschatology*, 3rd ed. (Akron OH: OSL Publications, 2002) 73.

7. Ibid.

8. *Baptism, Eucharist and Ministry*, "Eucharist," paragraph 20.

9. Nancy Duff, "Pauline Apocalyptic and Theological Ethics," in *Apocalyptic and the New Testament: Essays in Honor of J. Louis Martyn*, ed. Joel Marcus and Marion L. Soards, Journal for the Study of the New Testament Supplement Series 24 (Sheffield: JSOT Press, 1989) 281; Richard B. Hays, *First Corinthians*, Interpretation: A Bible Commentary for Teaching and Preaching (Louisville: John Knox, 1997) 196. Of course, I could make the same argument by way of creation or incarnation. For a eucharistic theology indebted to these themes, see Norman Wirzba, *Food and Faith: A Theology of Eating* (New York: Cambridge University Press, 2011) 144–78.

10. Miroslav Volf, *Exclusion and Embrace: A Theological Exploration of Identity, Otherness, and Reconciliation* (Nashville: Abingdon, 1996) 129.

11. Socioethical obligations can also be characterized as covenant obligations.

12. In articulating the disconnect in this way, it is important to grasp what I do *not* claim. The problem of the gap is not that of the church unsuccessfully applying moral lessons from a "spiritual" ritual to "social" settings. On this point, see John Howard Yoder, *Body Politics: Five Practices of the Christian Community before the Watching World* (Nashville: Discipleship Resources, 1992) vi–xi. Likewise, I do not hold, in contrast to an instrumentalist account of the Lord's Supper, that the primary importance of the Supper is its capacity to

empower Christians to achieve a particular social or political outcome through the liturgy. In this regard, see William T. Cavanaugh, *Torture and Eucharist: Theology, Politics, and the Body of Christ*, Challenges in Contemporary Theology, ed. Gareth Jones and Lewis Ayres (Oxford: Blackwell, 1998) 11–14. My emphasis on the social significance of the Lord's Supper is not a myopic perspective that erases the Supper's soteriological meaning; to the contrary, its social pertinence presupposes the saving efficacy of Christ's death, which itself is a social event.

13. Wainwright, *Eucharist and Eschatology*, 84.

14. Ibid.

15. See *Baptism, Eucharist, and Ministry*, "Eucharist," paragraph 1, for its discussion of the relationship of the Lord's Supper to other meals of God's reign.

16. Robert J. Karris, *Luke: Artist and Theologian, Luke's Passion Account as Literature* (New York: Paulist, 1985) 66.

17. *Baptism, Eucharist and Ministry*, "Eucharist," paragraph 1.

18. Stassen and Gushee, *Kingdom Ethics*, 29.

19. For a comprehensive account of the meals of Jesus in Luke–Acts, see John Paul Heil, *The Meal Scenes in Luke Acts: An Audience-Oriented Approach*, Society of Biblical Literature Monograph Series 52, ed. Sharon H. Ringe (Atlanta: Society of Biblical Literature, 1999).

20. Karris, *Luke*, 47.

21. Ibid., 56.

22. Ibid., 58–59.

23. Wainwright, *Eucharist and Eschatology*, 34.

24. Karris, *Luke*, 63–64.

25. Ibid., 70.

26. Ibid.

27. Wainwright, *Eucharist and Eschatology*, 21.

28. Ibid., 2. Later, Wainwright asserts that what is at stake in reclaiming the meal as an interpretive category for the Lord's Supper is the church's ability to envision the eschatological banquet through the form of the Lord's Supper. Insofar as the Lord's Supper no longer resembles a meal, "it is correspondingly difficult to see in it the sign of the banquet in the final kingdom" (158).

25. J. Frederick Holper, "'As Often as You Eat This Bread and Drink the Cup,'" *Interpretation* 48 (January 1994): 70.

26. Anthony C. Thiselton, *The First Epistle to the Corinthians: A Commentary on the Greek Text*, New International Greek Testament Commentary (Grand Rapids: Eerdmans, 2000) 761–64. See Thiselton's helpful discussion of *koinonia*.

27. Michael Haykin points to eighteenth-century English Baptist hymnody as a resource for uncovering a historic Baptist perspective of communing with Christ during the Lord's Supper. He cites, for example, the following stanzas from a hymn by English pastor Benjamin Beddome (1717–1795) that speak of communion with Christ as a profound feeding in which Christ is present, although Beddome holds to an understanding of the Supper as an ordinance: "Come then, my soul, partake, The banquet is divine: His body is the choicest food, His blood the richest wine. Ye hungry starving poor Join in the sweet repast; View Jesus in

these symbols given, And his salvation taste" (187). The meal imagery helps to convey the deep spiritual communion between Christ and the believer. See Michael A. G. Haykin, "'His soul-refreshing presence': The Lord's Supper in Calvinistic Baptist Thought and Experience in the 'Long Eighteenth Century,'" in *Baptist Sacramentalism*, Studies in Baptist History and Thought, ed. Anthony R. Cross and Philip E. Thompson, vol. 5 (Carlisle UK: Paternoster Press, 2003) 185–87.

28. In *Kingdom Ethics*, 25–28, Stassen and Gushee identify these characteristics as marks of God's reign.

29. Wainwright, *Eucharist and Eschatology*, 73.

30. *Baptism, Eucharist and Ministry*, "Eucharist," paragraph 20, italics added.

31. Gerd Theissen, *The Social Setting of Pauline Christianity: Essays on Corinth*, ed. and trans. John H. Schütz (Philadelphia: Fortress, 1982) 69, 73.

32. Hays, *First Corinthians*, 196.

33. Jerome Murphy-O'Connor, *Keys to First Corinthians: Revisiting the Major Issues* (Oxford: Oxford University Press, 2009) 182–83.

34. Ibid., 184.

35. Ibid.

36. See Anders Eriksson, *Traditions as Rhetorical Proof: Pauline Argumentation in 1 Corinthians*, Coniectanea Biblica, New Testament Series 29 (Stockholm: Almqvist & Wiksell International, 1998) 175–76; See also Otfried Hofius, "The Lord's Supper and the Lord's Supper Tradition: Reflections on 1 Corinthians 11:23b-25," in *One Loaf, One Cup: Ecumenical Studies of 1 Cor 11 and other Eucharistic Texts*, Cambridge Conference on the Eucharist, August 1988, ed. Ben Meyer (Macon GA: Mercer University Press, 1993) 89–96.

37. David Garland speaks of the well-known practice of "basket dinners" or contribution (*eranos*) dinner parties in which persons prepared a dinner for themselves and packed it in a basket to take to the event. The comparison to contemporary potlucks is misleading because the intention of potluck dinners is that each person will bring something to share. See David E. Garland, *1 Corinthians*, Baker Exegetical Commentary on the New Testament (Grand Rapids MI: Baker Academic, 2003) 541.

38. Theissen, *Social Setting of Pauline Christianity*, 154; Ben Witherington III, *Conflict and Community in Corinth: A Socio-Rhetorical Commentary on 1 and 2 Corinthians* (Grand Rapids MI: Eerdmans, 1995) 243–45.

39. Hays, *First Corinthians*, 196.

40. Theissen, *Social Setting of Pauline Christianity*, 158, 162.

41. See Gordon Fee, *The First Epistle to the Corinthians*, New International Commentary on the New Testament (Grand Rapids MI: Eerdmans, 1987) 540–43, for a helpful overview of the debate.

42. Garland, *1 Corinthians*, 540-41; Hays, *First Corinthians*, 197. Scholars who defend the alternate view, which I find less persuasive, argue that the problem of verses 17-22 is a temporal one in which wealthier Christians begin eating their own meal before others arrive for the ritual meal. These interpreters hold that higher-status Corinthians would have greater flexibility over their time as a result of their social standing and therefore could arrive earlier and, more important, begin eating without their poorer counterparts. The Greek word *pro-*

lambanei in verse 21 is translated as "each of you goes ahead with your own supper" (NRSV) or "each of you goes ahead without waiting for anyone else" (NIV) to render this temporal sense. The importance of this exegetical option is that if the issue that Paul addresses is primarily one of some not waiting for all to gather, then one might interpret the communal problem as one of a breach in etiquette.

43. Hays, *First Corinthians*, 197.

44. Fee, *First Epistle to the Corinthians*, 542.

45. Garland, *1 Corinthians*, 541–42.

46. Thiselton, *First Epistle to the Corinthians*, 145.

47. See Otto Knoch, "'Do This in Memory of Me!' (Luke 22:20; 1 Cor 11:24-25): The Celebration of the Eucharist in the Primitive Christian Communities" in *One Loaf, One Cup*, 8. Knoch, through identifying an "expiation motif" in the words of institution in 11:24, argues that the meaning of the Last Supper tradition is rooted in Jesus' interpretation of his own death as having soteriological significance. Jesus imparts salvific meaning to his death by drawing upon Old Testament themes found in Exod 24:8, Isa 53, and Jer 31:31-34, and he anticipates his death through the ritual acts of the breaking of the bread at the start of the meal, the sharing of the cup that follows the meal, and the relating of their significance through interpretive sayings. According to this reading, Jesus, through an act of obedience to God's will, dies "for others," and through this self-giving death initiates a new covenant with God's people. See also Garland, *1 Corinthians*, 546–47, for a representative illustration of this reading.

48. Suzanne Watts Henderson, "'If Anyone Hungers . . .': An Integrated Reading of 1 Cor 11.17-34," *New Testament Studies* 48 (2002): 198.

49. Henderson quotes from a sermon by John Chrysostom on this passage: "Paul reminds us that the Master gave up everything including himself, for us, whereas we are reluctant even to share a little food with our fellow believers" (Henderson, "'If Anyone Hungers . . .,'" 203, quoting John Chrysostom, *Homilies on the Epistles of Paul to the Corinthians* 27/5).

50. The traditional or majority reading is found in the NRSV, REB, NIV, and NJB, as cited by Thiselton, *First Epistle to the Corinthians*, 899.

51. Henderson, "'If Anyone Hungers . . .,'" 196.

52. Theissen, *First Epistle to the Corinthians*, 163–64.

53. Dennis Smith, "Meals and Morality in Paul and His World," in *Society of Biblical Literature 1981 Seminar Papers* 20, ed. K. H. Richards (Chico CA: Scholars Press, 1981) 328.

54. Henderson, "'If Anyone Hungers . . .,'" 201.

55. Ibid., 201–202.

56. Ibid., 202.

57. Ibid., 205.

58. Ibid., 203–206, esp. 205–206. Henderson notes that by the time of Paul's writing, the term "house" (*oikia*) had acquired a wider semantic range in the Greek language that includes the communal or collective sense of "house" as a household or community.

59. Ibid., 206, brackets added.

60. Ibid., 207. Henderson suggests that Paul draws on the prophet Isaiah as a framework for his reprimand of the community's table fellowship. In Isa 5:8, the prophet condemns the wealthy's misuse of the homes of others for unjust purposes, and denounces the isolation and divided community that follow as a consequence: "Ah, you who join house to house, who add field to field, until there is room for no one but you, and you are left to live alone in the midst of the land!" (205). Likewise, she cites a segment from Isa 58 that highlights "house" as a place where hungry members of the community should be fed: "Is not this the fast that I choose? . . . Is it not to share your bread with the hungry, and bring the homeless poor into your house? . . . [Isa 58:6,7]" (Henderson, 207). Stassen and Gushee emphasize the prophetic tradition of Israel as a primary source for Jesus' teachings and note that Isaiah is the primary prophet from whom Jesus appropriates his teachings on God's reign.

61. Henderson, "'If Anyone Hungers . . .,'" 208.

62. See Sara Miles, *Take This Bread: The Spiritual Memoir of a Twenty-first-century Christian* (New York: Ballantine Books, 2007).

63. Ibid., 58: "Communion" refers to Holy Communion or the Lord's Supper. In lower case, "communion" has the meaning of fellowship or relationship.

64. Miles, *Take This Bread*, 97.

65. Miles met with one of the priests after she envisioned the pantry as a food-sharing ministry. She shared how she had been inspired by the inscriptions on the church's new altar table. One quotation in Greek was from the Gospel of Luke: "This guy welcomes sinners and eats with them." The other quotation was indebted to the seventh-century mystic Isaac of Nineveh: "Did not our Lord share his table with tax collectors and harlots? So do not distinguish between worthy and unworthy. All must be equal for you to love and serve" (*Take This Bread*, 95). Later recalling the conversation, the supportive priest who anticipated opposition to the church's welcoming of poor strangers into the sanctuary during the week stated, "I thought, wow, this will be interesting. We just spent all this money on an altar [nearly $6,000 dollars], and now we're gonna bring in people who will scuff it?" (111–12).

66. Miles, *Take This Bread*, 127.

67. Ibid., 129.

68. Ibid.

69. Ibid., 99. Old Testament scholar Ellen Davis has helped me to see that Communion functions prophetically for Miles. It leads and enables her to decisively enact God's community-restoring justice on behalf of the marginalized and to confront unjust powers or structures that denigrate the poor. Miles's profound love for the poor in her community leads her to act justly for and with them. The importance of food pantries, in contrast to soup kitchens that encourage dependency by having people come to be fed two or three times a day, and which often lead to humiliation—is choice. In a pantry, those in need of food get to choose their own groceries. More important, families are enabled to cook and eat together in their own homes.

70. Ibid., 77.

71. Ibid., 81, 96.

72. See William T. Cavanaugh, "Dying for the Eucharist or Being Killed by It? Romero's Challenge to First-World Christians," *Theology Today* 58 (July 2001): 187–88; "Consumption, the Market, and the Eucharist," in *Hunger, Bread and Eucharist*, ed. Christophe Boureux, Janet Martin Soskice, and Luiz Carlos Susin (London: SCM Press, 2005); "The

World in a Wafer: A Geography of the Eucharist as Resistance to Globalization," *Modern Theology* 15 (April 1999): 186–88.

73. L. Shannon Jung, *Food for Life: The Spirituality and Ethics of Eating* (Minneapolis: Augsburg Fortress, 2004) 75–92; see also Wirzba, *Food and Faith*, 71–109.

74. See United States Department of Agriculture's Economic Research Service, www.ers.usda.gov/topics/food-nutrition-assistance/food security-in-the-us. It documents that 50.1 million people lived in food-insecure households in 2011. "Food insecurity" refers to households at certain times during the year that were "uncertain of having, or unable to acquire, enough food to meet the needs of all their members because they had insufficient money or other resources for food." The definition includes households classified with low food security and very low food security. Households with low food security were able to avoid disrupting their food patterns or reducing food intake because of their use of federal food assistance, food pantries, or eating a less varied diet. In households with very low security, the eating pattern was disrupted and food intake was reduced because of insufficient resources. In reports prior to 2006, these particular households were described as "food insecure with hunger." I cite this government figure because it is used by advocacy groups such as Bread for the World. I use "hunger" throughout the article, for, although I appreciate the precision of the definition, I struggle with the term "food insecurity." I also recognize that those who hunger may have incomes that place them above the federal poverty line.

75. See verses 27-32 that deal with the issue of judgment in conjunction with the practice of discernment. Although misunderstandings of judgment in this context have led to unfortunate readings of this passage, the topic falls outside the scope of my present inquiry.

76. Hays, *First Corinthians*, 200.

77. Ibid.

78. Cavanaugh, "Dying for the Eucharist," 187.

79. Ibid., 188.

80. William H. Willimon, *The Service of God: Christian Work and Worship* (Nashville: Abingdon, 1983) 133–34.

81. Ibid., 131, italics added.

Chapter 6

Delivering Love

LAURA RECTOR

Introduction

Faith is passed on in communities. Glen Stassen once explained to a class that another student and I were like his grandchildren because he had also taught our undergraduate professor, David Gushee. Certainly, Glen Stassen has been a theological grandparent, but he is also a mentor, close friend, colleague, teacher, and even sometimes a rescuer to me. He has passed on a legacy of faith rooted in love and justice to his students and his colleagues, but what were Stassen's theological influences? As a student at Union Theological Seminary, Stassen received an academic legacy to develop and pass on to others. The words of 2 Timothy 2:2 come to mind: "And the things you have heard me say in the presence of many witnesses entrust to reliable people who will also be qualified to teach others" (TNIV). This has been his pattern. One of the Union professors who contributed to the theological legacy that Glen Stassen inherited, developed, and passed on to others was Daniel Day Williams.[1] This essay shows how Stassen was influenced by Williams when he developed the concept of delivering love, even as he grounded the concept in Scripture.

A Student's Praise for His Teacher

Williams was a well-known process theologian who taught at the University of Chicago, Chicago Theological Seminary, and Union Theological Seminary. His publications spanned almost four decades, but it is *The Spirit and the Forms of Love,* published in 1968, that concerns Stassen's work on delivering love.[2] As a process theologian, Williams believes that God is moved by what happens in history, and in this work he looks at what that means for how we understand both divine and human love. Williams writes, "The history of the conception of love is also the history of the conception of God."[3] Williams believes that God enters with compassion into the human situation and can be moved by human love, and, therefore, human loves reflect the Creator's love.[4] He writes, "God's dealing with his world does involve his own suffering. His love manifests itself in the communication of his longing, his agonizing over his world. His power remains sovereign, and its work will be done, but God does not live untouched by what happens."[5] Humans can, in fact, "become occasions of his suffering."[6] God acts and is acted upon in history, and, therefore, "The new ethical relationship demanded by the action of God's love in Christ is the giving of concrete help to the neighbor, the spirit of mercy and compassion, the creative concern which is the human analogue of what God has shown to man. It is an analogue that means the imitation of a divine pattern through participation in history."[7]

When Williams writes of God's *suffering,* he seeks to correct the Neoplatonic ideas that God is impassable and that love and justice are polarized.[8] He uses *suffering* to show that God can be moved, changed, or affected by others, although his participation does not have the limitations of suffering, finite humans.[9] This understanding shapes Williams's theory of the atonement, which he grounds in the experiences of "reconciliation in human life"[10] and the concrete experiences of Jesus revealed through the New Testament. Unlike atonement theories in which human beings have no involvement except as passive recipients, Williams's theory involves both divine and human actions, and these actions create the church—as a new community founded in reconciliation.[11] In *Kingdom Ethics,* Stassen calls Williams's book "profound,"[12] and he praises Williams for understanding love's meaning through "a narrative of the Hebraic concept of covenant "and in "the atonement as the action of God's community-creating love,"[13] while not setting love "over against justice."[14]

In *Kingdom Ethics,* Stassen discusses major definitions of love in theological ethics. He offers Williams's concept of mutual love as a contrast to Anders Nygren's view of sacrificial love, and offers his own work on delivering love as a way to deepen Gene Outka's concept of love as equal regard.[15]

Stassen praises his former teacher for showing a mutual love characterized by five qualities.[16] First, it affirms the "Real otherness or individuality" of both loving parties. No one is "destroyed or absorbed" by the other. Second, he points out that love has "Freedom with limits." Love does not coerce, but love also involves limits when we make commitments. Third, love involves "Acting and receiving, or suffering." The fourth quality Stassen lists is the "Power to change the other and be changed by the other." Finally, love involves "Impartial judgment and justice."[17] This last quality means that love includes a realism that can appraise needs and respect truthfulness.[18] This quality also tilts Stassen's scales in Williams's favor against Nygren, because Stassen, too, wants to correct a false split between love and justice.[19]

In contrast, when Stassen discusses Nygren's concept of sacrificial love, he is mostly critical.[20] In Nygren's understanding, humans are "passive recipients of what God does for us, with passive righteousness given by grace, without any calculation of our merit."[21] Love does not flow back and forth between the Creator and the created. Rather, only God truly loves.[22] Stassen recognizes that sacrificial love has value, because it can show compassion even when that path is wrought with pain. Further, it can "interrupt the vicious cycle of mutual recrimination."[23] But he points out "some very damaging liabilities."[24] For instance, sacrificial love can be so idealistic that people cannot live up to it. It also has no room for self-concern or protection. Perhaps most important, it creates a false dichotomy between love and justice. Stassen argues that sacrificial love has been used to keep the marginalized from opposing oppression, and along with that, when someone assumes they know the good for others without involving them, it creates paternalistic and dependent relationships. Finally, it mischaracterizes the work of the cross and, therefore, falls short of the biblical narratives because it makes self-sacrifice, rather than deliverance into God's kingdom community, the purpose of Jesus' death.[25]

Stassen more softly criticizes Gene Outka's concept of "love as *equal regard*," but he prefers Williams.[26] Outka understands that we love everyone without regard to "their special traits, actions, merits or what they can do for us."[27] Stassen sees more potential for justice in Outka's definition than he does in Nygren's self-sacrificial love because "all are equal." Further, he praises Outka for having a place for "self-regard." But he calls Outka's definition "incomplete"[28] because self-regard can easily become a rationale for ignoring the needs of others. He also criticizes Outka's view for its foundation in "Kant's 'categorical imperative' (always treat persons as ends-in-themselves and never merely as means to an end)," rather than Scripture.[29] Stassen believes that it fails to take in special obligations to family members and other loved ones. Moreover, it stays at a philosophical level instead of grabbing us "deep down, where our unspoken motivations come from."[30] He then turns to his own concept of delivering love to offer a biblical corrective to Outka's more philosophical love.[31]

Love Tied to the Trinitarian Reality of the Living God

Both Stassen's appreciation of Williams's work and his criticisms of Outka and Nygren set the stage for understanding Stassen's theory of delivering love in his influential ethics textbook.[32] It is first important, however, to understand that some of Stassen's other influential works bear witness to his understanding of delivering love. Although Stassen writes most clearly about delivering love in *Kingdom Ethics,* his ideas about God the deliverer can be traced throughout his scholarly career. What Stassen believes about the character and reality of the living God is crucial to understanding the way he thinks about love. As former student David Gushee writes, Stassen asks us to believe in "a certain kind of God: one who is present and active in the world, bringing deliverance and healing into our wounded lives and broken relationships."[33] In *Living the Sermon on the Mount,* Stassen writes, "To be in God's presence is to be in the presence of the one who redeems us, *who delivers us.* This is certainly the case in Exodus 3 and 6, when the hallowed name of God is revealed to Moses, and it means 'God is our deliverer.'"[34] He argues, "The Ten Commandments are about God's presence, and God's delivering love for the vulnerable."[35] This delivering love, in turn, is crucial to understanding the Sermon on the Mount, to which Stassen has devoted much of his scholarship. He writes, "Jesus gives a way of deliverance for people who need it."[36]

In an earlier work, "Concrete Christological Norms for Transformation," Stassen developed a Trinitarian understanding of love, although there he refers to movements characterized by delivering love as historic periods of "transformative, prophetic faith."[37] In this response to the work of H. Richard Niebuhr, Stassen shows that key movements of deliverance or prophetic transformation were movements characterized by a three-fold concept of God: (1) "the sovereignty of God over all of life," (2) the "living, dynamic, eternal Judge and Redeemer," and (3) the God who "is known with structure and content"[38] through Jesus Christ.[39] Stassen associates each of these understandings with a person of the Trinity.[40] This Trinitarian understanding is key to Stassen's understanding of God as deliverer. Using Niebuhr, Stassen points out that such ideas influenced the democracy of the early Puritans, the Great Awakening and the antislavery movement that grew out of it, the Social Gospel movement, and the American civil rights movement. In other words, this understanding of God points to a God who delivers people living in oppression.[41] The ideas Stassen found in H. Richard Niebuhr's writing are also present in Daniel Day Williams, who co-wrote at least one project with Niebuhr.[42]

The Responsive Love of a Sovereign God

When it comes to the sovereignty of God, Williams asks, "Is not the heart of faith the recognition that God is utterly different from man? God is creator and not creature; *Lord and sovereign, not dependent and limited by the conditions of our existence.* Our knowledge of the love of God must come from his self-disclosure. It is not a projection from our human loves."[43] Williams's understanding of God's sovereignty has a different nuance than the impassability sometimes assigned to that doctrine.[44] Just as in Stassen's essay, however, the idea of God's sovereignty leads to trust.[45] Williams argues, "If Yahweh is not in control of the heavens and the earth, he cannot be the saving God. If there really are other gods, the claim for absolute trust in Yahweh breaks down. The doctrine of creation is essential to the relationship which Israel has with him."[46] Elsewhere, he undergirds the theme of God's sovereignty with his discussion of Augustine, Calvin, and the age-old tension between people's freedom and God's rule, as well as a discussion of whether God is "unchangeable." Williams wants to avoid Neoplatonic and Augustinian misunderstandings of God as unchangeable and impassable.[47] Rather, he teaches that historical realities affect God.[48]

God's rule also does not free people from responsibility. A proper understanding of God's rule should not result in determinism, but allows people freedom to act in love.[49] People interact with the Creator, bearing the *imago dei* as "the will to belong."[50] They were made for communion with God and others, but also for autonomy.[51] Humans still retain their individuality and freedom within the reign of God.[52] As Williams notes, "One of the marks of authentic love is growth in freedom to acknowledge the realities, and to keep the integrity of the self within those realities."[53] Freedom has both negative and positive possibilities, of course. Williams writes, "Radical freedom may be man's possibility of shaping his future, but also of destroying his life."[54] God's eternal reign also offers a focus for humanity's creative endeavors.[55] The *imago dei* is a checkpoint for helping people become loving and just, even as God is loving and just, rather than allowing people to destroy themselves and others.[56] For this reason, the eternal finds meaning in the temporal, but the temporal could very well focus its vision and nurture love by looking to the eternal quality of God's reign, without falling into the Neoplatonic metaphysics that Williams warns about.[57] This understanding of God's sovereignty gets at several of the qualities that Stassen admired in Williams's work: individuality, freedom with limits, the ability to act and be acted upon, or to change and be changed. Most important, it has implications for justice.[58]

Stassen has a strong commitment to justice, shaped by this understanding of God. Love requires justice.[59] The fact that God rules and God is free to respond to people's pain gives people comfort that allows them to take action. As Stassen points out, civil rights leaders like Martin Luther King, Jr., were able to act precisely because of belief that God ruled over earthly history and could respond to the human plight.[60] In his later work, *Kingdom Ethics,* Stassen says that the Beatitudes show this "participative grace" and that this is key to understanding his approach to ethics.[61] He explains that "Grace is God's deliverance, his transforming initiative and not our human-effort, high-ideal, hard-striving achievement."[62] Grace also empowers humans.[63]

The Redemptive, Dynamic Love of a Just God

Niebuhr's understanding of God as a dynamic judge who transcends human institutions correlates with the work of the Holy Spirit.[64] This helps root love in justice, because it adds a correction of truth and realism to our understandings of human works—including the work of the church.[65] This idea of God as "dynamic" also highlights at least two of the qualities Stassen praised in Williams's work, because these things get at God's creativity: the ability to respond, to act, to receive, and to suffer in love, and the ability to change and be changed.[66]

Williams emphasizes the importance of the Holy Spirit's work in his discussion of love. As a process theologian, Williams views God "in historical-temporal terms" and hopes to "recapture aspects of the biblical message which have been obscured throughout the history of the tradition."[67] The Holy Spirit, although an eternal being, illustrates best God's ability to meet the changing reality in which humans dwell. Williams calls love "spirit"[68] and describes the Holy Spirit as "the spirit of unqualified love."[69] He also describes God's ability to share with his creatures "the power of his being, allowing them a measure of freedom and spontaneity."[70] This points to both the power and movement in the adjective Stassen applies to the Holy Spirit: "dynamic."[71] Williams adds, "To love is to act. Loving involves feelings, emotions, cravings, valuations and sharing, and all these require a movement toward the other, whether it be overt physical movement or the movement of the spirit."[72]

The Spirit also seeks truth and acts as judge. As Williams says, "The judgment of God transcends our judgments in history."[73] This quality of the Spirit highlights both the individuality and the justice that Stassen admires in his teacher's book.[74] It respects individuality, because people's needs receive genuine, truthful, and personalized assessment. Williams writes, "It is not loving concern alone which tells us what needs are; the structures of human existence, and their discernment require impartial, loving judgment, united with critical reflection."[75] This discernment in turn makes justice possible. The rational component of humankind's existence, often associated with images of justice, is also subject to love. Williams writes, "Reason needs the spirit and impetus of love to realize itself and to become the servant of the Kingdom of God."[76] Love must respect justice.[77] Not only that, love must "struggle for justice."[78]

Williams emphasizes that God is independent from human institutions, just as Stassen does.[79] This, too, helps create a community of just love. Williams points out that "The Holy Spirit and the human spirit remain two, not one."[80] He later shows that community-forming aspects of just love mean a "positive appreciation" of group loyalties, such as family bonds or patriotic love.[81] This conforms to the communal nature of humans' *imago dei*.[82] Yet at the same time, just love must guard against group idolatry.[83] Christian love means that humans must "live in an ambiguous and difficult relationship to every concrete form of group loyalty."[84] Hence, in works involving love and justice, "We never identify what God is doing with what we are doing."[85] Therefore, even the church cannot become an idol, because "One of the marks of the presence of the Holy Spirit is the acknowledgement by fallible men that the pure love of God cannot be claimed for any human community, even the Church."[86] Such humility makes changes in social structures possible, instead of merely associating the church with God's will.[87] At the same time, such humility means recognizing that God transcends the best-wrought human endeavors.[88]

The Delivering Love of a God who Is Manifested in History

Finally, the delivering God can be known with "structure and content"[89] through "the redemptive manifestation of God in Christ, within our real history."[90] Christ is the particular way in which God's love is known, and the prophetic movements that Stassen describes received their structure and content through him.[91] As we will see, the particular, concrete details of Stassen's delivering love fill out our understanding of how Jesus makes God known in history.

First, though, observe that, like the other Trinitarian concepts, this idea is also present in the work of Stassen's teacher.[92] Williams says, "God is known through his acts in which he discloses his power, his purpose, and his gracious intent."[93] In other words, God discloses through the concrete realities of history in order to form a community. Jesus is key to this divine self-disclosure. For example, reiterating the ideas of the process philosopher Alfred North Whitehead, Williams writes, "The Gospel presents the figure of the Christ as the expression of a non-coercive love which draws the world in its freedom toward a finer community of being."[94] Our faith can have content and structure for forming communion, because Christ gives concreteness to the analogue between God's love and human love.[95] As noted, Williams develops a theory of the atonement that expands on this idea of God creating community.[96] Jesus was divine self-disclosure of love because "Jesus revealed the love of God in a bloody first-hand encounter with the sin and evil in the world."[97] Later, he ties humanitarian love to "participation in the history of the love that gives itself for sinners."[98] Such love concretely points to what Stassen describes as "the redemptive manifestation of God in Christ."[99]

Williams's Influence on the Norm of "Delivering Love" in Kingdom Ethics

With this Trinitarian understanding of God in mind, we turn to Stassen's discussion in *Kingdom Ethics* and look at the particulars of Stassen's personal theory of delivering love.[100] Here, Stassen builds on the previously mentioned "structure and content" from Jesus—specifically from the parable of the Good Samaritan (Luke 10:25-37), the Sermon on the Mount, and the atonement.[101] While Stassen carefully presents delivering love through the lens of biblical interpretation, he also embeds his teacher's concepts in his norm of delivering love, even while he establishes his own distinctive definition. Williams's influence on Stassen's concept of delivering love is not limited to the section of *Kingdom Ethics* on mutual love.[102] In some ways, Stassen "thickens" the things he learned from his teacher through his biblical interpretation.[103] For example, Williams writes, "The love of God and the response of man create a new history in which the forms of love's expression cannot be identified with only one pattern or motif."[104] Similarly Stassen believes that "love is not just a single principle, like a song sung in a monotone."[105] Just as Williams writes that there is room for Christians to understand the atonement in multiple ways including his own, Stassen also presents a new understanding of the atonement. Williams writes, "All these metaphors have been worked into theories of the atonement in Christian history: but it is remarkable that no single doctrine of atonement has ever become the accepted theory to the exclusion of the others. It is as if at the centre of the Christian faith the redemptive action of God explodes all theories and formulas."[106] Likewise, Stassen writes, "The once-for-all drama of the cross has far deeper meaning than any one interpretation of the meaning of the atonement can exhaust."[107] Both authors' theories of the atonement point to God's formation of a community.[108] Stassen's delivering love also shows the relationship between love and justice that Williams asserts.[109]

In Stassen's understanding, love is a four-act drama.[110] In this drama of delivering love, Stassen discovers a theme that unifies the story of the Compassionate Samaritan, the teachings of the Sermon on the Mount, and the meaning of the atonement. In the next section of this essay, I describe each component of delivering love and point out the ways in which Williams influences them.

Love Sees with Compassion and
Enters into the Situation of Persons in Bondage[111]

The first act of delivering love involves seeing the situation of a person in bondage and responding with compassion. As mentioned, Stassen's understanding of delivering love is built initially around the parable of the Good Samaritan (Luke 10:25-37).[112] The original audience of the story would have "identified with the man in danger."[113] Likewise, Stassen sees this pattern of delivering love in the Sermon on the Mount when Jesus taught his followers to show compassion to enemies (Matt 5:43-48).[114] Stassen's theory of the atonement emphasizes that "God shows love for us by *entering incarnationally into our situation of bondage.*"[115] The first act in the four-act drama of delivering love involves seeing the plight of others with such heartfelt love that one enters into their situations of pain.[116]

Discussing the parable of the Good Samaritan, Stassen points out that the man who was robbed not only lost his physical belongings but was also dehumanized and stripped of his group identification. Stassen sees this as key to understanding sin in this situation and how the man was delivered:

> People had their security from membership in an ethnic group that would take care of them. Each ethnic group had its distinctive dress and speech. To be stripped naked and left unconscious and unable to speak was to be both shamed and unrecognizable as a member of any ethnic or religious community, and therefore removed from group loyalty and help.[117]

The barriers this put between the robbed man and the priest and the Levite were much like Williams's understandings of sin and group loyalties.

> Any non-conformity is a warning signal that my group is challenged. In the resulting anxiety we are tempted to reject the other's claim to our concern, and to absolutize ourselves. The will to belong becomes the will to preserve our way against every other. Since this can never be wholly justified rationally, we seek justification by identifying our way with the absolute good.[118]

Deliverance for the robbed man came from someone entering into his plight and restoring him to the safety of community instead of giving in to such anxiety.

Writing against the sacrificial love of Nygren that severs love from justice and the "thin ethic of *equal regard*" of Outka that has philosophical rather than biblical roots, Stassen uses the parable to point out that "love has special regard for those who are in bondage to others or to their own sin."[119] Perhaps this is because Williams, too, insists, "To love is to respond to what is present in history, with these specific people and their needs, their sin and their hope, and our sin and our hope."[120] This reflects the "impartial judgment and justice" that Stassen praises because it involves rationally assessing the other person's needs.[121] Significantly, Williams ties love to social justice just as Stassen does.[122] God's justice includes his compassion "toward the hurt, the weak and the oppressed."[123] This correlates with the Trinitarian understanding of God embedded in both authors' beliefs. The Spirit's dynamic nature meets humans' changing needs. The sovereign God who acts in history gets involved in the robbed man's plight through another human, and Jesus reveals God's love with "structure and content" through the parable.[124]

Love Does Deeds of Deliverance[125]

Delivering love is concrete, not abstract or impersonal. Again Stassen shows this through the parable of the Good Samaritan, the Sermon on the Mount, and his theory of the atonement.[126] For example, he points out that the compassionate Samaritan did nine deeds that were neither "unselfish" nor "sacrificial," but rather "precisely what is needed to deliver the half-dead victim in the ditch from his helplessness."[127] He argues that the Sermon on the Mount contains concrete "transforming initiatives" that are "the way of deliverance from vicious cycles of bondage and judgment."[128] As with Williams, Stassen's theory of the atonement is grounded in concrete, historic acts of God.[129] He writes, "The delivering love offered in the cross has continuity with the mighty works of God in the history of Israel and in *the deeds of deliverance,* healing, feeding, reconciling and confronting that Jesus did even before the cross."[130]

With different examples, Williams also embeds delivering deeds in his work on love. For example, Williams suggests that there are better forms of love than "elaborately dramatized and perverse examples of romanticism"[131] and advocating "faithfulness and integrity" in sexual ethics.[132] Love also can be closely tied to political justice (acts of deliverance) if such justice delivers people from bondage. As Williams says, "Since love is the spirit at work in the community of reconciliation, the work which love prompts is to be done in actual history where the neighbor is met. This means that to love is to be involved in the issues of political justice."[133] The American civil rights movement is an example of this.[134]

For Williams, this concreteness goes back to human imitation of the delivering God. He writes,

> In the Hebrew scripture God is known by Israel as the loving God who reveals himself in his actions toward the people with whom he has bound himself in a personal community of loving concern. His love takes on new expressions with the waywardness of his people. It becomes compassion, patience, a mourning for one who has turned away and the longing for this return. It takes form as the merciful concern and the will to restoration of the familial bond. In consequence, man's concern for the other person, the giving of what is needful, and a just and merciful regard for every person are the human expression of love as ethical responsibility.[135]

Once again the communion-creating purpose of both divine and human love is present, the second imitating the first. When people give "what is needful," they do acts of deliverance that restore community. As noted, both Williams and Stassen advocate a community-building love. This leads us to the next component of delivering love.[136]

Love Invites into Community with Freedom, Justice, and Responsibility for the Future[137]

The purpose of deliverance from bondage is the creation of a community characterized by justice. Stassen states, "Throughout the biblical story, deliverance is not only from sin but also into community. God not only liberates the people from Egypt but delivers them through the wilderness to the covenant community of Israel with specific practices and institutions of justice."[138] Deliverance into community is crucial to Stassen's understanding of the Samaritan's provision for the wounded man's ongoing needs. "Establishing community on into the future is itself a crucial deed of deliverance from the hostility, alienation, and aloneness that trap Jews and Samaritans in death-dealing bondage. . . . Jesus is calling Jews to have community with Samaritans."[139] In a similar fashion, the Sermon on the Mount "teaches that we are to make our enemy a member of our community."[140] Stassen also clearly sees God doing for us in the atonement. God's delivering love "is God suffering, bringing us into community with God and each other, community that we ourselves could not create."[141] Suffering creates community as God becomes vulnerable to human responses.[142] Williams argues repeatedly that love gives birth to community. His understanding of the atonement includes a renewal of "loyalty to the broken community in spite of the rupture of disloyalty."[143] With an atonement theory that includes human participation, Williams paves the way for community and the third emphasis of delivering love. He demonstrates how Stassen's Trinitarian understanding achieves concreteness. He writes,

> We have seen how the history of God's action in the world becomes reinterpreted in the New Testament as a history to be understood with Jesus Christ at its centre. It is now the history of humanity as lived under the impact of the new faith which is born out of response to Jesus, and through which a new "people" has come into being which lives by the mercy God has shown in him.[144]

Stassen's idea of a suffering God vulnerable to human response first took shape as he read Williams's book.[145]

Williams also reiterates this idea of community in his repeated discussion of the "will to belong."[146] He says that the "will to *belong*" is "the key to human action and feeling."[147] Human nature has a deep need for "belonging, or communion which constitutes its heart."[148] The will to belong can be self-protective and result in sin with the "refusal to trust in the giver of life and the greater community he is creating."[149] Conversely, appropriate trust in God led to movements of justice in the early Puritans, the Great Awakening, the American civil rights movement, and the Social Gospel movement.[150] Love directed toward God leads to a love that is delivering love, because those working toward justice trust the Creator,[151] who wants to bring others into a "*just* community."[152] Jesus' suffering restored the possibility of just community.[153]

Like Stassen, Williams weds love to justice in community. He writes,

> Love is not an alternative to involvement in the struggle for the rough justice of the world, but the love revealed in the Gospel leads to a distinctive view of the problem of justice. That view does not separate love and justice. It sees them as interrelated aspects of God's work of creating a community between himself and man and between man and man.[154]

Williams points to the importance of community when he writes that we need both intimate familial love and relationships outside the home. He argues, "The person is fulfilled in the world where God's work is being done. We have to find a union of love in its obligation to those with whom our lives are immediately bound; and love which calls upon each to become a creative member of a full society." Love leads us into community under the auspices of human freedom and God's reign, and yet it finds boundaries in justice. Stassen appreciates that Williams presents a freedom that accepts boundaries. For Williams, both freedom and love are informed by justice: "We see why in the strongest human loves concern for the other will be tempered with concern for the larger causes of justice which both must respect."[155]

Love Confronts Those who Exclude[156]

Part of building a just community, however, includes the fourth component of delivering love: confrontation.[157] Stassen believes that the entire parable was Jesus' way of confronting his listeners about their acts of exclusion. "It is such a strong confrontation that when Jesus asked the lawyer, 'Which of these three, do you think, was a neighbor to the man who fell into the hands of robbers?' the lawyer could not say, 'The Samaritan.' He spoke indirectly: 'The one who showed him mercy.'"[158] In a similar manner, the Sermon on the Mount was a confrontation of others. Stassen explains, "In his teaching on peacemaking, Jesus was confronting those who nursed anger and called others fools, those who excluded outcasts, those who sought revenge, those who wanted to kill Roman soldiers, those who hated their enemies and loved only those who love them, and those who judged others."[159] As with the other three emphases of delivering love, Stassen's atonement theory also supports this idea. He writes, "God discloses and confronts the sin that we had been hiding, and establishes community with us even where we commit the worst sin we can imagine—which stands for all other sins of rejection, injustice and violence against God and our fellow humans."[160]

This confrontational aspect of love reminds us of the Spirit who speaks truth and who gives discernment.[161] Williams speaks to this type of truth when he recognizes that sin hurts men as well as women in casual sex acts.[162] More important, Williams ties Jesus' love directly to social justice and a critique of those who exclude. He writes, "Jesus was not crucified for preaching a pure love unsullied by contact with social issues, but for relating the message of love to the critique of social power and privilege."[163]

Conflict is understood within the context of vulnerability, risk, and the creation of community:

> Love does not resolve every conflict; it accepts conflict as the arena in which the work of love is to be done. . . . Love seeks the reconciliation of every life so that it may share with all the others. If a man or a culture is finally lost, it is not because love wills that lostness, but because we have condemned ourselves to separation and refuse reconciliation.[164]

This openness to the risk of confrontation is important for grounding community in reality rather than self-deception. Williams reminds us, "It is a fair proposition that all sin involves some kind of dishonesty, a self-deception about our real motives, and a distortion of truth about others."[165] He then adds concreteness to this thought through the actions of Jesus. He writes, "The human spirit is a proving ground for the truth against the lie. We should remember that a not inconsiderable part of Jesus' ministry was spent in controversy over specific questions of law and ethical practice."[166] Confrontation for the sake of truthfulness in community has a place in the imitation of Jesus.

Conclusion

Daniel Day Williams believed that "the mystery of love creates its own difficulties, for the truth is that since the loves are not wholly separate the meanings shade into one another."[167] Williams's thoughts about love definitely "shade into" Glen Stassen's delivering love. Certainly, he was not the only influence on Stassen's concept of love, but Williams was an important contributor to delivering love. In turn Stassen has passed his understanding of love on to a community of students who study and develop his concepts in academic works such as this one, but who also practice them in concrete acts of social justice. May they entrust their own theological "children" and "grandchildren" with a legacy of appreciation for the love of God the deliverer.

NOTES

1. Williams uses gender-exclusive terms like "man" and "mankind" in the quotes that follow. I retained them for the accuracy of the quotations.

2. See Stassen's discussion of this book, as well as his own work on delivering love, in Glen Stassen and David Gushee, *Kingdom Ethics: Following Jesus in a Contemporary Context* (Downers Grove IL: InterVarsity, 2003) 327–44.

3. Daniel Day Williams, *The Spirit and the Forms of Love* (New York: Harper & Row, 1968) 104.

4. Ibid., 5.

5. Ibid., 33.

6. Ibid., 128.

7. Ibid., 45.

8. Ibid., 53–63.

9. Ibid., 127–29.

10. Ibid., 177.

11. Ibid., 173–91.

12. Stassen and Gushee, *Kingdom Ethics*, 330.

13. Ibid., 332.

14. Ibid., 331.

15. Ibid., 327–44.

16. Ibid., 330–32.

17. Ibid., 331.

18. Williams, *The Spirit and the Forms of Love*, 120–22.

19. Stassen and Gushee, *Kingdom Ethics*, 345–47.

20. Ibid., 328–30.

21. Ibid., 328.

22. Ibid.

23. Ibid., 329.

24. Ibid.

25. Ibid., 329–30.

26. Ibid., 332.

27. Ibid.

28. Ibid.

29. Ibid.

30. Ibid., 333.

31. Ibid.

32. Ibid., 327–44.

33. David Gushee, preface to Glen Stassen, *Living the Sermon on the Mount: A Practical Hope for Grace and Deliverance*, by Glen Stassen (San Francisco: Jossey-Bass, 2006) Kindle e-book.

34. Stassen, *Living the Sermon on the Mount*.

35. Ibid.

36. Ibid.

37. Glen Stassen, "Concrete Christological Norms for Transformation," in *Authentic Transformation: A New Vision of Christ and Culture*, ed. Glen Stassen et al. (Nashville: Abingdon Press, 1996) 133.

38. Ibid., 134.

39. Ibid., 135, 139.

40. Ibid., 141.

41. Ibid., 133–37.

42. See H. Richard Niebuhr, Daniel Day Williams, and James Gustafson, *The Advancement of Theological Education* (New York: Harper & Brothers, 1955).

43. Williams, *The Spirit and the Forms of Love*, 122, italics mine.

44. See Williams's discussion of Augustine and those like Luther and Calvin who repeated his neoplatonic ideas in *The Spirit and the Forms of Love*, 90–110.

45. Stassen, "Concrete Christological Norms for Transformation," 135.

46. Williams, *The Spirit and the Forms of Love*, 27.

47. Ibid., 90–110, 53–63.

48. Ibid., 5.

49. Ibid., 116.

50. Ibid., 205.

51. Ibid., 205–206.

52. Ibid., 114–16.

53. Ibid., 116.

54. Ibid., 103.

55. Ibid., 135.

56. Ibid., 134–35.

57. Ibid., 106–108, 90–110.

58. Stassen and Gushee, *Kingdom Ethics*, 331–32.

59. Ibid., 337–38, 345–47.

60. Stassen, "Concrete Christological Norms for Transformation," 136–37.

61. Stassen and Gushee, *Kingdom Ethics*, 35.

62. Ibid., 36.

63. Ibid., 36–37.

64. Stassen, "Concrete Christological Norms for Transformation," 134, 138–39, 141.

65. Ibid., 138.

66. Stassen and Gushee, *Kingdom Ethics*, 331.

67. Williams, *The Spirit and the Forms of Love*, 107.

68. Ibid., 3, 249.

69. Ibid., 4.

70. Ibid., 109.

71. Stassen, "Concrete Christological Norms for Transformation," 134, 141.

72. Williams, *The Spirit and the Forms of Love*, 117.

73. Ibid., 271.

74. Stassen and Gushee, *Kingdom Ethics*, 331.

75. Williams, *The Spirit and the Forms of Love*, 121.

76. Ibid., 288.

77. Ibid., 122.

78. Ibid., 275.

79. Stassen, "Concrete Christological Norms for Transformation," 138–39.

80. Williams, *The Spirit and the Forms of Love*, 191.

81. Ibid., 256.

82. Ibid., 205.

83. Ibid., 256–58.

84. Ibid., 258.

85. Ibid., 248.

86. Ibid., 274.

87. Ibid., 274–75.

88. Ibid., 248.

89. Stassen, "Concrete Christological Norms for Transformation," 134–35, 139–40.

90. Ibid., 131.

91. Ibid., 139–42. Such movements also did not divorce love and justice. Stassen also calls this "redemptive love." See pages 136–37.

92. Williams, *The Spirit and the Forms of Love*, 34–51.

93. Ibid., 276.

94. Ibid., 107–108.

95. Ibid., 45.

96. Ibid., 173–91.

97. Ibid., 172.

98. Ibid., 262.

99. Stassen, "Concrete Christological Norms for Transformation," 131.

100. Stassen and Gushee, *Kingdom Ethics*, 333–44.

101. Ibid.

102. Ibid., 330–31.

103. See Glen Stassen, *A Thicker Jesus: Incarnational Discipleship in a Secular Age* (Louisville KY.: Westminster John Knox, 2012). In PhD seminars, he regularly assigns Michael Walzer's *Thick and Thin: Moral Argument at Home and Abroad* (Notre Dame: University of Notre Dame, 1994).

104. Williams, *The Spirit and the Forms of Love*, 5.

105. Stassen and Gushee, *Kingdom Ethics*, 333.

106. Williams, *The Spirit and the Forms of Love*, 39.

107. Stassen and Gushee, *Kingdom Ethics*, 342.

108. Williams, *The Spirit and the Forms of Love*, 173–91; Stassen and Gushee, *Kingdom Ethics*, 342–44.

109. Williams, *The Spirit and the Forms of Love*, 243–75; Stassen and Gushee, *Kingdom Ethics*, 337–38.

110. Stassen and Gushee, *Kingdom Ethics*, 333.

111. Ibid., 334.

112. Ibid.

113. Ibid.

114. Ibid., 340.

115. Ibid., 342.

116. Ibid., 334–36.

117. Ibid., 335.

118. Williams, *The Spirit and the Forms of Love*, 147–48.

119. Stassen and Gushee, *Kingdom Ethics*, 335.

120. Williams, *The Spirit and the Forms of Love*, 247.

121. Stassen and Gushee, *Kingdom Ethics*, 331.

122. Williams, *The Spirit and the Forms of Love*, 201–202, 243–75.

123. Ibid., 245.

124. Stassen, "Concrete Christological Norms for Transformation," 130–41.

125. Stassen and Gushee, *Kingdom Ethics*, 336.

126. Ibid., 336–37, 340–41, 343.

127. Ibid., 336.

128. Ibid., 341.

129. Williams, *The Spirit and the Forms of Love*, 173–91.

130. Stassen and Gushee, *Kingdom Ethics*, 343.

131. Williams, *The Spirit and the Forms of Love*, 230.

132. Ibid., 231.

133. Ibid., 249.

134. Ibid., 268–69.

135. Ibid., 33.

136. For their treatments of the atonement, see Williams, *The Spirit and the Forms of Love*, 173–91, and Stassen and Gushee, *Kingdom Ethics*, 337–38.

137. Stassen and Gushee, *Kingdom Ethics*, 337.

138. Ibid.

139. Ibid.

140. Ibid., 341.

141. Ibid., 343.

142. Ibid. Stassen admires this emphasis on community in Williams's understanding of the atonement (332).

143. Williams, *The Spirit and the Forms of Love*, 180.

144. Ibid., 41.

145. Ibid., 180–86.

146. Ibid., 205, 209.

147. Ibid., 146.

148. Ibid.

149. Ibid, 207.

150. Stassen, "Concrete Christological Norms for Transformation," 130–37.

151. Ibid.

152. Stassen and Gushee, *Kingdom Ethics*, 338.

153. Williams, *The Spirit and the Forms of Love*, 186.

154. Ibid., 244.

155. Stassen and Gushee, *Kingdom Ethics*, 331,122; Williams, *The Spirit and the Forms of Love*, 240, 250.

156. Stassen and Gushee, *Kingdom Ethics*, 338.

157. Ibid., 338–44.

158. Ibid., 339.

159. Ibid., 341.

160. Ibid., 343.

161. Stassen, "Concrete Christological Norms for Transformation," 134, 138–39, 141; Williams, *The Spirit and the Forms of Love*, 271, 121.

162. Williams, *The Spirit and the Forms of Love*, 237.

163. Ibid., 201–202.

164. Ibid., 138.

165. Ibid., 177.

166. Ibid., 178–79.

167. Ibid., 2.

Chapter 7

Holistic Character Ethics
An Ethics for a Social Gospel?

Elizabeth M. Bounds

Introduction

I first met Glen Stassen at a session on Michael Walzer's work at the Religion and Social Sciences section of the American Academy of Religion in 1991. Of course, Glen himself had put the session together and had invited Michael Walzer to respond to a conversation that engaged liberalism, communitarianism, and, occasionally, religion.[1] The setting of our meeting is an appropriate start for this essay because it wonderfully illustrates Glen Stassen's complexity. He is an ardent Baptist comfortable both in Christian evangelical circles and in academic discussion of political philosophy. Someone who never backs away from scriptural authority in more "secular" or "modernist" contexts *and* never backs away from the knowledge present in modern(ist), natural, and, in particular, social sciences. Someone who, like Walzer himself, could be called both a "communitarian" and a "liberal"— and neither label on its own would be quite right.[2]

To honor Stassen, I chose to focus on his notion of a holistic character ethics, found most clearly in chapter 3 of the volume *Kingdom Ethics* that he and David Gushee co-authored.[3] The model he lays out in this chapter stretches back to one of his early works, "A Social Theory Model for Religious Social Ethics," published in 1977.[4] In the earlier article he argues that Christian social ethics should turn to political or social theory rather than analytic philosophy when it engages in public or policy discourse. Although the audience and context of *Kingdom Ethics* is quite different (no one is championing analytic philosophy!), his emphasis on the importance of social theory has remained constant.

I am not one of Stassen's evangelical conversation partners, and thus I don't think I am the primary audience for a good amount of his work, including *Kingdom Ethics*. But from the moment we met, Glen Stassen and I knew that we shared a deep commitment to the heritage of Christian social ethics, including, in particular, a conviction that serious engagement with social theory is necessary for ethical work that wants to maintain a commitment to Christian traditions of justice. Both of us have allegiance to the social gospel/social liberal heritage that has been central to Christian social ethics in the United States. Glen comes by this by parentage—his father, Harold Stassen, was a Republican from a time when liberal republicanism did not seem profoundly contradictory. He had a long political life, was one of the eight United States signers of the United Nations Charter, and marched in the 1963 March on Washington as president of the American Baptist Convention. I come by it both from parentage, since my father was a lifelong member of the Liberal Party of New York, of which Reinhold Niebuhr was a co-founder, and by context, growing up in the Upper West Side of Manhattan and attending Union Theological Seminary in New York City.

We also connect through our instinctive peacemaking/facilitating personalities that put us both relationally and intellectually in mediating positions. For example, Stassen has taken leadership in the development of models of just peacemaking that have enabled Christian ethics to overcome what had become an irrelevant just war/pacifism division. Indeed it was his work with just peacemaking that helped me to engage questions of violence and conflict transformation. And each of us is a "both/and" rather than "either/or" thinker, seeking to avoid dichotomies such as context/virtues vs. principles, liberalism vs. communitarianism, sacred vs. secular, private vs. public, and so forth. Both of us have understood the need to revise the liberal framing that has been the mainstay of Christian social ethics for many decades, even though I do this work from a postmodern framework, while Stassen is more clearly connected to communitarianism. Yet, simultaneously, both of us refuse simply to reject all forms of modernist liberalism; rather, we see key strengths in parts of that tradition that need to be retained.

So I am deeply attuned to Glen's project of developing a holistic character ethics. I will show how Glen's model wonderfully combines both liberal and communitarian dimensions as part of continuing the work of Christian social ethics. I will conclude by asking whether there are some tensions or frictions in the mix.

Problems in Christian Social Ethics

Gary Dorrien writes that Christian social ethics is "a tradition that began with the distinctly modern idea that Christianity has a social-ethical mission to transform the structures of society in the direction of social justice."[5] In the days of social gospel and for a good part of the twentieth century, this mission could depend on some sort of tacit assumptions of audience, agents, and authority that were ultimately framed by the institutions of the liberal or mainline Protestant churches.

That assumed frame is no longer there, which has meant that these presuppositions no longer hold. The decline in the membership and role of mainline churches has reduced both audience[5] and authority.[6] By the later twentieth century, a variety of critiques had challenged assumptions about the nature of the agent or actor of Christian ethics who was no longer assumed to be male, white, middle-class/educated. These challenges particularly arose out of claims made on the basis of the experience of those persons and groups who had been marginalized from the production of mainline Christian ethics. However, their projects in ethics generally shared the mission of mainline Christian social ethics named by Dorrien as "transforming structures of society in the direction of social justice," although they gave more varied accounts of power than the economically oriented ones found in Rauschenbusch, Niebuhr, or John Bennett.

As these voices emerged from the late 1960s onward, contestations for authority in Christian social ethics were inevitable. Paul Ramsey's *Who Speaks for the Church?* which attacked the World Council of Churches' position opposing the Vietnam war, is a significant example. His worries about the ways churches should be involved in policy and politics highlighted key themes that would play out over the next decades. There was the concern for the proper role of the church, the caution about politics and policy (no "specific partisan proposals"), and the reservations about a focus on justice.[7] In the world of Reinhold Niebuhr, the nature of the church and its engagement in public policy was simply assumed. H. Richard Niebuhr, a profound influence on Stassen (who was the first person to urge me to read him), did take the church much more seriously due to his engagement with Troeltsch's understanding of the ways church exists in historical form. His historicism shaped both the sociology of the church done by the early Gustafson[8] and the emergence of the character and community emphasis of Stanley Hauerwas.

The concern about virtue and character in Christian ethics emerges out of this context. Stanley Hauerwas has, of course, been the most visible of the character ethicists in the arena of US academic Christian ethics. Jennifer Herdt remarks that "Hauerwas turns to the category of character because he finds in it a corrective both to characteristically Protestant and characteristically secular modern ailments."[9] But Hauerwas is only the most visible Christian ethicist within a broader "communitarian turn" that seeks these correctives.

Common among all of these Christian communitarian ethicists is, first, the focus on the church as the arena where ethics is carried out. Indeed, in Hauerwas's work, the church is audience, authority, and agent all in one. The turn to the church is understood as reclamation of the particularity of Christian identity, in contrast to "secular" society. But the degree of distinction and separation varies among communitarians; the church may be its own public or it may offer its own distinctive voice within that public.

The authority and identity of the church is found both in tradition and, in particular, in scriptural authority. The way this scriptural authority functions varies, however, from the more generalized "story" approach of Hauerwas to more specific engagements with texts found in Yoder and others. This (re)assertion of scriptural authority has been strengthened by the new prominence of evangelical churches and evangelical scholars where the primacy of Scripture has always been central.

Second, the method engaged is virtue ethics with its emphasis on character and virtues rather than rules and principles. An ethics of character is seen as the answer to what Gilbert Meilaender has called "a wide dissatisfaction with an understanding of the moral life which focuses primarily on duties, obligations, troubling moral dilemmas and borderline cases."[10] Aristotle, usually read through Alasdair MacIntyre, is seen as offering a richer account of ethical practice that focuses on goods rather than rights and on the nature of the actor rather than the properties of the act. The actor is not an isolated individual but one morally formed by the surrounding community and its practices.

While all versions of an ethics of character share the focus on Christian identity (church and Scripture) and on character, they nevertheless can be distinguished by what their authors see themselves as opposing or preserving. While there is a general reaction against modernity, different dimensions of modernity are highlighted. Often, modernity is read as liberalism and defined as individualism or as Enlightenment rationalism. For some there is particular concern about the method of universal rules and principles or about the role of social theory, which is seen as trumping Christian identity. For others it may include a reaction against justice and any kind of public social engagement, seen as characteristic of earlier liberal Protestant social ethics.

Stassen understands well that a correction of some of the modernist forms of Christian ethics does not necessarily require all of the different "oppositions" to modernity. He especially resists a kind of distinctively "Christian" way that requires disengagement from the public moral engagement or a dismissal of social theory. This difference from much communitarian ethics lies at the heart of the holistic character ethics he develops.

Glen's Way

Glen Stassen's model of a holistic character ethics navigates skillfully among the dimensions of this turn to character/virtue. In the introduction to *Kingdom Ethics*, he and Gushee establish their location, suggesting that they are eager to avoid "theological/political labels and categories" since "[w]e think we are offering a Christian ethics that seeks to follow Jesus' lead as faithfully as possible." They place their Baptist standpoint within a broad tradition, saying they are "the kind of Baptists who connect both to the Anabaptist and to the Reformed strands of Baptist tradition, as well as to the Great Awakening, revivalist, and Pietist heritage of North American Baptist life." There is also acknowledgment of engagement with the historical black church tradition, the Protestant churches of Europe, Catholicism, and the mainline heritage of theological education.[11]

The richness of Stassen's approach is evident in the breadth embraced in the four dimensions of holistic character ethics described in *Kingdom Ethics,* which include critical perception, critical thinking, deep particularity, and deep faith.[12] Characteristically, Stassen has avoided any simple "liberal" vs. "communitarian" choice but has sought to transcend dichotomies. While he follows Hauerwas and other communitarian-oriented Christian ethicists in rejecting appeals to thin Kantian rationalism and in criticizing "the corrosive force of modern atomistic individualism,"[13] he refuses to accept the all-out ban on modernity. Instead he insists that some of the tools deemed "modernist" (particularly the use of social theory) can be encompassed as part of an ethics based in Jesus' teachings and in scriptural authority.

This balancing is evident in the way the four dimensions of character ethics are laid out as practices of incarnational discipleship: Way of Seeing; Loyalties, Trusts, Interests, Passions; Way of Reasoning; and Basic Convictions. These dimensions nicely balance the modernist ("Seeing" and "Reasoning") and communitarian/traditional ("Loyalties" and "Basic Convictions"). While Stassen affirms reason as one dimension, it is "reasoning *with and through holistic character, which includes the virtues.*"[14] Reason, it is implied, does not have to be a narrow rationalism. Instead, it functions in partnership with the other dimensions, particularly the dimension of convictions.

This point is made even more clearly in another chapter in *Kingdom Ethics* also primarily drafted by Stassen, "The Form and Function of Moral Norms." There he insists that Christian ethics must draw upon a full range of moral forms, with the proviso that rules are principles that are "*embodied* in narratives . . . they get their meaning and have their context in the realistic, embodied, Hebraic narrative of both Testaments, and in their analogous function in a realistic, embodied way of living in our social context."[15] Rules and principles are one of the necessary ways narratives are "incarnated" and enable consistency and order in moral living.[16]

Reason is also expanded through the dimension of passions or loyalties (to other persons, to community, to God), as these shape our "interests" or the foci that we bring to our moral lives. This insistence on contextuality is one place where appeals to experience can appear. *Kingdom Ethics* is cautious about experience. In the chapter on "Authority and Scripture," where Gushee is the first author, it says, "The problem with religious experience as a source of authority is its radical subjectivity."[17] The danger of a modernist individualism or relativism, that is, of a distorting self-interest, is checked by the communal aspect of this dimension, along with the understanding of an ultimate loyalty to God.

Experience is also part of the way of seeing. For me, this dimension is the one that best shows Stassen's commitment to a truly social Christian ethics. In his discussion of "perception," he manages not merely to bring in critical social analysis but also to insist that it is a tool essential for Christian ethics of character. As he points to the ways in which our perceptions can be distorted, a traditional theme of Christian teachings on sin, he suggests that we need social theory to correct these distortions, to develop "self-critical understanding."[18] This is particularly the case because Christian ethics is not only an ethics of the personal life but also an ethics for all aspects of the world since our characters are the product of the social order in which we are embedded. If we do not understand this, we "lack awareness of how [. . .] participation in various economic and political structures promotes destructive policies, institutions, and social practices. Character ethics desperately needs critical social theory or it can misuse people to turn them into virtuous supports of an unjust society."[19] Critical social theory is not a source of distortion but is, in fact, key to enabling a "self-critical understanding of how we perceive *authority, change, threat, and truthfulness* in our society,"[20] balancing the embeddedness of tradition and character with modernist critical capacities.

Authority on the Ground

Stassen's holistic character ethics is galvanizing as a way of living out the concrete incarnational discipleship he sees as the mission and purpose of the church. It is an ethics that calls for full engagement in the world, without retreat to individualism or communal sectarianism. It insists that forms of modern knowledge and experience are part of this mission. And, to return to Dorrien's definition, it claims justice as central to the work of the church. This justice is a full biblical justice, seeking "an end to unjust economic structures, unjust domination, unjust violence, and unjust exclusion from community."[21] In all of these ways, Stassen is passing on the heritage of Christian social ethics.

This acceptance of "modernist" ideas is balanced, as I have suggested, by a strong affirmation of scriptural authority. The weighting in this direction is apparent in the model of the four dimensions.[22] While you could work through the dimensions in any order, or make them into the kind of hermeneutical circle used in liberation theologies, the arrows in the diagram require a particular order (see The Four Dimensions of Character diagram on p. 45). While "Seeing" and "Reasoning" may be shaped by "Loyalties" and "Basic Convictions," the reverse is not possible.

While the order of the ethical process does preserve the authority of church and Scripture, it does not reflect the way modern knowledge has profoundly affected both our convictions and our passions. Surely the process is more circular or interactive. For example, does not an understanding of the scientific accounts of the universe and its formation, or of the processes of evolution, require us to engage seriously our understanding of Scripture? Claiming scriptural authority does not mean claiming the authority of a particular interpretation of Scripture. This question becomes particularly compelling when the Christian authority invoked may lead to the very forms of injustice that biblical justice opposes.[23]

Thinking about these arrows also led me to further reflection on what it might look like to "do" Glen Stassen's ethics. Even though there is an emphasis on practices, the ways issues are actually engaged seem sometimes heavily cognitive, which always favors academics over the broader range of persons in the church. Yet the way Glen lays out the four dimensions could lead to a much fuller process, one that might, in fact, range among the four dimensions more freely than the arrows suggest. A key question is how to engage constructively with the realities of power and conflict that inevitably mark our ethical processes. It takes leadership and skill and commitment to keep the community truly working together around issues of disagreement and/or avoidance. All of us who are scholars and teachers of Christian ethics have much more work to do to engage the way Christians actually *do* ethics, especially as most of us do not live in the thick communities that produced, for example, the French Huguenots who rescued Jews in Le Chambon during World War II.

As it happened, while working on this piece, I had the opportunity to sit in on a class at a women's prison discussing the very chapter that has been the core of this reflection. I was fascinated to hear the resistance expressed by many of the women to Glen's communal-oriented norm—indeed to the very notion of ethics! These women had only experienced negative judgment from systems of morality and ethics. They were reflecting on experiences of church where they were told "how bad you are." For them, affirming the value of their own self was critical, especially in a place where "you are a number in a number." As one woman said, "You might need to *disconnect* from community" to find this affirmation.[24] As I sat there, I remembered again that even though community, authority, and tradition are all vital resources, especially for the Christian heritage, there can be no simple affirmation of these goods without recognition of the concrete realities, marked by power, pain, and suffering, in which these moral teachings are being lived out.

I wished that Glen Stassen had been in the room—I know he would have engaged the women with his characteristic gentle intensity, seeking to find a collective place that would enrich us all. For him, this is all part of following the path laid out for us by Jesus.

NOTES

1. This session was eventually published in the *Journal of Religious Ethics* 22/2 (Fall 1994).

2. Walzer himself described communitarianism as internal critique of liberalism in "The Communitarian Critique of Liberalism," *Political Theory* 18/1 (February 1990): 6–23.

3. As the authors note in the introduction, chapter 3 is one of the chapters Glen drafted first, and, as I will discuss, it derives particularly from Glen's work.

4. Glen Stassen, *Journal of Religious Ethics* 5/1 (1977): 9–37.

5. Gary Dorrien, *Social Ethics in the Making* (Malden MA: Wiley-Blackwell, 2010) 1.

5. Since the 1950s, mainline churches declined from more than 80,000 churches to about 72,000, one-fifth of all Protestant congregations today (Bama Group, "Report Examines the State of Mainline Churches, https://www.barna.org/barna-update/article/17-leadership/323-report-examines-the-state-of-mainline-protestant-churches#.UexAhY04uSo [accessed 13 July 2013]).

6. Methodists, who made up nearly one in five members (18%) of the 87th Congress, which was seated in 1961, make up a little less than 10% of the 112th Congress. Some other largely mainline Protestant denominational families also have seen a decline in their numerical representation in Congress. For example, Episcopalians have gone from 12% to 8% and Congregationalists from 5% to less than 1% during this period (Pew Research, Religion and Public Life Project, "Faith on the Hill: the Religious Composition of the 112th Congress," http://www.pewforum.org/Government/Faith-on-the-Hill—The-Religious-Composition-of-the-112th-Congress.aspx [accessed 21 July 2013]). I should note, however, that newer scholarship tells a more complicated story, such as the recently published *After Cloven Tongues of Fire: Protestant Liberalism in Modern American History* by David Hollinger, which argues for continuing mainline *cultural* influence.

7. Ramsey framed his points as issues of method, but they were also claims for authority to counter the claims made by the two-thirds world voices that were becoming more prominent in the World Conference of Churches (Paul Ramsey, *Who Speaks for the Church?* [Nashville: Abingdon, 1967]).

8. James Gustafson, *Treasure in Earthen Vessels* (Louisville: Westminster John Knox, 2008).

9. Jennifer Herdt, "Hauerwas Among the Virtues," *Journal of Religious Ethics* 40/2 (2012): 208.

10. Gilbert C. Meilaender, *The Theory and Practice of Virtue* (Notre Dame IN: University of Notre Dame Press, 1984) 4–5. The turn to virtue ethics within communitarian Christian ethics is connected to a larger turn within academic ethics against limits of Kantian idealism "at the expense of the material, embodied, emotional, or practical" (Michael Lambek, *Ordinary Ethics: Anthropology, Language, and Action* [New York: Fordham University Press, 2010] 14).

11. Glen H. Stassen and David P. Gushee, *Kingdom Ethics: Following Jesus in Contemporary Context* (Downers Grove IL: IVP Academic Press, 2003) 15.

12. Ibid., 59.

13. Ibid., 56.

14. Ibid., 60; emphasis original.

15. Ibid., 117; emphasis original.

16. Ibid., 117, 70–71.

17. Ibid., 89.

18. Ibid., 75.

19. Ibid., 74.

20. Ibid., 75.

21. Ibid., 365. This quotation comes from the chapter on Justice, which was first authored by Glen Stassen.

22. Ibid., 59.

23. Ibid. The chapter on sexuality, primarily authored by David Gushee, illustrates this point. In the discussion of homosexuality, it is apparent that no understanding of scriptural authority can countenance full affirmation of LGBT persons. Yet this is exactly where experiences and modern knowledge push hard on how we interpret Scripture and understand what its authority means. Of course, this is also precisely the place of contention in both mainline and evangelical Christian communities.

24. Wonderfully, this class was being taught by a student of David Gushee's at the McAfee School of Theology. She encouraged the women to see that the issue might not be "community" vs. "self" but the kind of community they might be able to find and form.

Chapter 8

Nuclear Jesus

TINA PIPPIN

But in those days, after that suffering, the sun will be darkened, and the moon will not give its light, and the stars will be falling from heaven, and the powers in the heavens will be shaken. Then they will see "the Son of Man coming in clouds" with great power and glory. Then he will send out the angels, and gather his elect from the four winds, from the ends of the earth to the ends of heaven. (Mark 13:24-27, NRSV)

The first angel blew his trumpet, and there came hail and fire, mixed with blood, and they were hurled to the earth; and a third of the earth was burned up, and a third of the trees were burned up, and all green grass was burned up. The second angel blew his trumpet, and something like a great mountain, burning with fire, was thrown into the sea. A third of the sea became blood, a third of the living creatures in the sea died, and a third of the ships were destroyed. The third angel blew his trumpet, and a great star fell from heaven, blazing like a torch, and it fell on a third of the rivers and on the springs of water. (Rev 8:7-10)

The theme of this paper is *fire*—from the biblical apocalyptic fire from God that rains down on earth in the last days of judgment to the governmental apocalyptic fire that surrounds me as I write these words within the "nuclear triangle" of Georgia: Oak Ridge Reservation, Savannah River Site (SRS), Vogtle nuclear power plant. I am also interested in where to find Jesus in the midst of these fires. Glen Stassen passed on to me his knowledge of fire—from the fire of his own passion for teaching ethics to his anti-nuclear activism and hope that the chances of an earth-ending fire from a nuclear apocalypse would become zero. He inspires me to keep track of all these fires and potential apocalypses and to work for a different future.

The Bible pushes against this hope of a fireproof future. In the first passage above, from the so-called "Little Apocalypse" of Mark's Gospel, Jesus warns of a sudden and soon end of the world. Whatever hope people have in the return of the messianic Son of Man is overshadowed by a completely scorched earth. This description of the Big Crunch of the universe draws readers into a form of onlooker syndrome; we cannot look away from the horror, even as we attempt to glance toward the hope of heaven. The second passage, from the Great Big Apocalypse of John, confirms the tragic ending of the earth by fire mixed with blood. At face value, these fiery events seem inevitable. Even if one is not a Bible believer, the inevitability of human evil could eventually triumph. With Hiroshima and Nagasaki, Chernobyl and Three Mile Island and Fukushima, the End will eventually catch up to us, and it will be of our own creation. Is this the End the apocalyptic Jesus prophesied? Must there be a cleansing of the earth by fire, like the previous cleansing by flood in the biblical myth? Does Jesus join the ranks of genocidal deities that began with Noah's God? Stassen confesses a different faith and envisions a different ending. In this article, I want to wrestle with the link he makes between his commitment to anti-nuclear activism and his assurance in the nonviolent message of Jesus.

Living within the Unholy Trinity

The unholy trinity of the Oak Ridge Reservation in Tennessee, the Savannah River Site in South Carolina, and the Vogtle nuclear power plant in Burke County, Georgia, just across the river from the SRS, provides urgent boundaries for my ethical and theological thinking. This setting in which I am situated, in work and in family life, is a dangerous cauldron of nuclear accident possibilities. The main concerns are, of course, nuclear war (accidental or terrorist initiated) and nuclear power plant accidents. My house sits well within ground zero in a major city. But there are other threats as well: a transport accident of nuclear waste from Rocky Flats to the SRS, and the pollution of ground water from the Savannah River to three states—South Carolina, Georgia, and Florida from the SRS or Vogtle.

In the midst of such apocalyptic anxiety are groups that monitor and call for accountability. Georgia WAND (Women's Action for New Directions) educates and activates against all forms of war, especially nuclear war and nuclear power. Recent work includes seeking Weapons of Mass Destruction (a term from the George W. Bush administration that falsely helped fuel the Iraq War) at the SRS and monitoring the Vogtle nuclear power plant in southwest Georgia.[1]

One of National WAND's founders is Helen Caldicott. She continues her campaign, from her time as a co-founder of Physicians for Social Responsibility, of calling attention to the dangers of nuclear weapons and nuclear power. Caldicott is a true prophetess of doom about the threat to the southeastern United States and elsewhere. In one example of her doom scenarios, she shows at once a present and a future threat at the Oak Ridge Reservation:

> Since 1943, the plant has released thousands of pounds of uranium into the air, and radioactive and chemical wastes have been improperly stored or buried on site. There is extensive ground water, soil, and surface water contamination with isotopes such as plutonium, uranium, Americium 241, cobalt 60, cesium 137, radium 228, and others.[2]

Like her scary scenario of a bomb dropping on whatever city she is speaking in, Caldicott paints a broader picture of the production of uranium and the waste of the nuclear industrial complex.[3] One look at the Google Earth nuclear fallout simulator on my city, Atlanta, although I think it underestimates the range and effects of any size bomb, is enough to convince me that zero weapons is the only sustainable goal.[4]

The situation of the South as a nuclear dumping ground hit crisis mode in 2001 when South Carolina governor Jim Hodges, a Democrat and a United Methodist, threatened to lie down in the middle of Interstate 20 or send the South Carolina Highway Patrol to block a shipment of plutonium waste from Rocky Flats to the SRS.[5] He lost his appeal, and the SRS remains a dumping ground for waste from nuclear weapons production; the recent victory holding off more waste is only a temporary fix. The interstate is two miles from my house, so nuclear waste, on trains or in unmarked trucks, is a huge concern to me. The Southeast, and especially South Carolina, is stuck in this vicious cycle of production of nuclear materials, for weapons and for energy, and nuclear waste. What is a Christian ethical response to this range of issues—from the continued creation of Cold War bombs and deadly deterrents to environmental pollution and racism?

Stassen's ethical thinking on these nuclear issues provides a base as I think about how to live in this triad. His ethical method emerges out of his own work in nuclear research, drawing from his college degree in nuclear physics.[6] He understands the world and theology through the lens of nuclear physics; science and faith are necessarily compatible for him, and a responsible theology demands a scientific base. Unlike Caldicott, Stassen's focus is almost solely on nuclear weapons. His work in the Nuclear Freeze Campaign in the early 1980s influenced his theology of "transforming initiatives."[7] This concept comes from several sources. The main source is psychologist Charles E. Osgood's idea of a "reciprocal initiative" that is needed as an alternative to war ("Graduated Reciprocation in Tension Reduction" or GRIT).[8] Stassen also draws from the nonviolent theology of Martin Luther King, Jr., and Jesus' teaching in the Sermon on the Mount in Matthew 5–7.[9] Stassen sets key steps in creating a nuclear-free world:

• Halt all production of nuclear fissile materials.
• Ratify the Comprehensive Test-Ban Treaty.
• Agree with Russia to cut numbers of nuclear weapons in half, and then with other nations to cut further.[10]

Independent initiatives to reduce the threat of war and violence are part of Stassen's ten practices of just peacemaking, along with "reduc[ing] offensive weapons and weapons trade."[11] Taking the first step to transform a potentially violent situation is central to his peace plan. Stassen finds inspiration in the model of Jesus: "The Sermon on the Mount, as well as all of Jesus' ministry, seeks not to give people a guilt trip but to deliver them from the vicious cycles that cause our bondage to guilt, hostility, and injustice."[12] When facing the apocalyptic deity, what initiative will stop the apocalypse?

Jesus on Fire

Was Jesus an apocalyptic prophet? Did he preach about the end of the world by fire? Was he the apocalyptic Son of Man who scares the seer John with fiery eyes, feet of bronze, and a two-edged sword in his mouth (Rev 1:12-16)? Jesus cannot shed his apocalyptic skin, whether it is his own or a cloak laid on him by the Gospels, Paul, the early church, and tradition. The answer about who Jesus was depends on the part of the New Testament where you land. Whether or not Jesus' teachings are apocalyptic has a basis in how you define apocalyptic and how you determine the authenticity of sayings and representations of Jesus in the New Testament. A central question in the debate is, did Jesus use the apocalyptic Son of Man sayings about himself, or were the Gospel writers reflecting early apocalyptic connections in their communities? Scholars continue to argue this issue, lining up passages to support each thesis. There are strong opinions on either side. Dale Allison summarizes one argument, ". . . our choice is not between an apocalyptic Jesus and some other Jesus; it is between an apocalyptic Jesus or no Jesus at all."[13] The debate is grounded in a search for the historical Jesus—for the use of the historical-critical methods to uncover, as closely as possible, the message of Jesus. The approach is ultimately a modernist one, a quest for certainty.

What is this apocalyptic message of Jesus in the Gospels? The roots are of course in Jewish apocalyptic, full of destruction and fire. Central to the end-of-the-world action is the Messiah. Gershom Scholem relates, "Jewish Messianism is in its origin and by its nature—this cannot be sufficiently emphasized—a theory of catastrophe . . . the catastrophic and destructive nature on the one hand and the utopianism of the content of realized Messianism on the other."[14] Apocalyptic literature is about the end of days, and these days are filled with a final, all-consuming (except for a holy remnant) war. Jesus said, "When you hear of wars and rumors of wars, do not be alarmed; this must take place, but the end is still to come. For nation will rise against nation, and kingdom against kingdom; there will be earthquakes in various places; there will be famines. This is but the beginning of the birth pangs" (Mark 13:7-8). This Jesus does not fit Stassen's view of the peacemaker who out of love confronts the authorities to urge them to repent.[15] In the scenario of biblical apocalyptic, the earth is part of the sacrifice, part of the final cleansing. Jesus' sacrifice on the cross is a precursor to an unrestrained destruction.

The last book of the Christian Bible is all about this earth-ending war. In the Apocalypse of John (Revelation), Jesus is one of the ringleaders of the violence. The text calls for a nonviolent but faithful resistance to the Roman Empire of the late first century CE; certainly there are martyrs (Greek, "witnesses").[16] There is the redemption of the elect, but at what cost? The genocidal fantasy is unbearable.

Stassen sees a consistent and concrete Jesus, in both preaching and actions. His Jesus is incarnate, in flesh and blood and word and walk, and calls on believers (past and present) to be incarnate disciples for transformative justice in the world. What did Jesus teach? Can we ever really know for sure? Political judgment on the Roman Empire? An imminent end? A restored kingdom on earth? Eternal life in a heavenly kingdom? His role as the apocalyptic Son of Man? Destruction of the planet? We will never know for certain. Of all the alternatives in Jesus scholarship, I like Stassen's Jesus the best—a Niebuhrian, Gandhian peacemaker who stands against the status quo of a violent, war-mongering empire. Yet, as a scholar of apocalyptic literature and culture, these other texts and other Jesuses nag at me.[17] These plural Jesuses wreak all kinds of havoc—from disrupting the powers and authorities to wiping them off the face of the earth for all eternity. These Jesuses seem counterproductive to a peacemaking program. Jerry Falwell was right; his Jesus would have a nuclear arsenal, controlled by humans on his behalf, of course.[18] How must we confront these biblical texts and these tyrants?

Conclusion: Confronting the Angel of Death

When I was a graduate student in the 1980s at the Southern Baptist Theological Seminary (SBTS) in the days before its apocalyptic end (or B.F., Before the Fall or Before the Fundamentalists), Stassen showed us how a response to nuclear weapons and power necessarily fit into a Christian social ethic. SBTS had its own Cold War remnant: a fallout shelter underneath the main administrative building. I imagine that this shelter is still intact; an odd Cold War relic in the midst of an institution now full of premillennialist, Rapture believers. Does this shelter now serve as an additional insurance policy, in case of a timing glitch on some nuclear firestorm? Falwell had certainty of a global nuclear war, but also that the true believers would be raptured before the bombs fell.[19] Such a shelter provides an ironic hole in this faith stance, but it also exposes the real fear of the weapons that we are told will be a deterrent to war and a protector of our nation.

The existence of this shelter, with its understated sign on a door in the main hall, caused unease for some of us. In the 1980s, the city of Louisville became a "Nuclear Free Zone" for both nuclear weapons and nuclear power, part of a movement to create nuclear-free spaces starting with one's self and going outward from home to work to city to county to state to country. The underground bunker is a haunted space. Helen Caldicott exposed such spaces as extremely unsafe because they become vacuums when all the air is sucked out by the nuclear blast. Still, the false hope of safety triumphs in the dual spaces of the shelter and the Rapture to heaven.

In this context, Stassen gathered a group of his graduate students to write a response to the nuclear madness of the time. The nuclear freeze movement SANE/Freeze, later known as Peace Action, was a voice of reason; it called for a mutual and verifiable freeze on testing and building of new nuclear weapons. The confession our small group created is as current now as in the time of the Reagan presidency. We confessed to the insanity of "shelter" in a nuclear age and in direct opposition to the biblical apocalyptic message. In a way, we were responding to the apocalyptic texts—and Jesuses—however and by whomever they were created. We were deciding, as late twentieth-century Christians caught in the Cold War, to take our stand with a certain Jesus of the New Testament, against the doom-enacting others. In doing so, we acknowledged the reality of nuclear war, with its "apocalyptic peril and historic opportunity" (see document below). The confession of sin, of complacence, of culpability, and of accountability was a way to stand against the apocalypse and to turn toward hope through concrete, transformative action.

A Confession of Faith in a Nuclear Age

We, the undersigned members of the Southern Baptist Theological Seminary community, believe that people of faith are called to discern the signs of the times and to act in obedience to God's present will. We believe this is a time of apocalyptic peril and historic opportunity. We have long known that nuclear war means untold tragedy, the massacre of hundreds of millions of human beings, and unprecedented sin. Now scientists warn that the use of one-third the present nuclear arsenals will create an icy winter death for the whole Northern Hemisphere and perhaps the world.

We must respond not with fatalism but with obedient, transforming initiative. There is worldwide support for a mutual and verifiable halt in the nuclear arms race; there are unprecedented offers of reductions in nuclear weapons; and there is the almost unanimous concern of experts that the nuclear arms race needs to turn away from destabilizing first-strike weapons toward greater stability, peace, and justice. We are at a turning point in history for the peoples of the world. We fear, however, that our leaders and the peoples of the world are losing the historic opportunity now before us. Now is the time when we are called to let our light shine before the world, through our actions, so that the world may see God's guidance leading us from apocalypse to hope.

We who follow the Prince of Peace are called now to repentance. We confess our reluctance to obey Christ's lead as ministers of reconciliation. We confess our lack of faith in God who raised Christ from the dead. We have trusted not the God of the Universe, but the Titans of the Trident. Because Jesus Christ has liberated us from the Principalities and Powers of the age, we accept the challenge to move beyond our former despair, guilt, and hopelessness. It is we ourselves who condemn the world to hostility; it is God who works among us for peace.

Because we are not destined to perpetual hostility with the Soviet Union, we urge our leaders to press now for a bilateral and verifiable nuclear arms halt; and then to negotiate mutual arms reductions and a more stable nuclear balance. We believe that the U.S. should also pursue aims beyond military deterrence and thus encourage fundamental change in the relationship between the U.S. and the Soviet Union. We pledge ourselves to work for a problem-solving rather than blame-pointing relationship between the U.S. and the Soviet Union. We encourage all Americans to participate in the political process through which we may begin to realize our hopes for peace.

We call on churches to pray for peace and pray for our enemies at the time of the coming of the Prince of Peace (Advent and Christmas), on Memorial Day Weekend (Peace Sabbath and Peace and Justice Week), on the Day of Prayer for World Peace (the first Sunday in August), and at

other appropriate times. We call on churches to form Christian Life com-
mittees and Peacemaker Groups, which pursue the inward journey of
prayer and study and the outward journey of appropriate Christian citizenship in transformative peacemaking.

We commit ourselves to a relentless moral address to the present arms
race. We offer ourselves in fervent prayer for healing and peace among all
nations. We call on all people of faith literally to join hands, uniting in
mutual vulnerability, hope, prayer, and commitment to work as one people for peace.

This framed confession hangs in my office as a reminder to me of my
complicity, responsibility, and call to action. And it reminds me that, like
the nuclear issues, to understand the Jesuses of the New Testament requires
"a relentless moral address."

NOTES

1. An example of one of their recent victories is their work to halt further storage of
nuclear waste at SRS: http://gawand.org/2013/07/23/srs-cab-votes-to-reject-interim-
storage-at-the-site-support-communitys-recommendation/ (accessed 6 August 2013).

2. Helen Caldicott, *Nuclear Madness: What We Can Do* (New York: W.W. Norton, 1994)
170.

3. For nuclear winter scenarios, see Helen Caldicott, *Missile Envy: The Arms Race and
Nuclear War* (New York: Bantam, 1986); Jonathan Schell, *The Fate of the Earth and the Abolition* (Stanford CA: Stanford University Press); Paul Halpern, *Countdown to Apocalypse: A
Scientific Exploration of the End of the World* (Cambridge MA: Perseus Publishing, 1998)
135–53; Lynn Eden, *Whole World on Fire: Organizations, Knowledge & Nuclear Weapons Dev-
astation* (Ithaca NY: Cornell University Press, 2004) ch. 1.

4. The Google Earth map is found at http://nuclearsecrecy.com/nukemap3d/# (accessed
6 August 2013). The Yucca Mountain, Nevada, nuclear waste transport is on hold, but if
the site did ever get approval, the transportation route would go directly in front of Agnes
Scott College on the railroad tracks through Decatur, Georgia, a major residential area. For
the route, see http://www.state.nv.us/nucwaste/states/georgia.htm and the factsheet from the
Nuclear Information Resource Center: http://www.nirs.org/factsheets/road.pdf (both
accessed 6 August 2013).

5. David Firestone, "Governor Threatens to Bar U.S. Plutonium Shipments," *New York
Times,* 11 August 2001, http://www.nytimes.com/2001/08/11/us/governor-threatens-to-
bar-us-plutonium-shipments.html (accessed 6 August 2013).

6. Glen Harold Stassen, *A Thicker Jesus: Incarnational Discipleship in a Secular Age*
(Louisville KY: Westminster John Knox, 2012) 84.

7. See Glen H. Stassen, *Just Peacemaking: Transforming Initiatives for Justice and Peace*
(Louisville KY: Westminster/John Knox, 1992) 37–88; 98–102.

8. Charles E. Osgood, *An Alternative to War and Surrender* (Urbana IL: University of Illinois Press, 1962). For a discussion of Osgood's independent initiatives, see Stassen, *Just Peacemaking: Transforming Initiatives*, 98–102.

9. Stassen, *A Thicker Jesus*, 203.

10. Ibid., 212.

11. Stassen and Gushee, *Kingdom Ethics*, 172–73. See also Stassen, *Just Peacemaking: Transforming Initiatives*, 98–102.

12. Stassen, *Just Peacemaking: Transforming Initiatives*, 249.

13. Dale Allison, *Constructing Jesus: Memory, Imagination, and History* (Grand Rapids MI: Baker, 2010) 46–47.

14. Gershom Scholem, *The Messianic Idea in Judaism and Other Essays on Jewish Spirituality* (New York: Schocken Books, 1971) 7.

15. Stassen, *A Thicker Jesus*, 162.

16. Examples of martyrs in the Apocalypse of John include Antipas, the Two Witnesses, the souls under the altar, and the 144,000.

17. For a creative example of a postmodern imagining of Jesus, see the novel by A. J. Langguth, *Jesus Christs* (Los Angeles: Figueros, 2003).

18. Jerry Falwell, "The Twenty-First Century and the End of the World," *Fundamentalist Journal*, May 1988, 11.

19. Jerry Falwell, *Nuclear War and the Second Coming* (Lynchburg VA: Old Time Gospel Hour, 1983).

Chapter 9

Economic Justice
A View from Outside the Vineyard

RICK AXTELL

A key insight from my first Christian Ethics course with Glen Stassen was the degree to which ethical deliberation is shaped by one's "loyalties"—the allegiances, perspectives, passions, and interests that arise from one's participation in identity-shaping groups and contexts.[1] The study of economic justice from the campus of the Southern Baptist Theological Seminary, a peaceful enclave in the comfortable Crescent Hill area of Louisville, highlighted the degree to which perception is colored by context. Course readings on economic justice convinced me to move from a wealthy suburban congregation to an inner-city fellowship whose members included public housing residents, homeless men and women, and social activists who modeled committed discipleship. Later, I moved into the building as a ministry resident, living in community with other church members and ten homeless men.[2]

I soon became aware of personal and systemic realities that kept these men homeless. This chapter examines one of those realities, the growing phenomenon of *contingent employment*. I explore *day labor* contracted through temporary staffing agencies, a type of contingent work that affects those at the economic margins. I draw upon firsthand experience of working through temp agencies in Louisville and from interviews with homeless day laborers.[3] Day labor practices reveal deep flaws in a labor economy insufficiently structured to meet the needs of its most vulnerable participants. Like those standing outside the vineyard in Matthew's parable (Matt 20:1-16), these laborers subsist at the margins of a consumer society to which they are almost invisible. Day labor violates Stassen's concept of "delivering justice" that restores the marginalized to community.[4] Incarnational discipleship consistent with a "thicker Jesus"[5] calls for *systemic* change.

Contingent Work

Before the sun is up, they are already at the temp agency after a walk from the shelters, sitting on hard benches in a cold cinder-block room, wrapped in well-worn coats to ward off the morning chill. They are looking for work, just for today. And they'll be back tomorrow, hoping to get a work ticket at the same company twice in a row. They are the workers who package the vegetables we buy at the grocery store. They process the chickens we eat. They send our CDs through the shrink-wrap machine, remove trash from the construction site, and wash soiled linens from the local hospital. They never use the word *career* to describe their work, for this word suggests a narrative that proceeds through hiring, training, and hard work to raises, promotions, and retirement with a pension. Their expectation is limited to today's check, not health coverage, not benefits or pensions, and certainly not work that gives a sense of worth, identity, or connection to community.

In the midst of a renewed commitment to efficiency and competitiveness, the United States labor picture changed considerably at the end of the twentieth century. In particular, the growth in "contingent" forms of employment is seriously eroding commonly accepted labor standards, including job security, health and pension benefits, workplace safety, wage and hour expectations, and the capacity to organize and bargain collectively.[6]

As a case manager in men's shelter programs, I argued that residents would not get on their feet by working irregular jobs with no benefits in which the temp agency retains a portion of the salary paid for the work, deducts a portion for services rendered, and exercises daily control over who is chosen for jobs. Yet these jobs fill an employment gap for those with problems related to drugs and alcohol, criminal backgrounds, sporadic work histories, disabilities, or undocumented immigration status.

Temporary help firms arose in the 1920s to supply clerical workers to the growing service sector. Temp work isn't new. But the increase in temp work over the last thirty years has been startling; businesses now use it as a routine staffing strategy. In the early 1970s, 200,000 people worked through temporary and contract staffing services (0.3% of the workforce). In 1990, there were more than 1 million temporary workers (1%).[7] By 1993, *TIME* magazine called the "disposable" workforce "the most important trend in business today," one that is "fundamentally changing the relationship between Americans and their jobs."[8] From 1990 to 2008, temporary staffing employment grew from 1.1 million to 2.3 million,[9] now representing almost 2 percent of US jobs, totaling 3 million workers on an average business day.[10] In Kentucky, temp workers grew from 14,000 in 1990 to 32,500 in 1997.[11]

By 2011, Kentucky's average daily employment in temp jobs was 43,006, involving a total of 198,688 individuals.[12]

Agencies I visited in Louisville illustrate the growth in client businesses and workers. Labor Ready, for example, employs primarily unskilled manual laborers, reflecting the trend toward temp work in industrial settings (surpassing clerical) that once offered permanent jobs with benefits. Founded in 1989, Labor Ready grew from eight branches in 1991 to more than eight hundred in 2012.[13] A profitable corporation traded on the New York Stock Exchange, Labor Ready is now "the nation's leading provider of blue-collar staffing," connecting 400,000 people to temp jobs with 225,000 businesses in "construction, manufacturing, hospitality, events, restoration, auto services, logistics and warehousing, retail support, waste and recycling."[14]

The term "contingent labor" was coined by labor economist Audrey Freedman in 1985 to describe the "management technique of employing workers only when there is an immediate and direct demand for their services." It came to describe all kinds of "flexible work arrangements" designed to control labor costs in a competitive global economy.[15] The term now refers to temporary services; some self-employed workers; seasonal, casual, contract, on-call, freelance, and leased employees; and part-time workers.[16] But studies show that many part-time workers choose that status as a permanent option for various personal reasons.[17]

To highlight its impermanent nature, the Bureau of Labor Statistics (BLS) defines contingent labor as "any job in which an individual does not have an explicit or implicit contract for long-term employment."[18] The Bureau's *Current Population Survey* also measures four types of "alternative work arrangements," defined as employment arranged through an employment intermediary (temporary staffing firm) or employment whose place, time, and quantity are unpredictable:[19]

1. *Independent contractors, consultants, and freelance workers* are the largest, best-educated, and best-paid group (sometimes identified as self-employed, but distinguished from business owners). This category includes 10.3 million workers or 7.4 percent of total employment (construction workers and farm hands but also computer programmers, consultants, paralegals, and accountants who may be highly skilled and highly compensated).

2. *On-call workers* are called to work only when needed. These make up 1.8 percent of the workforce or 2.5 million workers (e.g., substitute teachers, registered nurses, performance artists).

3. *Contract company workers* are paid by an agency that contracts their services with one customer/worksite. These workers make up 0.6 percent of the workforce or 813,000 workers (e.g., janitorial or landscaping services).

4. *Temporary help agency workers* are "paid by a temporary help services agency that supplies them, upon request, to employers looking to fill a temporary full- or part-time staffing need."[20] Many *day laborers* fit into this category, but many remain uncounted. In 2005, BLS estimated 1.2 million temp help agency workers (0.9% of total employment). The American Staffing Association puts the figure at 1.9 percent of the non-farm workforce in 2012.[21]

These four categories make up about 11 percent of the employed. Such alternative arrangements do not necessarily mean inferior jobs with low compensation. Contingent work arrangements have produced two classes: skilled workers in high demand who command fat contract fees and thrive on the wealth and flexibility afforded by their employment choices, and the mostly unskilled laborers who are struggling to survive in low-paying jobs with no benefits.

Day labor fits partly into the fourth alternative work arrangement now making up almost 2 percent of the workforce. But it also fits into an informal segment of the economy that does not register on many official surveys.[22] Many of these workers are homeless men and women, immigrants (documented or undocumented), extremely poor, uneducated, unskilled, mildly disabled, depressed or mentally ill, chemically dependent, or returning to society after periods of incarceration. They usually represent a combination of several of the above. These workers are some of the most vulnerable and marginalized people in America. They are disconnected and disposable, hired when companies need them and shifted elsewhere as the vagaries of corporate demand dictate. They may work through a temp agency, or they may wait on street corners or at shelters for contractors or farmers to pick them up and pay them in cash.

Working Day Labor Jobs

The day labor jobs I worked for this project were manual labor jobs contracted through temporary staffing agencies. For my first job, I arrived at the cinder-block waiting area of Labor Works at 5:45 a.m. Forty men were sitting on wooden benches. Some had slept there overnight. Staff communicated with applicants from an elevated platform behind a seven-foot wall, their heads looking down from above. I was called to work at Jones Plastic. After receiving goggles and one work glove, I passed a Breathalyzer test and got on a van. Only on our way to an east-end industrial park did I learn that I'd work a twelve-hour shift.

Working alone, I produced 490 plastic "lazy susans" for kitchen cabinets, removing each from a machine at shoulder level, poking holes, trimming edges, and boxing them in cartons of 22 each. I got four fifteen-minute breaks, one of which was my lunch break. I breathed chemical odors for twelve hours and had no earplugs. It was exhausting work. I had little human contact throughout my day, except for managers who checked my work five times for quality and quantity of output. Gross pay was $63.00 or $5.25 per hour,[23] but I received only $40.92 after deductions. Deductions included $4.00 for the van; $1.00 for the goggles and glove; $12.26 for federal, state, and local taxes; and $4.82 for Social Security and Medicare. I paid for my transportation, goggles, and glove with my first hour of work, about 41 "lazy susans."

At One Force Staffing, the agency most interviewees considered Louisville's worst, I arrived at 5:00 a.m. at the concrete structure downtown. About seventy men and ten women filled the rows of seats. A foul-mouthed dispatcher handed down sign-up sheets and applications over an elevated counter. I got my work ticket at 6:00. When my name was yelled, I entered a door and lined up. The ticket advised that the client company with whom I was placed agreed not to hire me as a permanent worker for thirty days.

I got on a van that dropped me off at Crenshaw Distributors. I waited (unpaid time) until someone showed up at about 6:45. Four workers then unloaded a semi-truck of carpet matting. The rolled mats were six feet long, a few feet across, and very heavy. You get one onto your shoulder, balancing it with neck bent to the side and arms holding end and middle, then carry it to the end of the warehouse, stack it on a pile, and return for the next. It was backbreaking labor, and I was sweaty and filthy within minutes. After an hour I was faltering, occasionally unable to lift heavier rolls above head level. At one point I fell and scraped an arm, which bled while I worked.

After the first truck, which took two hours, another was unloaded with a forklift. The owners waited for orders to reload their own trucks for re-tailers, but with fewer orders in a depressed market, they needed me for only four hours (the required minimum). For someone counting on a full day's pay, this would be a tough blow. The agency van came back for me. I waited for my check for almost two hours. I'd arrived at 5:00 and left after 12:30—seven and a half hours of my time.

My check for four hours of actual work time amounted to $12.20. The hourly rate for this job was $7.50, for gross pay of $30.00 before deductions. (Minimum wage at this time was $5.85 per hour.) In addition to taxes and Social Security, One Force had deducted $7.00 for transportation ($7 from *each* worker on *each* fifteen-passenger van), $1.00 for (unneeded) gloves, and $4.75 for a boxed lunch. Agency deductions alone (beyond taxes) amounted to $12.75 off the top, in addition to the agency's gain from paying me less than it charged Crenshaw for my labor, which covers overhead and profit.

Business Advantages of Temporary Employment Arrangements

For companies contracting with a temp agency, the advantages are obvious. First, this alternative cuts costs.[24] Businesses can save money in a competitive and unpredictable market and leave the personnel headaches to others. Employers using a temp agency avoid the expensive burdens of health care costs and pension plans. The most recent BLS survey of alternative work arrangements shows that only 8 percent of temporary help agency employees have employer-provided health coverage, compared to 56 percent in traditional work arrangements.[25]

The temporary staffing industry serves a key role for businesses restructuring in the face of global competition and technological change. It also allows for the flexibility businesses need as they respond efficiently to shifts in demand.[26] A buffer against cyclical fluctuations, temp workers are the first to be discarded in economic contractions and the first to be hired as recessions move toward recovery. Hence, temp workers are most affected by market cycles, accounting for 20 percent of the job losses in the 2008–2009 recession. Similarly, the temporary staffing industry created more jobs in the three years after the Great Recession (June 2009–July 2012) than any industry (786,000 jobs).[27] A climate of uncertainty related to Congressional paralysis (budget and debt ceiling standoffs), major changes in health care requirements, weak demand in the recessionary economies of trade partners, and slow return to pre-recession levels of demand indicate growth in temporary labor as businesses delay permanent hires.

Another benefit to companies is the ability to dampen union demands for better wages, benefits, and working conditions.[28] According to Paul Whiteley, then-director of Kentucky Jobs with Justice, contingent labor has a destabilizing effect in union shops. Temp workers resent regulars who earn more money for doing similar jobs or who won't perform work reserved for temps. Union workers see day laborers as a threat to job stability and permanence. They are intimidated from pushing for concessions from management in contract negotiations, reasoning that their jobs could become temp jobs. Because there is no consistency to a constantly changing workforce that rotates individuals in and out of the plant, workers are unlikely to act as one bargaining unit. Further, companies routinely contract with temp agencies when unions strike. Whiteley claims that companies believe it is in their interests to keep these workers divided.[29]

Advantages to Temporary Workers

Clearly this arrangement is advantageous for client businesses. What about workers?[30] Why do homeless men and women work day labor jobs for a temp agency instead of finding full-time, permanent jobs?

Daily Cash

The most common answer in my interviews was that day laborers get paid daily. Eighty-eight percent (36 workers) cited this as the primary positive feature of the arrangement. Several said that daily money pays fees required by some shelters, plus food (since workers often miss soup kitchen hours), bus fare, gas, cigarettes, phone minutes, and other day-to-day expenses. While only 17 percent (7) said they frequently used their money to buy alcohol or drugs, 63 percent (26) had self-reported history of substance abuse, with 22 percent currently addicted. Several cited as a disadvantage that daily pay can fuel addiction. These responses suggest that more workers buy alcohol and drugs than admitted it. The only nearby places that cash checks after hours are liquor stores, and most interviewees reported routinely cashing checks at liquor stores for a $1 charge. Nevertheless, using words like "daily needs" and "survival," workers reported that daily cash was their primary reason for working these jobs.[31]

Flexibility and Variety

Forty-four percent (18) cited the flexibility of day labor as an advantage, noting that they could work when they want to or when they cannot work permanently for reasons related to health, disability, medical appointments, school or vocational training, preferences for lower levels of responsibility, or obstacles presented by homelessness. Seven workers mentioned the variety offered by day labor, valuing the ability to test different kinds of employment and the stimulation offered by diverse occupations.[32]

Skill Development

Sixteen workers (39%) reported that day labor was a way to learn new job skills such as carpentry, power-washing, roofing, and machinery operations, or social skills such as following instructions, developing positive work habits, or getting along with others. Responses were mixed, however. One hoped to learn construction skills, but jobs were "nothing but sweep all day, pick up after workers' trash" (13J).[33] "Most of the time," one reported, "it's washing dishes, warehouse work, cleanup, like there's nothing really to it" (16R).

Bridge to a Permanent Job

Although most interviewees knew of contracts forbidding client companies from hiring temporary workers for permanent jobs,[34] 53 percent believed client companies would hire a good worker anyway. Nine workers (22%) had been hired for a job originally done through a temp agency. But many workers said they worked temp day labor because they could not get other jobs for a variety of reasons, including physical or psychological health (27%), addiction (22%), criminal record (15%), or lack of transportation (15%). Other obstacles to permanent employment included lack of skills, low education levels,[35] scarcity of job openings, sporadic work history, SSI restrictions, undesirable military discharge, lack of proper clothing, or lack of documentation (ID, Social Security card). Seven respondents mentioned special obstacles presented by homelessness: "It's sort of a catch-22 because if you are homeless you can't get a permanent job, but you can't get a home if you don't have a permanent job" (9R). They worried about the two-week wait for the first check when one gets permanent work: "There's no use getting a job when I have no food, hardly any clothes, no shelter, and I would have to work two weeks straight just to get a first paycheck. No, no, no. I would fall out and die before then" (8J). Thirty-four percent said they would take a permanent job if offered.

Worker Complaints

Low Pay and Paycheck Deductions

Low pay was the primary complaint, mentioned by 68 percent (28) of the workers, most of whom work for just above minimum wage.[36] Related to dissatisfaction with pay is widespread outrage about paycheck deductions perceived as excessive. Thirty-six respondents (88%) emphasized this point with extensive stories reinforced with pay stubs showing deductions for van rides (usually $5 to $7), helmets, gloves, safety glasses, work boots, lunches, and even check-issuing charges.[37] Often these charges were daily, even if issued equipment was unnecessary. Workers labeled these practices "outrageous," "heartless," and "crooked" and commented, "they're getting rich off us," "it's a scam," "they take too much for themselves," "it defeats the whole purpose," and "you forfeit $12 before you even get out the damn door." One asked, "You worked 8 hours for what? About $30 . . . . How can they get away with that? There's gotta be a labor law" (7R).

The difference between what workers get paid and what the agency charges the company for their labor was a sore spot for 41 percent of my interviewees, although many recognized the agency's right to profit from the service they provide: "It may be $14 or $15, but I ain't gonna make more than $8, and you know I think that's just a little unfair. They can make a profit; they gotta operate. They got salaries to pay, I understand that, but it's just kind of hard to swallow sometimes" (17R).

Lack of Benefits

Seventy percent mentioned the lack of health benefits. Most workers I interviewed did not have health coverage of any sort unless they were eligible for Medicaid or receiving SSI disability or veteran's benefits.[38] Others mentioned unaffordable health insurance options for those working steady tickets. A few reported that although you can qualify with full-time hours, "They're gonna see to it that they don't do that. You're not gonna get the hours to get those benefits. I don't know anybody that's receiving any benefits" (17R). One added, "When you've worked enough time to get benefits, they'll send somebody else there to keep the cycle going; save the company money" (4J).

Similarly, workers did not trust Workmen's Compensation, insisting that agencies regularly fight claims, even for serious injuries. Several told stories of dismissal as a result of injury, noting that addiction history or immigration status can deter claims. This comment was representative: "You don't expect them to pay for it, do you? That's the chance you take . . . if you get a lawyer or something, which half of them we can't afford no way, you can get a common lawyer that don't charge and he might get you some kind of Workmen's Comp, but no settlement. Labor places don't settle with homeless people" (7R).

Uncertainty

Another complaint involved uncertainty about getting a work ticket. More than half of these workers had frustrating stories of long waits before placement, and many sat for days without getting work: "I went for five days a week for two weeks and didn't get a ticket; . . . got there at 4:30 in the morning and left at 4:30 in the afternoon. . . . It's like goin' to the casino . . . it's a gamble on whether you get out or not. If you don't get out you don't get to eat that day" (2R). The gamble is significant for those whose housing depends on being present for shelter check-in times. Exasperating waits (for placements, rides, and checks) frequently require exhausting twelve- to fourteen-hour days for eight hours of work.

Fifty-six percent objected to perceived favoritism at the agencies that exercise ultimate power over who is chosen for jobs. "I sat up to ten hours a day for as many as nine days in a row. They'll call their friends and pick them over you, even if you were there on time. Pass right over you" (10R). This is especially galling when agencies send vans to the shelters: "They'll come here to the shelter and promise people to work and pick them up and take them there, but they don't ever get out [on jobs] and they don't bring them back; you gotta walk back" (20R). Several argued that filling the benches was a strategy "so that when somebody calls, they got people" (4J).

Types of Jobs

Workers complained about getting the worst work—work they see as demeaning, demanding, and dangerous. Day labor jobs were described as "the cruddiest work," "stuff regular people wouldn't necessarily do," "like sweatshops," "no-brainer jobs," "slave labor," "excruciating," and "just pretty much stuff a monkey could do." Workers described jobs in trash dumps, work with discarded body parts, toil in sewers, disaster cleanup, jobs at incinerators, and labor in "hazard conditions." Such work seems to reinforce low self-esteem: "We go out to the job; they try to find the nastiest things the regular workers don't wanna do, all the nasty filthy stuff, let the temps do that. We just temps" (21R). One commented, "I'm just kind of envisioning the ones calling the temp service being like 'none of my workers want to do it; send me some of the scum ya got, they'll do it for us'" (8J).

Commenting on safety conditions, ten interviewees told stories of scaffolds with no tie-downs, cleanup at construction sites without helmets, poorly maintained machinery, extreme heat without drinking water, hands crushed in machines, fingers cut off, days inhaling incinerator ash, and hours of repetitive motion. Eleven workers, however, affirmed that companies they had worked for took safety seriously. Other common workplace complaints included long shifts and inadequate breaks, resentment or disrespect from regular workers, and unwarranted suspicion (e.g., drug tests, work checked more often, assumptions about addiction or criminal tendencies).

These men and women have little power and few social connections. They are not union members and unions often resent them. For diverse personal reasons, they may be unlikely or unable to secure other types of work. Their circumstances leave them vulnerable to exploitation in a marketplace that sees laborers as business expenses rather than persons-in-community with inherent rights. If Christian responses do not go beyond charity, they will not reflect the "delivering justice" consistent with the "thicker Jesus" Glen Stassen proposes as a resource for ethical action.

Justice Considerations

The concept of economic justice is crucial in the writings of Glen Stassen. Justice is an indispensable condition for genuine peace/shalom and an essential element of "just peacemaking."[39] Economic justice is fundamental to a comprehensive concept of human rights, with a "trilingual" grounding in reason, Scripture, and experience.[40] At the deepest level of basic convictions,[41] initiatives for justice are an inescapable emphasis in the Sermon on the Mount and the "prophetic hermeneutic" of Jesus,[42] and therefore central to Stassen's presentation of a "thicker" Jesus. In the Beatitudes and other passages of the Sermon on the Mount, understood from the perspective of the Hebrew prophets, the emphasis on *righteousness* (Greek: *dikaiosyne*— Matt 5:6; 6:33) is a prophetic call to *justice* (Hebrew: *tsedaqah*). Stassen understands these terms as "*delivering justice* (a justice that rescues and releases the oppressed) and *community-restoring justice* (a justice that restores the powerless and the outcast to their rightful place in covenant community)."[43] His work intends to rescue the Sermon on the Mount from evasions that interpret it as spiritual rather than political, as inward dispositions rather than concrete public actions, or as abstract universal ideals rather than modeled virtues and practices arising in particular community contexts. Arguing against secularizing dualism,[44] Stassen sees the Sermon as relevant for a public ethic that can be persuasive in a pluralistic context.

For Stassen, then, the grounding of a Christian public ethic arises from New Testament texts, particularly the Sermon on the Mount, read through a prophetic lens.[45] The ethic is *communal* and *covenantal*,[46] emphasizing *character* shaped by particular contexts.[47] Principles of justice can provide clear guidance, but these "are not suspended in midair"; they derive power and grounding in identity-shaping community narratives, especially the grand narrative of grace (God's transforming initiatives, i.e., the exodus, the cross). An ethic of "incarnational discipleship," then, is *a response to grace.* Rules and principles are embodied (incarnated) in narratives, and narrative ethics must "be concretely expressed, *embodied,* in principles, rules, and concrete judgments about particular cases."[48] As such, the teachings of the Sermon on the Mount are concrete images of what it means to participate in the ever-advancing Reign of God.[49]

The content of the resulting ethic of *delivering justice that advances the Reign of God* highlights compassionate action "that delivers the poor from poverty and restores them into community."[50] Stassen and Gushee elaborate this ethic of justice in terms of the universal destination of goods that must consider *distributive fairness* (reflected, for example, in Jubilee principles[51] intended to redress imbalances):

> It is one of humanity's cardinal sins . . . —this division into have and have-not, those who have a chance at earning their fair share and those who die of hunger, sleep in the streets or succumb to preventable diseases. The fight for distributive economic justice amidst varying levels of injustice is (sadly) a perennial aspect of human responsibility and a key dimension of the Christian ethical task.[52]

Here, justice rejects both libertarian[53] and egalitarian extremes. It is grounded not in equality of outcome but in *human need,* partly because equality of outcome fails to take the theological mandate to work seriously. Here, I quote at length because of the (ir?)relevance to day labor realities:

> Work itself remains rooted in God's design for human life. Work reflects and advances human dignity as our vocations become an outlet for creativity, self-development and even joy, an avenue to contribute to the common good and means of providing for ourselves, our families and those we can bless with our generosity. The ability to keep, enjoy and de-velop the fruit of our labor as private property enhances the incentive to work and is legitimate as long as we also meet our public ethical respon-sibilities. . . . A just society creates wealth, including that found in adequately remunerative work to all who are able to work. Its number one priority in wealth-creation, however, is not extravagant bounty for the few but access to economic opportunity and participation in economic community for the many.[54]

Coupled with an adequate theological view of human freedom and responsibility, distributive justice relies on both the individual responsibility to
work and the responsibility of the community as a whole ("first private and
then public efforts") to "meet the needs of those who cannot care for themselves."[55]

Kingdom Ethics articulates principles pertinent to this world of tough
economic realities, but they remain curiously abstract in terms of application
in economic matters (in contrast with concrete chapters on racism and creation care). While the work reviews systemic critiques of advanced capitalist
societies in a globalized economy, it does not take a position in debates about
"the mix of, and nature of, public and private relief and empowerment ven-
tures."[56] The authors decry an "ends-justify-the-means" work culture in
which "profits are all that matters,"[57] but they offer no analysis of labor
exploitation. Yet they denounce a "free market ideology" that believes
"corporations should be free to do whatever they calculate is in their self-
interest."[58]

Nevertheless, the principles in *Kingdom Ethics* point us to concrete actions. Stassen outlines four dimensions of biblical justice: (1) delivering the
poor and powerless; (2) liberating the dominated from domineering power;
(3) stopping violence and establishing peace; and (4) restoring the excluded
to community.[59] Principles must be embodied in concrete practices and actions. Because sin is both personal and structural, deliverance occurs on the
individual behavioral level and the broader systemic level. What might this
mean for day laborers?

Countering domination requires realistic balancing of power. *Kingdom
Ethics* proposes a covenant ethic that checks and limits corporate power.[60]
But organizing for fair wages and benefits is difficult for this transient population. It will require allies in the labor movement, the churches, and the
larger community. The challenge to collective bargaining for day laborers
in the economic realm suggests that justice also requires action in the political realm, including advocacy for increased minimum wage,[61] expanded
Earned Income Tax Credit, mandated equal pay and benefits for day laborers, and guaranteed universal health insurance as a community obligation
beyond the responsibility of employers. Legislative advocacy must ensure
that temporary staffing firms are licensed and regulated, including limits on
paycheck deductions and mechanisms to transition workers toward permanence after sixty days with the same company. Legislation should include
codes of conduct for employers contracting day laborers and for employers
operating overseas whose labor practices fuel the race to the bottom.

For churches, this work requires a revitalized commitment to working people and renewed outrage about practices that offend human dignity and exclude others from community. When they learn about the strong tradition of labor activism in the rich narratives of our past,[62] churches can offer a liberative tradition based on a theological understanding of the dignity of the human person created in the image of God and entitled to share in the abundance of creation. Day labor trends challenge us to ask whether we do indeed believe in the notion of community. Are humans merely isolated individuals at the mercy of the market, or are they social creatures entitled by virtue of their inherent worth and dignity to participate meaningfully in the life of the community?

Action consistent with incarnational discipleship must go beyond charitable "ministries to the poor." Such language indicates a failure of community, implying that "the poor" constitute some group outside "the church." "They" are recipients of "our" ministry. Praxis consistent with Stassen's covenantal concept of justice understands that the poor and vulnerable among us need community, not merely charity. Certainly, church activists can document and publicize the experiences of day laborers in their communities, establish temp worker centers, boycott companies that counter strikes with temp laborers, and advocate for legislative improvements. But churches can also model genuine alternatives. After all, systemic abuses continue because we cooperate. Our consumption fuels the system. Hence, churches can withdraw participation (and investment) from corporations that exploit labor. In addition to connecting unemployed members with employers within congregations, churches might consider creating non-profit labor pools that refuse to profit from the vulnerability of others, ensuring that profits now taken by staffing agencies go instead to workers.

Modeling powerful examples of covenantal alternatives, churches can enter the public square with confidence. And because delivering justice focuses on human need, it is consistent with discourse on human rights that is viable in a pluralistic context.[63] The emphasis on need leads to a fulsome concept of rights, thoroughly grounded in biblical warrants.[64] But Stassen's "trilingual" grounding for human rights (Scripture, reason, and experience) prevents the imposition of a religious worldview in the public square. The concurrent use of the languages of reason and experience allows for a Christian ethic that can function as "salt and light"[65] in public debate, strengthened by the complementary witness of alternative community models.

Prior to the religious grounding in particular Scriptures or the rational public discourse of human rights is the narrative of human experience, which may be the most powerful language of all. Human rights discourse itself originates in a sense of deprivation and abuse. For this reason, this chapter has focused on the experiences of individuals. Stassen quotes Monika Hellwig: "The idea of human rights is surely first shaped by the sense of violation. It has its origin in an existential scream of pain or deprivation. When we hear the scream, we know what it means not because we can explain it but because we can feel it. It is by the capacity for empathy that we know what it means. But we have to hear the scream first."[66]

This language of experience brings us back to Stassen's insight about loyalties. Incarnational discipleship modeled on a "thicker Jesus" is indeed embodied in context, but what we see is determined by where we stand. Biblical texts do not stand alone with some fixed universal meaning/ethic to be discovered by the faithful seeker and then deductively applied. Hence, we must read content into a thickening portrait of Jesus while firmly situated alongside those at the margins. Here, I want Stassen's call for a thicker Jesus to be more explicit about the mutual illumination process of a continuing hermeneutic circle: the example and teachings of Jesus, understood through the lens of his prophetic hermeneutic, shape our commitment to and identification with those who are poor. But praxis alongside the poor continually reshapes our image of Jesus as we fill out a thicker understanding of this one who is the source of Christian ethics. And so on. Some sort of hermeneutic circle continues inevitably. But our thick Jesus will turn out to be meaningless for those who are poor if read from the confines of middle-class comfort from which those laborers who make that comfort possible remain invisible (and it won't be very motivating for the comfortable either).[67]

Perhaps it is significant for a "Kingdom Ethic" of incarnational discipleship that Matthew's parable about the profligate grace of the kingdom of God pictures day laborers outside the vineyard, clearly a first-century reality as well. It is a parable of inclusion no doubt grounded in the experience of marginalization or solidarity with the excluded. It was told by someone who must have understood the utter insecurity of those at the margins; someone who must have stood alongside them, comprehending the existential threat of a day without pay; someone who must have known the relief that a full day's wage would bring to those in great need. Who is this one? Perhaps we will only begin to understand from outside the vineyard.

NOTES

1. Glen H. Stassen and David P. Gushee, *Kingdom Ethics: Following Jesus in Contempo-rary Context* (Downers Grove IL: InterVarsity, 2003) 63–64. Loyalties to friends, mentors, and models; loyalties to the practices and means routinely employed in particular contexts to achieve goals; loyalties to communities that shape identity; and ultimate loyalties are the often-unexamined filters that shape or distort ethical deliberation.

2. Stassen often warns against the danger of irrelevance for armchair ethicists who are disengaged from real-world praxis, backing up this warning with an embodied model of the scholar-activist. I am grateful for his example and for his influence on my life.

3. Findings arise from a five-stage process: (1) 48 semi-structured interviews in 1999: 29 black males (60.4%), 14 white males (29.1%), 4 black females (8.3%), 1 white female (2%). (2) Using purposive nonprobability sampling, researchers conducted one-hour struc-tured interviews with 37 homeless men and 4 homeless women in 2007 (Centre College IRB approval, 6/19/07). Of these, 24 were black (58.5%), 14 were white (34.1%), 1 was Hispanic (2.4%), and 2 of dual ethnicity (4.9%). 26 reported addiction issues (63.4%) and 16 reported disabilities. (3) Day labor jobs worked in 1999 and 2007. (4) Interviews at 5 temp agencies in 2007 and 2008. (5) Interviews with day labor organizers in 2011. Formal interviews (stage 2) were tape-recorded and identified with interviewer's initials, interviewee number, and date. Transcripts of each interview were typed. Open-ended first-level coding identified meaning units, and excerpts were linked to coding categories and subcategories. My superb research assistant, Jennifer Siewertsen, conducted numerous interviews and tran-scribed and codified all tapes.

4. Stassen and Gushee, *Kingdom Ethics*, chs. 17 and 20.

5. Glen Stassen, *A Thicker Jesus: Incarnational Discipleship in a Secular Age* (Louisville KY: Westminster John Knox, 2012).

6. Union membership (11.3% of all workers) is at its lowest level since the 1930s (Bureau of Labor Statistics, "Union Members Summary," 23 January 2013).

7. Tian Luo, Amar Mann, and Richard Holden, "The Expanding Role of Temporary Help Services from 1990 to 2008," *Monthly Labor Review*, August 2010) 3–4.

8. Janice Castro,"Disposable Workers," *TIME*, 29 March 1993, 43.

9. Luo et al., "The Expanding Role," 3.

10. Steven P. Berchem, "Structural Shift?: Annual Economic Analysis Explores Data and Trends in Flexible Workforce Management," American Staffing Association, 2012, pp. 3–4, americanstaffing.net/digital (accessed 19 July 2013).

11. Wayne Tompkins, "More Employers, Individuals Find Temporary Work Fulfills Needs," *Courier Journal*, 1 November 1998, E1.

12. American Staffing Association fact sheet, "Staffing Firms Create Jobs in Kentucky," June 2012. These were contracted through 731 temporary staffing offices, generating $895 million in payroll in 2011.

13. www.laborready.com (accessed 4 Feb 2014). Labor Ready is a brand of a larger cor-poration called TrueBlue, Inc., in Tacoma WA.

14. "We'll supply the elbow grease to help your business grow," *Labor Ready*, www.labor-ready.com/How-We-Work (accessed 24 July 2013).

15. Anne E. Polivka, "Contingent and Alternative Work Arrangements, Defined," *Monthly Labor Review* 119/10 (October 1996): 3–9; Mark H. Grunewald, "The Regulatory Future of Contingent Employment: An Introduction," *Washington and Lee Law Review* 52/3 (1995).

16. Polivka, "Congingent and Alternative Work Arrangements, Defined," 3–4.

17. Ibid.

18. Ibid., 4.

19. Ibid., 5. In 1995, the BLS *Current Population Survey* provided the first official attempt to measure the prevalence of contingent labor, with additional surveys in 1997, 1999, 2001, and 2005. Figures here come from Bureau of Labor Statistics, "Contingent and Alternative Employment Arrangements," February 2005.

20. Luo et al., "The Expanding Role," 3.

21. Berchem, "Structural Shift?" 15.

22. Abel Valenzuela, "Day Labor Work," *Annual Review of Sociology* 29 (2003): 307–33. Valenzuela distinguishes between *formal* temp agency day labor and *informal* open-air day labor.

23. Minimum wage was $5.15 per hour. Regular Jones workers started at $7.55/hour or $8.05 (2nd shift).

24. Brenda Lautsch, "Uncovering and Explaining Variance in the Features and Outcomes of Contingent Work," *Industrial and Labor Relations Review* 56/1 (October 2002): 24–25, 36–38.

25. BLS *Current Population Survey*, 6.

26. Luo et al., "The Expanding Role," 4–6, 13; Lautsch, "Uncovering and Explaining Variance," 24–25, 37–38; Desmond King and David Rueda, "Cheap Labor: The New Politics of 'Bread and Roses' in Industrial Democracies," *Perspectives on Politics* 6/2 (June 2008): 284; Vicki Smith, "The Fractured World of the Temporary Worker: Power, Participation, and Fragmentation in the Contemporary Workplace," *Social Problems* 45/4 (November 1998): 414, 420, 423–24, 426.

27. Berchem, "Structural Shift?" 3–10. But these are high-turnover, short-tenure jobs.

28. King and Rueda, "Cheap Labor," 280, 293–94.

29. Paul Whiteley, author's interview, 22 February 1999.

30. All findings are from second-stage interviews with 41 day laborers in 2007.

31. Several cited the possibility of overtime pay as an advantage, showing that they had been paid for overtime work. Others experienced cutbacks if they got close to overtime. This disagreement may reflect the difference between billable and unbillable overtime. *Billable* overtime is paid for by the *client company* when an employee works for that same company for over 40 hours in a week. *Unbillable* overtime is paid by the *temp agency* for those who work over 40 hours at different worksites. Temp agencies discourage this latter situation.

32. 31 people (75%) worked for three or more agencies, and 16 worked at 10 or more job sites in the past decade.

33. To preserve guarantee of confidentiality, interview citations refer to the number of the taped interview and the primary interviewer (J for Jennifer Siewertsen and R for Rick Axtell).

34. Agency contracts include clauses that client businesses will not hire workers in permanent jobs for 30 to 90 days. 72% of interviewees knew of such clauses. Workers complained of being cut off just before reaching the limit. Several took permanent jobs without telling the agency, thereby saving new employers from fines or finder's fees.

35. Fifty-three percent (22) of interviewees dropped out of high school. Eight (19%) had a GED. Eight had vocational/technical training. Twelve had some college; none had graduated. One had an Associate Degree.

36. 80% reported that they made minimum wage, or just above, at their temp jobs, and 56% reported that their highest salary at a temp job was under $10/hour. Three workers reported high hourly salaries from $20 to $49 due to placement at "prevailing wage" sites or particular skills (electrician; bulldozer operator).

37. For some steady ticket worksites that pay weekly, One Force charges workers $5 to $8 to issue a daily check.

38. Thirty interviewees (73.2%) had no health insurance, including Medicaid. Single men without dependent children were ineligible for Medicaid in Kentucky.

39. Glen Stassen, ed., *Just Peacemaking: The New Paradigm for the Ethics of Peace and War* (Cleveland OH: Pilgrim, 2008) 18–19, 22–27, 132–52; Glen Stassen, *Just Peacemaking: Transforming Initiatives for Justice and Peace* (Louisville KY: Westminster John Knox, 1992) 103–104, 155; Stassen and Gushee, *Kingdom Ethics*, 171–72.

40. Stassen, *Just Peacemaking: Transforming Initiatives*, 138, 153–62. Stassen argues against definitions of human rights focused on civil and political freedoms to the exclusion of economic rights; cp. *Just Peacemaking: New Paradigm*, 25–27.

41. Stassen and Gushee, *Kingdom Ethics*, 59, 61. This is the "beliefs" or "ground of meaning" dimension in Stassen's adaptation of Ralph Potter's four dimensions of ethical deliberation. See Glen Stassen, "Critical Variables in Christian Social Ethics," in Paul D. Simmons, ed., *Issues in Christian Ethics* (Nashville: Broadman, 1980) 57–76.

42. Stassen and Gushee, *Kingdom Ethics*, 91–95. "Few issues are so thoroughly addressed in Scripture, including the teachings of Jesus" (409).

43. Stassen and Gushee, *Kingdom Ethics*, 42, 413.

44. Ibid., 61. "Secularizing dualism" is a distortion in which Jesus has no relevance for a public ethic, which is therefore derived from other sources. This was a key insight of John Howard Yoder's *The Politics of Jesus*, 2nd ed. (Grand Rapids MI: Wm. B. Eerdmans, 1994), a major influence on Stassen. Conversely, "secularizing domination" seeks to "impose one's understanding of the way of Jesus on the world," prompting a backlash that strengthens secularizing forces.

45. Stassen and Gushee, *Kingdom Ethics*, 91–94: Jesus interpreted Torah through a prophetic lens, thereby (1) highlighting covenant as a response to grace rather than as casuistic legalism; (2) emphasizing moral rather than cultic responses; (3) identifying righteousness as deeds of love, mercy, and justice; and (4) rooting actions in the wellsprings of character.

46. Ibid., 15, 43–44, 56-58, 63–64, 117, 131–32, 276, 371–72, 423.

47. It is therefore surprising that Stassen's work on the Sermon on the Mount doesn't discuss the situational context in the Matthean community influencing the evangelist's shaping of Q material.

48. Stassen and Gushee, *Kingdom Ethics*, 117–18.

49. I interpret this Reign as both present and future, breaking into this history, now; a history dynamically pulled forward by the eschatological Promise and those who align with it (consciously or not), although never fully achieving it. See Gustavo Gutierrez, *A Theology of Liberation: History, Politics, and Salvation*, 15th anniversary ed. (Maryknoll NY: Orbis, 1988) 91–105, 121–40.

50. Stassen and Gushee, *Kingdom Ethics*, 413. In Matthew 6:19-34, this public ethic is related to a personal ethic of gratitude, sufficiency, and generosity, reflecting deliverance from the vicious cycle of anxiety/greed that overvalues treasures on earth and seeks to serve two masters (410–18). Hence, the teaching on freedom from anxiety and greed "is a justice teaching, not a psychological teaching" (413).

51. Ibid., 347, 354, 358, 414, 442. These concrete redistributive practices in Leviticus 25 include forgiveness of debts, release of debt slaves, return of land gained by creditors to its original owners, and fallowing of land. This ethic entails a "great reversal" that is good news for the poor (e.g., Luke 1: 51-53; 4:18-21; 6:20-26; 14:15-24; see pp. 418–19). John Howard Yoder's discussion of Jubilee in *Politics of Jesus*, chs. 2 and 3, influenced Stassen's interpretation,

52. Stassen and Gushee, *Kingdom Ethics*, 420. The authors, on pages 39–39, discuss a preferential option for the poor in relation to the first beatitude (Matt 5:3) but apply it to public policy only implicitly in their chapter on economic ethics.

53. Libertarians argue that day laborers freely choose their work arrangements as advantageous. But day labor realities clarify that justice cannot be evaluated in terms of procedural arguments alone. The purely procedural view collapses the concept of justice into a commutative norm that accepts only "negative" human rights, emphasizing non-coerced voluntary choices but ignoring positive freedom (the actual wherewithal to choose alternative options). Purely procedural norms lack the balancing teleological concerns for equality (or well-being) and community that are constituent principles of an adequate notion of justice. Humans are social beings, and our inherent dignity requires some commitment to positive economic rights, including the rights of workers to organize to secure basic needs. See National Conference of Catholic Bishops, *Economic Justice for All*, 10th anniversary ed. (Washington, DC: United States Catholic Conference, 1997).

54. Stassen and Gushee, *Kingdom Ethics*, 421.

55. Ibid., 422.

56. Ibid.

57. Ibid., 371.

58. Ibid., 371; cf. 372, 437.

59. Ibid., 349–65, seen in the prophets (especially Isaiah) and in the example of Jesus. Ironically, the inclusive covenant community envisioned in *Kingdom Ethics* cannot yet extend welcoming arms to gay and lesbian Christians (who experience their sexual orientation as an existential given) *if* those Christians have chosen to commit themselves to a covenant of marital faithfulness. Here, the framing of the discussion, 307–11, ensures that some will remain "the excluded ones."

60. Stassen and Gushee, *Kingdom Ethics*, 372, 420. The authors affirm a mixed/balanced economy consistent with the covenant ethics approach of C. Eric Mount, Jr., *Covenant, Community and the Common Good: An Interpretation of Christian Ethics* (Cleveland OH: Pilgrim, 1999).

61. Arguments that minimum wage increases result in job losses can be tested historically; past increases resulted in few job losses. At the right levels, raising the minimum wage, especially when supplemented with the Earned Income Tax Credit, can increase economic activity as workers with more purchasing power create a virtuous circle, leading to more jobs. See Sheldon Danziger and Peter Gottschalk, *America Unequal* (Cambridge: Harvard Press, 1995).

62. See Perry Bush, "To Follow the Carpenter from Nazareth," and Bill Wylie-Kellermann, "The Power of Alliance: Why the Church and the Labor Movement Belong Together," in *Sojourners*, September-October 1998.

63. Jack Donnelly argues that human need is the rational and experiential basis of human rights notions about which differing political and economic systems have reached an "overlapping consensus." Hence, human rights, including economic rights, are grounded in our (constructed) moral sense of what is required for a life of dignity, and invoke state obligations to ensure those rights (*Universal Human Rights in Theory and Practice*, 2nd ed. [Ithaca NY: Cornell University Press, 2003] 7, 10–17, 40). For the US Catholic Bishops, human rights (negative and positive rights) are the minimum conditions required for life in community and the fulfillment of human dignity.

64. See Stassen's work on Richard Overton's Christian defense of human rights in the context of the 17th-century English Revolution in *Just Peacemaking: Transforming Initiatives*, ch. 6.

65. Stassen and Gushee, *Kingdom Ethics*, 473–83.

66. Stassen, *Just Peacemaking: Transforming Initiatives*, 160.

67. Stassen and Gushee, *Kingdom Ethics*, 370: "The biblical emphasis on justice . . . has been largely neglected in affluent white North American churches. Not being routinely victimized by injustice, the comfortable have tended not to notice the problem."

Chapter 10

Jesus and Justice
Confronting Viral Narratives of Racism

REGGIE L. WILLIAMS

In order for Christians to understand Jesus' commandment, "do to others what you would have them do to you,"[1] Glen Stassen highlights the connection between the way of Jesus and justice.[2] Stassen's claim is particularly important today for our national conversation about race. Indeed, Christians cannot have a meaningful conversation about race without understanding the connection between Jesus and justice. In *Kingdom Ethics,* the superb textbook co-authored by Stassen and David Gushee, the authors maintain that justice is central to Christian ethics, claiming that justice rather than reconciliation, must anchor the conversation about race: "justice rather than reconciliation is the better rubric under which to consider the issues of race. . . . [B]oth biblically and in the context of historical patterns of racial injustice in the United States, the concept of reconciliation is empty of content unless it is built upon a sturdy foundation of justice."[3]

That is not to say that, for Stassen, the conversation about reconciliation is bankrupt; Stassen's body of work, both in and out of the classroom, illustrates that his advocacy of the way of Jesus underscores restorative justice. And in the conversation about race, Stassen's interpretation of Jesus shows that any discussion of reconciliation that omits justice misunderstands the way of Jesus. Stassen's work provides us with a new narrative that can guide us toward genuine justice.

The Evangelical Race Divide

Christians typically don't agree about how to address the problem of race. The disagreement largely centers on worldviews formed within Christian groups that are predominately African American or predominately white. Michael Emerson and Christian Smith make this point in their book *Divided by Faith,* which tells the story of a black/white racial divide among evangelical Christians. They argue that the divide is fueled by divergent interpretations of the social role of faith for Christians. The factors contributing to the chasm include different interpretations of Jesus and salvation, emphasizing either personal salvation or salvation from sources of social and systemic sin.[4] White Christians, who see Jesus as a personal savior, view racism as individual overt actions stemming from sin in the hearts of individuals. Racism, in the individualist perspective, is miraculously erased when the convert accepts Jesus as personal Lord and savior.[5] But the salvation-as-social camp (in *Divided by Faith*, this group is primarily African American) sees racism as systemic and structural sin. Accordingly, Christian discipleship must include a social and political dynamic to oppose systemic injustice. The difference between the two camps is racial, and it reveals a chasm within our respective interpretations of faithful Christian living.

The two camps also represent different interpretations of a narrative of racial domination[6] and an appropriate Christian response to it. But loyalty to the perspective within one camp alone is also problematic. If we see racism as the rare but overtly objectionable behavior of individuals, we miss the social and systemic scope of the problem. But if we only see it as social and systemic, we miss critical attention to the way that harmful ideologies can distort individual character. The narrative of racial domination is deeper and broader than one interpretation alone can explain.

This essay is not a review of *Divided by Faith*, but it does ask a question that is latent within that book's pages: what role does our Christian faith play as an impediment to, or as motivation for, an appropriate Christian response to white racist domination? This question is especially salient in an America that is increasingly multicultural. Even if most Christians believe that their faith helps bridge the gaps in social interaction created by historic white supremacy, current social conditions in America betray a different reality; one's claim to be a Christian is often evidence of membership in one of the two rival camps identified by Emerson and Smith, depending on the color of your skin. That is no surprise, given the histories that we all inhabit. Our western world was shaped in a not-so-distant past of overt and violent white supremacy. The narrative of white supremacy is not only in the past. It remains embedded within the body-politic of American life like a virus, adapting to the antibodies we employ in our efforts to eradicate it, changing its method of operating within the western world, such that even when we seek to rid ourselves of it, we may even be availing ourselves of its use, only to perpetuate it. We are inside the racialized understanding of humanity so deeply that it appears impossible to escape.

A History of Confronting Domination

Stassen insists that Christians discuss justice precisely because reconciliation without justice avoids injustice and secures our places within the problem of white supremacy. Over more than fifty years of teaching, Stassen's careful exegesis of the way of Jesus has inspired active confrontations with racial injustice inside and outside the classroom. During his graduate student years at Duke University, from 1960 to 1964, Stassen was the co-founder of the Duke University civil rights organization, the Christian Interracial Witness Association.[7] Under his leadership, justice-minded students at Duke University partnered with justice-minded students from Shaw University to convince the Sears-Roebuck department store in Durham, North Carolina, to increase the numbers of African Americans on their payroll beyond the two night janitors they currently employed. By use of nonviolent protest, Stassen's group of students successfully persuaded Sears-Roebuck to hire African Americans in prominent positions where the store's numerous African-American customers could see them and buy from them. This was part of a city-wide nonviolent movement that filled Durham's jail, closed down inner-city businesses, and achieved the major civil rights goals of fair employment policies, school integration, and integration of public accommodations. For Stassen, nonviolent direct action was as creative as it was effective at confronting unjust laws in faithfulness to the way of Jesus.[8]

A Narrative Like a Virus

Resistance to Stassen's student protests came from people whom society considered to be good Christians, claiming faithfulness to Jesus while remaining hostile toward non-white people and cries for social justice. Stassen was confronting a history of Christian white supremacy, which continues to perpetuate a social narrative of humanity that is diseased, aligning that narrative with Christian opposition to social justice, and disproving the white evangelical notion of a miracle motif. But, if we are to learn from Stassen and confront the enduring social narrative of domination, what must we do? If we are to avoid perpetuating the diseased worldview of the Christian opponents of justice, what must we do today?

The answer to those questions requires full disclosure of the problem we seek to address.[9] The problem is the narrative of white supremacy and our response to its contemporary restatement. Narratives are stories that communities tell of their origins to make meaning of their existence and order their societies. The narrative of white supremacy is a meaning-making narrative of humanity, one that is still being written.

In the story of white supremacy, some of us are protagonists and some of us are antagonists. Historically, our role in this narrative has literally been written on our skin as the language of race. In 1903, W. E. B. Du Bois introduced the concepts of the veil and double consciousness with the publication of his book, *The Souls of Black Folk.* The veil is a construct that describes racialization; it is the forced attribution of racial identity by white folks on black bodies that works like a projector screen. The veil is lowered and the human drama is played out on black bodies like a movie in which the good guys fight to maintain law and order against the bad guys in an imagined reality packaged for mass consumption. Whites project an image on the veiled black body from the imagined drama, and they craft their white identity as protagonists, in distinction from the imagined one on the veil. But Du Bois argued that real black selves are hidden "behind the veil." That is the reason for double consciousness; blacks know themselves as whites see them, always a projected image from vivid imaginations, and sometimes blacks possess knowledge of their real black selves. That is the drama into which we are all born. It is a communal story played out in society and on our bodies. We are scripted as protagonists or antagonists, without any merit or any consent. What we know about our human capacities is handed to us in the script we are given at birth. Yet, because it is a dynamic story, constantly changing, we can also influence how this story is told today and what it tells us about the society we should want.

The Prequel: Invention, not Discovery

The introduction to the tragic story of racial domination began in the Age of Discovery. When explorers set sail from European empires for new and uncharted lands, they began to write the story that we have today as they sought to demonstrate the greatness of their respective empires. European explorers came to understand themselves as distinct from the various types of people they met in foreign lands. They used the language of discovery, but in reality it was invention; people who once knew themselves by stories connected to their communities and ancestral lands came to be redefined by explorers as indigenes. Their identity was placed on their skin. Their land became the property of the crown and was renamed according to what was familiar to Europeans. It was the colonization of land and of beings. African people of lands and communities all became black people as their identity and character were invented by imperialists who drafted them by force into the newly invented western story of humanity.

After the Age of Discovery, during the Enlightenment, scientists like the Swedish Botanist Carl Von Linnaeus gave us the name *homo sapiens* in 1758, and German naturalist/anthropologist Johann Friedrich Blumenbach sought to classify life on earth. According to Enlightenment scientists like Blumenbach and Linnaeus, all of life can be classified and categorized by types. That includes human beings and humanoid types. In 1767, Linnaeus penned his notable work *Systema Naturae*, in which he introduced the Linnaean Taxonomy, a rank-based scientific classification of living organisms. His taxonomy described five types of human beings categorized according to skin color and land of origin: the *Americanus*, the *Asiaticus*, the *Africanus*, the *Europeanus*, and the *Monstrosus*.[10] His work was the nascent stage of the scientific language of race, and it required a very active and creative imagination. According to Linnaeus, each race contained innate character traits. *Americanus* was copper colored or red skinned, obstinate, and without content. Stubborn of character and easily angered, they wore paint for clothing and were governed by customs. *Asiaticus* was sooty, melancholy, and rigid. Some accounts of the taxonomy say they were yellow skinned, easily distracted, haughty and covetous, covered with loose garments, and governed by opinions. *Europeanus* was fair skinned, sanguine and brawny, blue eyed, gentle of character, intellectually inventive, covered with close vestments, and governed by laws. *Africanus* was black skinned, with a relaxed, phlegmatic disposition, black frizzled hair, silky skin, and a flat nose; they were crafty, indolent, lazy, and negligent. Like the red-skinned type, *Africanus* was not described as wearing clothing; they merely anoint themselves with grease and are governed by caprice. Finally, the *monstrosus* types were the most obviously folklore. *Monstrosus* was described as mountain-dwelling, four-footed, hairy wild men, like the Yeti, Sasquatch, or dwarves.

This rhetoric worked as the foundation for understanding human beings wherever the reach and influence of European empires could be felt. Linnaeus did not invent the rhetoric; he and other notable Enlightenment intellectuals endorsed it. And with well-crafted character profiles like these in place, the philosophical, scientific, and religious foundation for white supremacy was firmly established. Our story moved forward with the creation of overtly racist regimes. For our purposes, we are paying attention to the segments that have to do with America.

Chapter One: Slavery and the Racial Bribe

Michelle Alexander's recent book, *The New Jim Crow: Mass Incarceration in the Age of Colorblindness*, illustrates that we are experiencing a new chapter in the tragic narrative of white supremacy.[11] Colonial America became a foundational chapter in the story of race in America. Alexander argues that race-based slavery in America served two needs for European colonists: it was a solution to the growing need for labor by wealthy plantation owners, and it served as a creative solution to the class conflicts between wealthy and poor whites, by soothing the discomfort that poor whites felt over the economic, social, and political agenda of the wealthy white planters. How exactly did that work? Alexander describes a "racial bribe" used by the wealthy white planter class to eliminate aggravation between poor whites and themselves over labor and social status. The racial bribe gave whites privileges that were not accessible to *Africanus*. The bribe established an arrangement of norms and laws that placed blacks in a fixed status as the anchor of the social hierarchy, while giving poor whites status and authority to police *Africanus*.[12] It was a logical arrangement given the character profiles that were already in place for *Europeanus* and *Africanus*. The use of those profiles at this point in the story of the West ensured that even the poorest *Europeanus* would have a scientific, philosophical, and religious validation for dominating the capricious Africans. But it was a bribe. The bribe worked because it fit the story, and at the same time it organized society to secure luxury for the small planter class at the expense of many poor whites and blacks.

But the slave arrangement worked only as long as *Africanus* was not recognized as fully human. Many years later, in a 1961 commencement speech at the University of Pennsylvania, Dr. Martin Luther King, Jr,. made an observation about the logic of black inhumanity:

> Aristotle brought into being the syllogism, which had a major premise and a minor premise and a conclusion, and one brother had probably read Aristotle and put his argument in the framework of an Aristotelian syllogism. He could say that all men are made in the image of God. That was his major premise. Then came the minor premise: God, as everybody knows, is not a Negro; therefore the Negro is not a man. And that was called logic![13]

That racist logic was clearly absurd and offensive. But it was not the offense of that false logic that brought an end to slavery and the next chapter in the story. The end of slavery was aided by the increasingly forceful argument that slavery was inconsistent with the larger story of an American democratic republic. That was the theme of Frederick Douglass's admonition to abolitionists in 1852, when he asked the question, "What, to the American slave, is your 4th of July?"[14]

Chapter Two: The Rise of Jim Crow

With its demise, the end of slavery did not bring about the end of the racialized narrative of the West. Like a new plot twist, or a virus that refuses to let an antibiotic win, the story of white supremacy adapted to the changes. Shortly after the end of slavery, twenty-two-year-old Ida B. Wells-Barnett was seated in the first class ladies' coach, dressed formally as she typically was when she rode on a train in Tennessee. She was three years old when the Thirteenth Amendment ended slavery in 1865, and she witnessed modest gains in civil rights for black people before 1883. That was the year the United States Supreme Court allowed southern states the freedom to engage reconstruction as they pleased. On the train that day, when the conductor came by to retrieve her ticket, he demanded that she remove herself to the newly established colored car. Wells refused to give up her seat to the new race laws, and she even sank her teeth into the white man's hand as he laid hands on her to yank her to her feet. When three men threw her from the train at the next stop, the remaining passengers applauded. Wells sued that railroad company successfully, only to have her victory overturned by the United States Supreme Court as another overtly racist regime was being assembled.[15]

Ms. Wells was an early witness to the systematic establishment of the Jim Crow South, as the character profile of black people was adapted to argue that a new racial organizing system was important for the well-being of a decent society. Michelle Alexander argues that this new chapter extended the sedating features of white supremacy for poor, working-class whites. "Immoral" and "dangerous" were adjectives that joined "lazy," "capricious," and "negligent" in the character profile for black people. Until Jesse Owens won four gold medals at the 1936 Olympics in Berlin, poverty, perpetual disease, and short lives within black communities were reasons to include "physically feeble" as an adjective to the black profile. After 1936, "possessing animal qualities in physical capabilities" replaced "feeble."[16] In schools, through various entertainment sources, from pulpits and pews, depictions of white communities as the safe and idyllic Mayberry, rife with iconic two-parent patriarchal homes, masked the reality of white racist terrorism infecting the health of society at every level.

In December 1955, Mrs. Rosa Parks was on her way home from work after a busy day of dealing with the crush of Christmas shoppers. She was tired. When she refused to give up her seat in compliance with an ambiguous race law, she refused to stand for unquestioned participation in the story of white supremacy. That story did not fit the reality of her own humanity that she knew to be true. Like Ida B. Wells-Barnett more than seventy years earlier, Mrs. Parks refused the veil and rejected the narrative of an idyllic place where blacks are terrorized subjects in a white supremacist world. When applied to Mrs. Parks, the narrative that backed the need for segregation proved woefully inconsistent, and there was loud dissonance.

Four days after Mrs. Parks's arrest, Martin Luther King, Jr., stood at the pulpit of Holt Street Baptist Church in Montgomery, Alabama, to amplify the dissonance for the world to hear. In essence, King was saying, "Your profile of us is wrong, the story doesn't work, we are tired of this role, and you picked the wrong lady for your narrative."

> Mrs. Rosa Parks is a fine person. And, since it had to happen, I'm happy that it happened to a person like Mrs. Parks, for nobody can doubt the boundless outreach of her integrity. Nobody can doubt the height of her character; nobody can doubt the depth of her Christian commitment and devotion to the teachings of Jesus. And I'm happy since it had to happen; it happened to a person that nobody can call a disturbing factor in the community. Mrs. Parks is a fine Christian person, unassuming, and yet there is integrity and character there. And just because she refused to get up, she was arrested. And you know, my friends, there comes a time when people get tired of being trampled over by the iron feet of oppression.[17]

The impeccable character of Mrs. Parks betrayed the lie in the character profiles that were foundational for the Jim Crow system to work. The need to oppress and marginalize black people permeated society through the story white supremacy told about good and safe communities. That story did not match the reality of what the African-American community knew to be true, and Mrs. Parks became the embodiment of a truer narrative.

Yet Mrs. Parks's arrest, as damning as it was for the Jim Crow system, proved nothing to the white community in Alabama. They were loyal to the narrative of white supremacy no matter what. But Mrs. Parks gave license to African Americans to remove the veil and stop cooperating with the society's toxic race narratives. Mrs. Parks also contradicted what is most damning about the *Africanus* character profile: its potential to convince blacks that it is telling the truth about them. When the pejorative narrative proves convincing for blacks, black people also wield the weapons of white supremacy against other blacks. The insidious nature of white supremacy includes the power to inflict its viral hatred on the psyche of the racialized subject as well, making black people unwitting co-conspirators in the planter-class efforts to organize and secure control over all of society like the whites who were hostile toward Stassen's nonviolent protest of Sears-Roebuck.

Mrs. Parks and Dr. King proved the lie of the narrative that allied poor whites with the economically powerful in political and economic schemes that worked against their well-being. The language of race, with its character profiles, was no longer seen as consistent with the narrative of a democratic republic. With the success of the civil rights movement, and in the wake of World War II, overt racism had received a black eye.

Chapter Three: The New Jim Crow

But like a virus mutating yet again to conquer a powerful antibiotic, or like another clever plot twist, the narrative of domination adapted. What Alexander describes as the New Jim Crow is a new chapter in the story of white supremacy as a continuation in the racialized system of social organization. Alexander argues that proponents of racial hierarchy found that they could install a new racial caste system without violating the law or the new limits of acceptable political discourse: by demanding "law and order" rather than "segregation forever."[18]

The adaptations came at the level of the individual. King addressed social and systemic structures, and the adaptation to King's structural analysis came as a turn to the individual as moral agent. Poverty, for example, a plague King described as a non-discriminating structural and systemic injustice, was racialized as black, and depicted by civil rights opponents as the result of individual moral choices alone.[19] The narrative's adaptation kept the racial profiles in place to aid the formation of a new racial organizing principle, one that uses language like "post-racial" and "colorblind," making appeals to individual character, morality, law, and order rather than to overt systemic racial imagery. By appealing to the character of individuals, the racialized profiles are invoked in the absence of explicit racist language. The appeal to character is a colorblind tactic, which served to divert attention from structures that are arranged for the benefit of racialized protagonists in the narrative at the expense of the racialized antagonists. Widely disproportionate incarceration rates in a covertly named "war on drugs" are indicators of natural character flaws in capricious, inferior people. We do not notice the profiles that are invoked in the "war" by the reference to law and order, because the rhetoric fits the story we are told about black character, going as far back as colonialism. We know the story by heart.

Glen Stassen and the Race Narrative

Fortunately, the diseased worldview of racial domination has always met with dissonance. The activist scholarship demonstrated by the narrative of the way of Jesus in Stassen's Christian ethics is academic and social dissonance to the lethal harmony of white racist domination in American Christianity. Stassen's argument for holistic character ethics and pluralist citizenship neutralizes the contentious pull toward a single, dominating voice.

Stassen's holistic approach to Christian ethics pays attention to multiple factors that influence the formation of our character as moral agents, while accounting for our life in the social systems to which we belong.[20] His Christ-centered approach identifies the need to link the way of Jesus to the pursuit of justice, understood primarily as restorative. A holistic analysis of pluralist moral agents provides the opportunity for justice and for honest contribution to wholesome dialogue from multiple participants who are not dominated by a single narrative; instead, they are empowered to participate in a diverse community with a sense of ownership while maintaining a healthy sense of themselves.

A Biblical Model

Stassen's model is helpful for avoiding the problems that occur when we fail to account for the strength of the racist narrative. In America today, the language of "post-racial" and "colorblind" commonly describes popular responses to the troubling narrative of white supremacy. But "post-racial" and "colorblind" belie a latent presence of white supremacy and the pull toward the dominating narrative.

As Stassen advocates in his discussion of pluralist citizens, we are the product of complex sources of community obligations, stories, customs, food, and music that make us who we are. We are cultures in families and communities with histories that parents pass to children over many years. We have made traditions, and traditions have made us. The language of "post-racial," and "colorblind" returns us to a single dominating narrative in which we ignore our innate complexities.

The Tower of Babel as a Dominating Narrative of Injustice

In his recent book, *A Thicker Jesus,* Stassen points to the story of the Tower of Babel as an explicit illustration of a dominating narrative that can advance us beyond the language of colorblind and post-racial.[21] After the great flood, Noah's sons emerge from the ark, and God tells them to "multiply and fill the earth" (Gen 9:1). But instead, they remain local. Soon, they become a large number. They want to be known as a great and unified people, and they indicate that a building plan would do that for them. "Come," they say, "let's build a great city with a tower that reaches to the skies—a monument to our greatness! This will bring us together and keep us from scattering all over the world" (Gen 11:1-4). But indeed, they were supposed to "scatter all over the world." Instead, they embark on a plan for unity and greatness with an unauthorized building plan.

But their building plans were not dreams of greatness for all of their community to share. Someone had to build it. Someone had to toil and sweat as dominated participants in the story of a great people that was crafted by the social, economic, and politically powerful. The builders were not privy to the proud unity that the powerful sought; that unity was assembled on their backs, and it rendered them invisible.

Babel and the Four Dimensions of Transforming Justice

The Tower of Babel narrative of a great people demonstrates what Stassen identifies as four dimensions of injustice: (1) the injustice of greed; (2) the injustice of domination; (3) the injustice of violence; and (4) the injustice of exclusion from community. The transforming justice of the way of Jesus confronts each of these dimensions of injustice. In an ironic move, God saw Babel's monument of a unified people reaching to the heavens and came down. They did not reach God's level with their efforts at greatness. Indeed, they could not be great by building on the backs of marginalized and oppressed people. God came down to their level to see what they were doing. God was not fearful of any future greatness they might pursue, but, because of multiple injustices, God struck down their dominating unity, gave the people different languages, and halted their building plans. Attention to the four dimensions of injustice provides deeper insight into God's actions at Babel.

First, the people who dreamed of greatness and the people conscripted to build the tower were on different sides of social, economic, and political power, a fact that implies a dominating greed. The lust for greatness maintains goods and privileges in the hands of a limited number, for whom greatness is reserved. The dominated workers were forced to build the monument to greatness in the heat of the day, out of bricks and tar rather than sturdier materials like stone and cement, leading to an unstable and wobbling structure. This is reticent of a bad and harmful plan. Thus God disrupted their greedy, harmful plans.[22]

Second, the building plan was carried out by a class of people dominated by the imagined story of a great people, with which they were permanently excluded from identifying. That narrative of a great people had nothing to do with them; it was about a higher social class, but it demanded the bodies of the subjugated. By giving them different languages, God disabled the link of communication that allowed the story to continue, literally disrupting the dominating narrative and liberating the oppressed.

Third, God put an end to the violence inherent in securing forced compliance to the dominating narrative. The narrative that secures compliance from a subjugated people is also intellectual violence. It is a colonization of the mind that forces compliance by the subjugated, relegating human beings to subhumanity with a story (Gen 11:5-9). The narrative may also include the use of physical violence, which is also legitimized for use on the bodies of the subhuman by the sick logic of the racist narrative.

Last, by giving them different languages, God recovered subjugated people from physical and psychological violence, imposed invisibility, and social exclusion by providing them with the building blocks for their own culture. In the next chapter, the call of Abram is narrated and the Jewish culture is born, from whom the world receives a savior who will restore unity to the human family based on the justice of God's reign.

Jesus and Transforming Justice

The story of the Tower of Babel illustrates the injustices associated with a single, dominating narrative. A dominating narrative excludes voices and normalizes injustice in multiple dimensions. Stassen's work cites recent developments in research about Jesus that identify a deep commitment to justice in the way of Jesus. These new developments lead Stassen to identify four dimensions of delivering justice: "1) Deliverance of the poor and powerless from the injustice that they regularly experience; 2) lifting the foot of the domineering power off of the neck of the dominated and oppressed; 3) stopping the violence and establishing peace; and 4) restoring outcasts, the excluded, the Gentiles, the exiles and the refugees to community."[23]

Each of these dimensions is descriptive of the way of Jesus, often by his confrontation with injustices. They are not abstract principles. Justice is not an abstraction; it is concrete experiences that are connected with Stassen's definition of agape as delivering love. The four themes of justice help us see clearly the depth of Jesus' compassion and love.

A Different Building Plan

Centuries after the Tower of Babel, God brings the languages back together in an intentional way. On the day of Pentecost, the Holy Spirit came from heaven "like a mighty rushing wind" and settled like tongues of fire above the heads of disciples gathered there. And everyone watching this event heard them speaking in other tongues. That is, they heard them praising God together, in the languages of many different cultures (Acts 2:1-13). On the day of Pentecost, God reversed the cause of disunity and language confusion, and brought people back together under a different building project—under a different "unity." They retained their language, and in their formative language, they praised God together without domination. The Spirit of God came on the day of Pentecost as endorsement of the ministry of justice that Jesus demonstrated by his life and witness and to empower Jesus' disciples to follow him in the work.

The Pentecost narrative illustrates the connection between Jesus and justice that Stassen highlights. It demonstrates a justice-oriented, participative community that is empowered to maintain their formative group identity, as participants within a cross-cultural population. It is a restorative narrative in which we are called to bring our whole selves into the community, to be advocates of delivering justice, recognizing our task as prophetic. This new narrative, then, is the remedy for the virus that has infected us. Indeed, the good news is that healing is possible. Joining with God in the work of restoration means participating in the way of Jesus that Stassen advocates, where delivering justice, rather than the narrative of racial domination, is normative.

NOTES

1. Matthew 7:12 (paraphrased).

2. Stassen developed a method of analysis that accounts for multiple dimensions of input in our ethical decision-making. In the model, Stassen's analysis of our basic convictions argues that one's moral life as a Christian is affected significantly by the connection we see between Jesus and justice. See Glen Harold Stassen and David P. Gushee, *Kingdom Ethics: Following Jesus in Contemporary Context* (Downers Grove IL: InterVarsity, 2002) 55ff. Also, Stassen argues that our interpretation of Jesus' social commandments as either high ideals or concrete commandments for Christian obedience is connected to our understanding of the connection between Jesus and justice. See Glen Harold Stassen, *Living the Sermon on the Mount: A Practical Hope for Grace and Deliverance* (San Francisco: Jossey-Bass, 2006) 184ff.

3. Stassen and Gushee, *Kingdom Ethics*, 390.

4. Stassen and Gushee refer to the study by Emerson and Smith in *Kingdom Ethics*, with affirmation, to make their point about justice rather than reconciliation (406).

5. See the description of "the miracle motif" in Michael O. Emerson and Christian Smith, *Divided by Faith: Evangelical Religion and the Problem of Race in America* (New York: Oxford University Press, 2000) 117ff.

6. I use racial domination and white supremacy interchangeably. I am working with an interpretation of white supremacy that Willie Jennings describes as a constituent of a diseased Christian imagination in a discursive practice of self-discovery within the modern practice of colonialism. See Willie James Jennings, *The Christian Imagination: Theology and the Origins of Race* (New Haven: Yale University Press, 2010). Also see Cornel West's description of a "normative gaze" (*Prophesy Deliverance!: An Afro-American Revolutionary Christianity*, anniversary ed. [Louisville KY: Westminster John Knox, 2002] 53ff).

7. Stassen's co-founder of the Christian Interracial Witness Association, Wally Mead, earned a PhD in Political Science, and was a committed Methodist. Stassen was and remains a committed Baptist.

8. Even at this early time in his life, Stassen was modeling one of the key practices he would later include in his just peacemaking theory, nonviolent direct action. See *Just Peacemaking: The New Paradigm for the Ethics of Peace and War* (Cleveland: Pilgrim, 2008) 42–56.

9. My narrative method includes public disclosure, one of the practices of nonviolent direct action outlined in just peacemaking theory. See *Just Peacemaking: New Paradigm*, 51–53. Public disclosure is "publicizing the complete facts or events that are relevant to a conflict but that are being kept hidden or falsified due to deliberate strategies of disinformation" (51).

10. See Emmanuel Chukwudi Eze, *Race and the Enlightenment: A Reader* (Malden MA: Blackwell, 1997) 15ff.

11. Michelle Alexander, *The New Jim Crow: Mass Incarceration in the Age of Colorblindness* (New York: New Press, 2010) 25ff.

12. I am using Linnaeus's Latin terms as he did, in the singular form, to demonstrate figuratively the characters created within his racialized narrative of humanity. Broadly speaking, *Africanus* is a character that every person of African descent plays in the western world's narrative of racialized humanity.

13. Martin Luther King, Jr., and James Melvin Washington, *A Testament of Hope: The Essential Writings of Martin Luther King, Jr.*, 1st ed. (San Francisco: Harper & Row, 1986) 211.

14. Frederick Douglass, *My Bondage and My Freedom* (New York: Washington Square Press, 2003) 343ff.

15. See Emilie Maureen Townes, *Womanist Justice, Womanist Hope*, American Academy of Religion Series 79 (Atlanta: Scholars Press, 1993) 8ff.

16. Changes within the dominating narrative of race are adaptations meant to rectify recently discovered inconsistencies. Edwin Black describes passive eugenics as the belief that certain races will naturally cease to exist, leaving only superior races. Passive eugenics rectified the narrative of race, accounting for large, impoverished, sickly communities of African Americans post-Reconstruction. See Edwin Black, *War against the Weak: Eugenics and America's Campaign to Create a Master Race* (New York: Four Walls Eight Windows, 2003). Jesse Owens's performance at the Summer Olympic Games in 1933 highlighted major inconsistencies in the eugenics re-adjustment to the narrative of race. See Guy Walters, *Berlin Games: How Hitler Stole the Olympic Dream* (London: John Murray, 2006) 166ff.

17. Martin Luther King, Jr., Clayborne Carson, and Kris Shepard, *A Call to Conscience: The Landmark Speeches of Dr. Martin Luther King, Jr.* (New York: Intellectual Properties Management, in association with Warner Books, 2001) 8.

18. Alexander, *New Jim Crow*, 40.

19. I am referring to the myth of the welfare queen, among other racialized images of government-dependent, lazy minorities. See Ange-Marie Hancock, *The Politics of Disgust: The Public Identify of the Welfare Queen* (New York: New York University Press, 2004).

20. See Michael Walzer, *Obligations: Essays on Disobedience, War, and Citizenship* (Cambridge: Harvard University Press, 1970) 147ff. I'm borrowing the language of pluralist citizens from the political philosopher Michael Walzer, whom Stassen holds in high regard. Walzer describes a pluralist citizen with reference to primary (involuntary) and secondary (voluntary) group memberships. For Walzer, an involuntary group is one we enter by virtue of birth and is our primary group, while we enter secondary groups intentionally, as volunteers. Within secondary groups, our obligations can be more stringent, potentially placing members in conflict with primary group obligations. This is the case with cross-cultural group participation motivated to oppose unjust laws. The interaction between secondary and primary groups describes pluralism and agency. Secondary groups offer concrete opportunities for personal formation in a way that primary groups cannot, by providing an environment where obligations are incurred voluntarily, and they aid the formation of conscience or patriotism within group members. Secondary groups also allow for community and obligations in the absence of primary group allegiance. The pluralist citizen is one who belongs to multiple groups in which obligations are voluntarily incurred, making claims upon the state. This citizen's largest group is the state, yet she has more than one group to which she is obligated. The pluralist citizen makes an honest contribution to public discourse from core principles formed within the context of secondary group membership. Moral agency is the duty of a pluralist citizen. This discourse is the sort of dialogue made possible by persons who maintain a sense of themselves and are obligated to the groups within which they share commitments. Simple compliance to the state can be a betrayal of self and group obligations as well as the denial of "public character." A pluralist citizen is one who risks a patriotism that opposes the authorities.

21. See Glen Harold Stassen, *A Thicker Jesus: Incarnational Discipleship in a Secular Age* (Louisville KY: Westminster John Knox, 2012) 131–36. I am building on Stassen's argument that the Babel story challenges sinful pretensions to domination, and the alienation and loss of community that results. For Stassen, Babel serves as a paradigm for sin as "the temptation of power and domination."

22. Stassen, *Thicker Jesus*, 135.

23. Stassen and Gushee, *Kingdom Ethics*, 349.

Chapter 11

Just Peacemaking and the Moro-Christian Problem in Muslim Mindanao

Aldrin M. Peñamora

Introduction

It is a great and humbling privilege to be part of this splendid *Festschrift* for Dr. Glen H. Stassen, whom I consider my mentor and friend. I have certainly learned and continue to learn much from him, but among those many things, I especially value the centrality of Jesus in Christian theology and ethics. The Filipino conception of Jesus as the "God of Struggle" is relevant in just peacemaking in Mindanao, where for more than four centuries Muslims and Christians in the Philippines have been engaged in violent conflict. Indeed, the resolution or perpetuation of the Muslim-Christian conflict in Mindanao will be shaped largely by the image of Jesus held by the majority Christian Filipinos.

Just Peacemaking Theory

Just peacemaking, as Lisa Sowle Cahill describes it, is a "new paradigm that cuts between traditional just war theory and pacifism, combines a biblical faith commitment with political engagement, and aims to unite persons of many faiths and cultures in actually diminishing war and other types of politically motivated violence."[1] The question the new paradigm seeks to answer is different from the core issue being debated by just war and pacifism, which is centered on the rightness of waging war. Rather, just peacemaking asks, what practices should be nurtured and supported in order to prevent—not unrealistically abolish—war?[2] According to the twenty-three scholars who developed just peacemaking theory, the practices are ethically normative because they were not derived from abstract ideals; the practices have historical and empirical evidence that they "do in fact prevent numerous wars and multitudinous misery and death."[3]

According to Stassen and company, undergirding just peacemaking are three theological convictions: (1) *Initiatives*, a concept of discipleship grounded on the person, life, and teachings of Jesus; (2) *Justice*, or the participation of the church in engaging issues of peace and justice in the broken world; and (3) *Love and Community*, which refers to the church as the eschatological sign of God's love in the world.[4] These convictions are demonstrated by the ten following concrete practices. The *initiatives* are (1) support nonviolent direct action; (2) take independent initiatives to reduce threats; (3) use cooperative conflict resolution; (4) acknowledge responsibility for conflict and injustice, and seek repentance and forgiveness. Under *justice* are the practices of (5) advancing democracy, human rights, and liberty and (6) fostering just and sustainable economic development. The practices contained in the dimension of *love* and *community* are (7) work with emerging international cooperative forces; (8) strengthen the United Nations and international efforts for human rights; (9) reduce offensive weapons and trade; and (10) encourage grassroots peacemaking groups and voluntary associations.[5] As a third paradigm, just peacemaking does not supplant either the ethics of just war or pacifism, both of which remain equally important resources in evaluating the morality of waging war.[6]

Theologically underpinning the initiatives of just peacemaking theory is the Sermon on the Mount—the "*locus classicus* for Christian peacemaking."[7] However, nineteenth-century idealism has often crept into interpretations of the Sermon and made its teachings appear lofty and unattainable.[8] To rescue the Sermon, Stassen convincingly points out that the consistent pattern of Jesus' teachings does not consist of twofold prohibitionist antitheses but of threefold, grace-filled, transforming initiatives. Matthew 5:21-26, for instance, has often been interpreted as Jesus commanding us—unrealistically—never to be angry. Stassen contends that in 5:22, "being angry" is not an imperative but a participle that is a realistic diagnosis of a vicious cycle from which people must be delivered. Jesus' commands are thus found in the transforming initiatives in Matthew 5:23-26, which speak of transforming the angry person into a person of peace, and the relationship of conflict to one of friendship.[9]

Justice forms the second theological conviction of just peacemaking theory. The practices informed by this conviction are necessarily intertwined, for in order to flourish, rights, liberty, and democracy require an economy wherein extreme differences in wealth and power are overcome.[10] Indeed,

Scripture attests to how justice is related to God's denunciation of unbridled devotion to acquisitive ends, and God's concern for the oppressed that finds expression in the Hebraic-Christian concept of human rights.[11] Far from being mere ideals, human rights arise out of the concrete struggle of love and justice for victims of oppression that Jesus demonstrated by his solidarity with society's outcasts.[12]

Finally, the practices under *love* and *community* aim to strengthen co-operative forces. This conviction repudiates an individualistic or isolationist culture and seeks to recover Jesus' way of love that is far more than mere sentimentality. As Stassen and company incisively contend, the love that Jesus so centrally shows in the gospel materials is a community-building love that embraces the outcasts, the oppressed, and even one's enemies.[13] Indeed, just peacemakers are to be communities of love first and foremost, and they are to understand, work with, and support other institutions and forces working toward justice and peace.[14]

Just peacemaking, therefore, aims to establish the conditions that will allow people to live in a society that is just, peaceful, and free. It presents a comprehensive vision of concretely incarnating God's reign through following Jesus in discipleship.

Following a "Thicker Jesus": the Heart of Just Peace-making

Discipleship presupposes a certain understanding of Jesus—what his person, his teachings, and his life, death, and resurrection mean. For the theorists of just peacemaking, Christology is not about abstract or idealized conceptions; it is an incarnational perspective that (a) sees Christ as sovereign over all of life; (b) defines the meaning of Christ in terms of discipleship; (c) interprets Jesus' teachings, especially the Sermon on the Mount, as intertwined with concrete practices that can guide us in daily life; and (d) understands Jesus' humanity as one that showed a way to be followed. In other words, the Christology of just peacemaking "stays close to the Jewish servant Lord of the Gospels who called his disciples humbly to follow his way of nonviolent love, community-restoring justice, and peacemaking initiatives."[15] Just peacemaking therefore emerged from perceiving what Stassen calls a "thicker Jesus" that is primarily a result of a concrete exegesis of the Sermon and from having an ethic of "incarnational discipleship," which calls believers to recognize Jesus not merely as Lord of one, or some, but of all dimensions of life.[16] Indeed, based on God's salvific actions within history, of which the exodus and Christ events are key exemplifications,

God's sovereignty is defined by grace and compassion. For Stassen, the Sovereign God is also the gracious and compassionate deliverer.

Such characteristics of God can be discerned in the Old Testament, says Stassen, especially in relation to Yahweh's self-disclosure of the divine nature on the occasion of giving the Ten Commandments to Moses at Sinai (Exod 20:1-17), which had the exodus deliverance as the immediate background. While the individual commandments yield ethical and life-giving insights, what holds them together is the very character of Yahweh as deliverer (Exod 20:2; cf. 6:2, 6-8). That is, the commands are crucial expressions of God as deliverer, who "sees the misery, hears the cries, knows the suffering of the powerless, the vulnerable, the victims of violations of their basic human rights, and calls us into covenant to protect them."[17] Thus, while God is undoubtedly transcendent, Stassen perceptively sees that transcendence is not about hiddenness or unknowability; it speaks of God's indomitable nature as one that exceedingly loves and is constantly present to hear and deliver the oppressed with justice.[18]

Similarly, the New Testament, particularly in the Sermon on the Mount where Jesus taught most extensively on peacemaking and justice-making, attests to God's character as gracious and compassionate deliverer.[19] For the commands in the Sermon are not centered on unattainable ideals or on human striving. Instead, they point to "God's gracious initiative in delivering us from sin, guilt, and oppression, into a new community of justice, peace, and freedom, including our enemies; and to our obedient participation in God's way of deliverance."[20] The notion that in participation, grace implies passivity and disempowerment is here rejected. Rather, "participative grace" affirms the Bonhoefferian perspective that believers, through Christ, become active participants in God's grace, and thus Christ takes shape in us.[21] The Sermon on the Mount, as Jürgen Moltmann remarks, "determines the *politics of discipleship* and also *discipleship in politics*."[22] Participative grace is therefore not amorphic; it is *Christomorphic*, for its shape, Stassen incisively argues, is ultimately revealed in Christ. The "shape of grace is Christ taking form in us. We participate by answering Jesus' gracious call: come follow me."[23]

Jesus as the God of Struggle: A Thicker Jesus in the Philippine Setting

A thicker conception of Jesus is indeed vital to the incarnational discipleship of just peacemaking. In the Philippine setting, conceiving Jesus as the "God of Struggle" can be appropriated as a thicker and contextual re-imagination to support just peacemaking in Mindanao, where for centuries the *Moros* (or the Muslims of the Philippines) and Christians have been locked in animosity and violent conflicts. While the idea of a gracious and compassionate deliverer, as we have just seen, is certainly a biblical portrayal of God, it is also important that God is understood through a specific community's social, cultural, and historical location. For conceptions of Jesus are not neutral; they are historically and culturally conditioned, and to claim otherwise is to render Jesus homeless.[24] This is what James Cone means by "there is no place in black theology for a colorless God in a society where human beings suffer precisely because of their color."[25] "Thickness" certainly denotes being rooted in community.[26] For this reason, Karl Barth said to Asian theologians, "it is your task to be Christian theologians in your new, different and special situations."[27] The Filipino Catholic scholar, José M. De Mesa, is certainly right in saying that "theology is never far from home."[28]

In the poverty-stricken situation of the Philippines, there are numerous notions of Jesus.[29] Understandably, to the suffering masses, a portrayal of God that approximates the Aristotelian "Unmoved Mover," who is eternally immovable, immutable, indivisible, self-absorbed, and apathetic,[30] would be a dispiriting construct; for it is paradoxical that an all-powerful being would choose self-exile from all creation, and thus be incapable of coming to anyone's aid. In this sense, to the oppressed Filipinos, God, as Nietzsche pointed out, is for all intents and purposes, dead.[31] But even without adhering to an Aristotelian "stone-faced God"[32] or without participating in a Nietzschean deicide, many Filipino Christians still find the idea of a dead God worthy of veneration. Thus, there are numerous devotees in the Philippines of the dead or entombed Christ (*Santo Bangkay* or *Santo Entierro*).[33] There is much truth to the observation that Filipinos attach a "disproportionate significance to the suffering and death of Christ over that of his life and teaching."[34] In this perspective, Jesus is the scourged, beaten, humiliated, defeated and dead Savior—the Victim Christ.[35]

Such a perception of Christ, especially expressed in the cult of images, is a prominent feature of Philippine folk Catholicism. According to Benigno Beltran's incisive analysis, the "Christology of the inarticulate" that overly emphasizes Christ as victim over the living and resurrected figure of the Incarnate One has potentially damaging effects. In the face of oppression and injustice, especially, the image of Christ "can evolve into a form of idolatry when it becomes an end in itself and is used to legitimize oppression and passivity in the face of injustice."[36] Furthermore, says Beltran, excessive attention "on the sufferings of Jesus might foster despair before tragedy . . .

numbness in the face of brokenness and the acceptance of alienation as an irrevocable decree of fate. . . . Jesus would then be relegated completely to the realm and become historically inoperative."[37] Speaking of the plight of oppressed women in the Philippines, Virginia Fabella also points out how most of them are unaware of Christ's image as liberator, and know Jesus only as one who passively understands the sufferings that they endure; such women are thus oblivious of their class and gender oppression and "live on a status quo Christology."[38] This issue was given an adequate treatment by Filipino theologians who adhere to the school of thought called "Theology of Struggle" (hereafter TOS).

Now, struggle surely is the essence of Philippine history. A Filipino historian, Renato Constantino, writes that "the most fundamental aspect of Philippine history is the history of the struggles of its people for freedom and a better life."[39] Such is reflected in TOS, for the context of its irruption was the struggle against "the life world created by the martial law years."[40] It was in confrontation with the dictatorship of Ferdinand Marcos, which sought to create a non-political and domesticated public that was bereft of a proper sense of citizenship and national consciousness, that TOS emerged.[41] Unlike theological reflections that were formed in safer confines and institutions, TOS was hammered from concrete situations by people who were fighting injustice, languishing in prison, on the run evading authorities, or meeting secretly for the purpose of advancing justice and the freedom of the Filipino people. "It was a theology that was forged out of desperation," says Levi Oracion, "and there was nowhere else to go but in utter helplessness cry out for God's liberation and God's leading."[42] The term "struggle" thus appropriately underscored a change from the prevalent Filipino attitude of *pakikisama* (smooth interpersonal relations)—which can be a debilitating form of passivity—to *pakikibaka* (struggle).[43] As such, TOS is not merely *about* the struggle of oppressed Filipinos, that is, it does not imply that theologians were the ones who defined it and gave it direction; it is primarily a theology "in" and "of" struggle, it is "servant-theology" generated through companionship with the struggling Filipino people.[44] Praxis intertwined with theological reflection is therefore the essence of TOS.[45] Mariano Apilado's remark is surely on point that the struggle for liberation, or *revolutionary spirituality* "amidst adversities and disparities is the only way to do theology in the Philippines today."[46]

In view of popular images of Jesus in the Philippines that show him as mainly a passively suffering or dead God, the bearers of TOS are surely iconoclasts, for they see God as creation's principal actor who cannot endure injustice and who intrudes in human history to embrace the righteous cause of the oppressed and bring about the downfall of oppressors.[47] That God struggles with and for the oppressed is thus the core of the biblical message for TOS. One community worker's remark is incisive: "the theology of struggle brings down God from a God in heaven to a God who is among us and walking with us . . . having hands and feet."[48] For theologians of struggle, God's solidarity (*pakikiisa*) with the oppressed was supremely revealed in the Christ event. The Incarnation was not about the metaphysical relation of the divine and human "substances"; rather, it was the definitive affirmation that—as expressed in Jesus' cry of dereliction—there is no place and condition of human wretchedness that the divine pathos will not go.[49] From this perspective, the cross is not symbolic of passivity in the face of oppression; it signifies "God's radical opposition to all powers and structures that exploit and dehumanize human beings."[50] Such essentially was the conviction of revolutionary Filipinos during the late 1800s when they rose up in struggle against foreign colonizers. Through an indigenous practice called the *Pasyon*, they re-imagined Jesus' passion, death, and resurrection merging with their own sufferings, struggles, and anticipated victories.[51] According to Karl Gaspar, it is indeed necessary to emphasize the human face of Jesus as "liberator" or as companion (*kasama*) in the struggle in situations of oppression; for it is Jesus' life and death that make the struggle for justice indispensable, and his resurrection is what confers to the struggle the promise of ultimate liberation.[52] Thus, the religiously oriented nonviolent People Power Revolution of 1986, wherein the Filipino people risked their lives without being willing to take the lives of others, and which ultimately toppled the Marcos dictatorship, also exemplified what it means for TOS to follow Jesus' call to take up the cross, which is the very "symbol of struggle."[53] Indeed, for TOS, "God is Struggle, and Struggle is the name of God."[54]

Just Peacemaking in Muslim Mindanao

As God struggles indiscriminately for and with the oppressed, Christian faith communities are called to struggle also against injustice and oppression—including struggling against the oppression of those considered enemies. Thus, Christian Filipinos must fight for the rights of the oppressed Moro people, who are among the poorest people in the nation.[55] However, the destitute and volatile situation in the Moroland is largely the outcome of the Christian colonization of Mindanao. Hence, for the church in the Philippines, joining the contemporary struggle against Moro oppression and injustice also points to an inward ecclesial struggle that seeks to liberate the church itself from its colonizing past and Constantinian tendencies. In struggling for and with the Moros, the church humbly recognizes that it is always in need of reform—*ecclesia semper reformanda est.*

The "Moro Problem" has several dimensions that encompass the economic, political, and religio-cultural oppression of the Moro people, which have led to more than four centuries of violent conflicts in Muslim Mindanao.[56] While from the colonizers' perspective the problem was mainly how they can successfully, even if oftentimes violently, govern the Moros,[57] for the Moros the predicament was created by the colonizers, who have sought to govern those whom they do not understand.[58] The Moro Problem is really a "Moro-Christian Problem," which is rooted in *injustice.*[59] This injustice has many dimensions: unjust economic development for the Moros; unjust loss of Moro political sovereignty; and unjust depiction of Moro identity.[60] After a brief overview of the dimensions of poverty and violence in Moroland, let's see how just peacemaking practices can address the Moro-Christian Problem.

While the spreading of Catholicism was a key impetus in the Spanish conquest of the Philippines, the economic exploitation of the country was also an important motivation. The Moro scholar Salah Jubair makes this pointed remark: "Spain came to the Philippines not so much for the Cross . . . religion was merely used to justify what otherwise was a satanic lust for worldly gain and glory."[62] Now, the economic destitution of the *Bangsa Moro* (Moro Nation) is related to their *ancestral land,* from whose best parts they were driven out as ownership was handed over to Christian Filipinos and foreign-owned corporations. Such policy fundamentally goes against the Moro Islamic belief on property, which upholds that ancestral domain is *waqaf* or property in trust. Losing their ancestral domain was certainly debilitating for the Moros, for their social existence directly revolves around those lands.[63] So central is this issue that the success or failure of peace negotiations hinges on its resolution, for the Bangsamoros' claim "for their rights to their ancestral lands had become the core of the expression of their right to self-determination."[63] Further aggravating Moro poverty is the fact that most development efforts by the Philippine government—which is composed of a Christian majority—have been directed to improve primarily the conditions of Christian settlers. Studies done in 1970 showed that regions inhabited by Moros were among those with the highest infant mortality and unemployment rates; they also had the fewest doctors to provide health services, and lagged far behind in terms of educational services and other necessities such as water and power systems.[64] More recent reports in 2006 and 2009 invariably demonstrated how Mindanao continued to have the highest poverty incidence in the country.[65] Called the "land of promise," Mindanao became a land of fulfillment, but mostly for Christianized Filipinos and foreign investors.[66]

Such dismal conditions of the Moros that were imposed by a majority Christian nation and its government inevitably led to violent conflicts in Mindanao. In the early 1970s, the contemporary Moro struggle broke out. By 1976, some 50,000 people perished due to the conflict. When in 1996 the Jakarta Peace Agreement was signed between the Philippine government and the Moro National Liberation Front (MNLF), more than 150,000 persons had died from the armed clashes; 300,000 buildings and houses burned; 535 mosques razed; 35 towns completely wiped out; and half of the entire Moro population uprooted.[67] In the year 2000 alone when the Philippine Government (GPH) launched an all-out offensive, 439,000 persons were displaced, 6,229 houses razed, and some 2,000 people were killed.[68] More recently from August to September 2008, immediately after peace talks broke down between the government and the Moro Islamic Liberation Front (MILF), a battle ensued that claimed more than 100 lives and displaced around 600,000 people.[69] Certainly, the Moro-Christian struggle exemplifies the deadly and cyclical nature of war.

Addressing the multifaceted grievances of the Moro people that have led to the perpetuation of violence and deep-seated animosity between Moros and Christian Filipinos is certainly a complex task. Encouragingly, in line with the principles and practices of just peacemaking theory that give us concrete "constructive alternatives,"[70] there have been important initiatives implemented by Christian communities that aim to foster just and peaceful Moro-Christian relations. Two such initiatives are herein discussed as examples of just peacemaking in Muslim Mindanao: the initiative undertaken by the Bishops-Ulama Conference of the Philippines, which conforms to the just peacemaking practice of *supporting nonviolent direct action*; and the initiative that was begun by the Silsilah Dialogue Movement, which corresponds to the sixth just peacemaking practice of *fostering a just and sustainable economic development*. Such initiatives exemplify what it means to follow Jesus, the gracious deliverer who struggles for the oppressed.

As mentioned above, the year 2000 saw a devastating conflict between the Philippine Government and the Moro forces in Mindanao. It was then classified as a Moro-Christian conflict, which was aggravated by kidnappings done by a Muslim terrorist group. Such a perception of the events would

have certainly led to deeper hatred and hostilities not only between the com-
batants, but also among the rest of the Christian and Moro populations.
Thus, the Bishops-Ulama Conference of the Philippines (BUC)—formerly
known as Bishops-Ulama Forum (BUF)—a group composed of leading sen-
ior religious leaders of the Muslim, Catholic, and Protestant faiths in the
country, issued an unequivocal condemnation of the violence that unfolded.
The BUC's proclamation contained in part:

> We recognize that . . . an all-out war will not bring peace to Mindanao.
> We question the use of force of armed groups in holding hostage innocent
> civilian populations for their own ends. Thus, we urge the government
> and the MILF . . . to return to the negotiating table and begin traversing
> the road to lasting peace in Mindanao. . . . On our part, we religious lead-
> ers in Mindanao . . . can start the healing process through prayer rallies,
> inter-cultural dialogues, and the creation of zones of peace.[71]

As the proclamation came during the period of violent confrontations, for
the adherents of the Moro and Christian traditions, the BUC stood as a bea-
con of hope of the unity they all longed for. For this reason, the BUC remains truly significant in promoting peace in society's various levels.[72]

The economic development of the Moro *ummah* (community) is vital
in resolving Moro-Christian conflict. Many development projects have
failed, however, as some Christian groups cleaved to a paternalistic mindset
and proceeded with their endeavors without involving the Moros; they thus
became ignorant of the real needs of the people.[73] It is well for Filipino
Christians to remember that constructive initiatives must not be limited to
merely addressing the economic and even political rights of the Moro
people; it is equally crucial that Christians—who have customarily held
un-Christian views and responses toward the Moros[74]—give due regard to
the Moro as a *person*. In Stassen's *Just Peacemaking: Ten Practices for Abolishing War*, David Bronkema, David Lumsdaine, and Rodger Payne underscore
this point and say that the chief concern of development is "building up
and cultivating human persons and communities as wholes."[75] The late
missionary to the Moros, Peter Gowing, affirms this point and incisively
remarks, "the nub of the matter, is disposition, attitude. Success in attracting
the Moros to become contented and contributing citizens of the nation will,
in the long run, depend on a fundamental reconstruction of the present
negative attitude of Christian Filipinos."[76]

Sebastiano d'Ambra, an Italian Catholic priest who founded the Silsilah Dialogue Movement, realized the importance of genuinely understanding the needs of the Moro community when in 1985 a fire gutted more than 500 houses in a depressed area in Zamboanga city, where he used to live among impoverished Moros and Christians. Seeing the hapless situation of the residents, Silsilah took part in rebuilding houses and encouraged the people to start all over again. D'Ambra recalls, "it was the first time that the movement took the initiative of actually being together with Muslims and Christians, in solidarity with the victims of the fire. Muslim and Christian Silsilah members joined hands to express in action the fruits of their prayer and sharing in dialogue."[77] The event led D'Ambra to form the "Solidarity Project" that aims toward the holistic development of the person. Specifically, the project seeks to "identify and develop common bases of unity between Muslims and Christians in all aspects of life."[78] This perspective has since led Silsilah to underscore in its dialogical approach—which links us to God, to ourselves, to others, and to all creation[79]—meeting the material needs of impoverished Moros. Thus, on the island of Santa Cruz, members of Silsilah, having lived with the people and understanding their expressed needs, built an elementary school. Without the school, children would have found it difficult to cross the sea daily in order to attend the nearest public schools. Such initiatives toward the Moros reflect the fourth beatitude of the Sermon on the Mount, says D'Ambra, which he sees as a prophetic utterance of dialogue that searches for modes of uprightness and justice. The beatitude also conforms with the fourth practice of just peacemaking, *acknowledging responsibility for conflict and injustice and seeking repentance and forgiveness,* for as D'Ambra further explains, it "means that one has to look at the past and the present with the spirit of responsibility, asking and giving forgiveness and recognizing the sins and mistakes of the past and the present."[80]

Summary and Conclusion

In situating Jesus, the gracious deliverer, as the foundation and impetus of just peacemaking theory, Stassen gives Christian communities a truly valuable contribution. For how Christians perceive Jesus is certainly vital to the way they will follow him in situations of war and violent conflicts. This is exemplified in the Philippines, where Filipino Christians are faced with the enormity of the "Moro-Christian Problem." Will they see Jesus merely as a helpless victim, who in life was unable to confront—much less triumph over—oppressive worldly powers, or will they, like the adherents of the

Theology of Struggle, perceive him as Lord who ushered in God's kingdom as a vigorous upholder of righteousness and justice in defense of the oppressed? Simply said, the Christian faith communities in the Philippines must continue to wrestle with and decisively answer Jesus' question, "Who do you say I am?" (Mark 8:29).

NOTES

1. Lisa Sowle Cahill, "Just Peacemaking: Theory, Practice and Prospects," *Journal of the Society of Christian Ethics* 23/1 (Spring 2003): 195.

2. Glen Stassen, ed., *Just Peacemaking: Ten Practices for Abolishing War* (Cleveland: Pilgrim, 1998) 8; Glen H. Stassen, "The Unity, Realism, and Obligatoriness of Just Peacemaking Theory," *Journal of the Society of Christian Ethics* 23/1 (2003): 177–78. In the latter article, Stassen emphasizes that just peacemaking does not claim that it will lead to the abolition of war (180). See also Glen H. Stassen and David P. Gushee, Kingdom Ethics (Downers Grove IL: InterVarsity, 2003) 150, 174.

3. Duane K. Friesen; John Langan, S.J.; and Glen Stassen, "Introduction: Just Peacemaking as a New Ethic," in Stassen, ed., *Just Peacemaking: Ten Practices*, 9.

4. Ibid., 15.

5. Glen H. Stassen, "Just Peacemaking as Hermeneutical Key," *Journal of the Society of Christian Ethics* 24/2 (2004): 177. The various theorists of just peacemaking discuss each practice comprehensively in Stassen, ed., *Just Peacemaking: Ten Practices*.

6. Stassen recounts discussing just peacemaking with John Howard Yoder, who agreed that it adds a "crucial dimension," i.e., *peacemaking action,* to just war and pacifism (John Howard Yoder, *The War of the Lamb: The Ethics of Nonviolence and Peacemaking,* ed. Glen H. Stassen et al. [Grand Rapids MI: Brazo, 2009] 24).

7. Friesen, Langan and Stassen, "Introduction," in Stassen, *Just Peacemaking: Ten Practices,* 17–19; Glen H. Stassen, *Just Peacemaking: Transforming Initiatives for Justice and Peace* (Louisville KY: Westminster John Knox, 1992) 36–37; Glen H. Stassen, "A New Transformative Peacemaking Ethic," *Review and Expositor* 82/2 (1985): 260–61.

8. Stassen and Gushee, *Kingdom Ethics,* 132–33; Glen H.Stassen, "Grace and Deliverance in the Sermon on the Mount," *Review and Expositor* 89/2 (September 1992): 229.

9. Stassen and Gushee, *Kingdom Ethics,* 135. Cf. Stassen, "Grace and Deliverance," 232–35.

10. Friesen, Langan, and Stassen, "Introduction," in Stassen, *Just Peacemaking: Ten Practices,* 19.

11. Paul W. Schroeder, "Work with Emerging Cooperative Forces in the International System," in Stassen, *Just Peacemaking: Ten Practices,* 137–63. Schroeder emphasizes that the church needs to appropriate not the Lockean version of human rights but the one rooted in Hebraic-Christian origins.

12. Ibid., 160.

13. Friesen, Langan, and Stassen, "Introduction," in Stassen, *Just Peacemaking: Ten Practices,* 24–25.

14. Schroeder, "Work with Emerging Cooperative Forces" in Stassen, *Just Peacemaking: Ten Practices*, 144. See Duane K. Friesen, "Encourage Grassroots Peacemaking Groups and Voluntary Associations," in Stassen, *Just Peacemaking: Ten Practices*, 186—98.

15. Friesen, Langan, and Stassen, "Introduction," in Stassen, *Just Peacemaking: Ten Practices*, 7.

16. Glen H. Stassen, *A Thicker Jesus: Incarnational Discipleship in a Secular Age* (Louisville KY: Westminster John Knox, 2012) 221.

17. Glen H. Stassen, "The Ten Commandments: Deliverance for the Vulnerable," *Perspectives in Religious Studies* 35/4 (Winter 2008): 370.

18. Ibid., 360.

19. Stassen, *Just Peacemaking: Transforming Initiatives*, 36–37.

20. Stassen, "Grace and Deliverance," 237. See Stassen, "A Theological Rationale for Peacemaking," *Review and Expositor* 79/4 (Fall 1982): 632–33.

21. Stassen and Gushee, *Kingdom Ethics*, 36; citing James Todd, "Participation: An Overlooked Clue," *Encounter* 34 (1973): 27–35.

22. Jürgen Moltmann, "A Response to the Responses," in *The Politics of Discipleship and Discipleship in Politics: Jürgen Moltmann Lectures in Dialogue with Mennonite Scholars*, ed. Willard M. Swartley (Eugene OR: Wipf & Stock, 2006) 131.

23. Stassen and Gushee, *Kingdom Ethics*, 36.

24. See Choan Seng Song, *Tell Us Our Names: Story Theology from an Asian Perspective* (New York: Orbis, 1984) 11. Song is here speaking of the theological task in general, which I applied to the conception of Jesus.

25. James H. Cone, *A Black Theology of Liberation*, 2nd ed. (New York: Orbis, 1989) 63.

26. A fine work on contextualizing theology in the Philippine setting was written by Rodrigo D. Tano, *Theology in the Philippine Setting: A Case Study in the Contextualization of Theology* (Quezon City, Philippines: New Day, 1981).

27. Karl Barth, "No Boring Theology," *South East Asian Journal of Theology* 11 (Autumn 1969): 4–5.

28. José M. De Mesa, *Why Theology Is Never Far From Home* (Manila, Philippines: DLSU, 2003) xv.

29. See Leonardo N. Mercado, *Christ in the Philippines* (Tacloban City, Philippines: Divine Word, 1982). Mercado does not limit the models of Christ to those that are accepted by the official Roman Catholic Church. He also includes models that come from local sects or indigenous religious movements.

30. *Metaphysics* 12.7, 9.

31. "God is dead" is a phrase made popular by Friedrich Nietzsche. See Nietzsche's *The Gay Science*, ed. Bernard Williams (Cambridge UK: University of Cambridge, 2001) 109, 119–20.

32. Jürgen Moltmann.

33. See Fenella Cannell, "The Imitation of Christ in Bicol, Philippines," *Journal of the Royal Anthropological Institute* 1/2 (1995).

34. Douglas J. Elwood and Patricia I. Magdamo, *Christ in Philippine Context: Course Textbook in Theology and Religious Studies* (Quezon City, Philippines: New Day, 1971) 7.

35. Elwood and Magdamo, *Christ in Philippine Context*, 7. See also Almario C. Santos, "A Study of the Effect of the Roman Catholic Portrayal of Christ as a Victim," MDiv thesis, ISOT-Asia, 1984, pp. 30–41.

36. Benigno P. Beltran, *The Christology of the Inarticulate: An Inquiry into the Filipino Understanding of Jesus the Christ* (Manila, Philippines: Divine Word, 1987) 135 ff.

37. Ibid., 138. On p. 37 of "Christ as a Victim," Santose affirms Beltran's perspective and remarks, "If the Filipino passes on to himself the failure and weakness of his savior, he will work out the same principles in his life."

38. Virginia Fabella, "Christology from an Asian Woman's Perspective," in *We Dare to Dream: Doing Theology as Asian Women*, ed. Virginia Fabella and Sun Ai Lee Park (Kowloon, Hong Kong: AWCCT, 1989) 10.

39. Renato Constantino, *The Philippines: A Past Revisited*, vol. 1 (Quezon City, Philippines: Constantino: 1975) 11.

40. Levi V. Oracion, *God with Us: Reflections on the Theology of Struggle in the Philippines* (Dumaguete City, Philippines: Silliman, 2001) 11.

41. Oscar S. Suarez, "Theology of Struggle: Reflections on Praxis and Location," *Tugon* 6/3 (1986): 51.

42. Oracion, *God with Us*, 210.

43. Edicio de la Torre, *Touching Ground, Taking Root: Theological and Political Reflections on the Philippine Struggle* (Quezon City, Philippines: Social-Pastoral Institute, 1986) 156.

44. Feliciano V. Cariño, "The Theology of Struggle as Contextual Theology: Some Discordant Notes," *Tugon* 9/3 (1989): 210–13.

45. Anne Harris, *Dare to Struggle, Be Not Afraid: The "Theology of Struggle" in the Philippines* (Quezon City, Philippines: Claretian, 2003) 148. See Oracion, *God with Us*, 210.

46. Mariano C. Apilado, *The Dream Need Not Die: Revolutionary Spirituality 2* (Quezon City, Philippines: New Day, 2001) 116.

47. Oracion, *God with Us* 61.

48. Interview of "Mario," in Harris, *Dare to Struggle*, 200.

49. Oracion, *God with Us*, 48.

50. Levi V. Oracion, "How Emerging Theological Consciousness Come to Expression," in *Currents in Philippine Theology: Kalinangan Book Series II*, ed. Rebecca Asedillo, Liliosa Garibay, and Nonie S. Aviso (Quezon City, Philippines: Institute of Religion and Culture, 1992) 98.

51. Karl M. Gaspar, "Doing Theology (in a Situation) of Struggle," in *Religion and Society: Towards a Theology of Struggle, Book I*, Mary Battung et al., ed. (Manila, Philippines: Forum for Interdisciplinary Endeavors, 1988) 70–71. See Reynaldo C. Ileto, *Pasyon and Revolution: Popular Movements in the Philippines: 1840–1910* (Quezon City, Philippines: Ateneo, 1997) 11ff. Ileto argues how some social movements that fought Spanish and even American colonizers drew from the spiritual tradition of the *Pasyon*.

52. Karl M. Gaspar, *Pumipiglas: Teyolohiya ng Bayan: A Preliminiary Sketch on the Theological Struggle From a Cultural-Liturgical Perspective* (Quezon City, Philippines: Socio-Pastoral Institute, 1986) 47.

53. Gaspar, "Doing Theology of Struggle," 64.

54. Fritz Penaranda, "God and Chaos: A Philosophical Contribution to the Theology of Struggle," *The Asia Journal of Theology* 3/1 (April 1989): 345.

55. See Rufa Cagoco-Guiam, "The ARMM and the Peace Process: Imperatives, Challenges, and Prospects," *Notre Dame Journal* 32/5 (June 2006): 123ff.

56. See Macapado A. Muslim, *The Moro Armed Struggle in the Philippines* (Marawi City, Philippines: MSU, 1994) 117-33; Thomas Michael Wallis, "The Bases of the Moro Problem," MA thesis, American University, 1966, pp. 28ff.

57. See the "classic" definition of the "Moro Problem" given by Najeeb M. Saleeby in *The Moro Problem: An Academic Discussion of the History and Solution of the Government of the Philippine Island* (Manila, Philippines: E.C. McCullough, 1913) 16.

58. Robert McAmis, "Muslim Filipinos: 1970–1972," *Mindanao Journal* 3/3–4 (January–June 1977) 56.

59. Salah Jubair, *The Long Road Road to Peace* (Cotabato, Philippines: PIBS, 2007) 5–6, citing a 2005 World Bank Report.

60. Ibid., 6.

61. Jubair, *A Nation Under Endless Tyranny*, 3rd ed. (Kuala Lumpur: IQ Marin, 1999) 54.

62. Lualhati Abreu, "Ancestral Domain—the Core Issue," in *The Moro Reader: History and the Contemporary Struggles of the Bangsamoro People*, ed. Bobby M. Tuazon (Quezon City, Philippines: CenPEG, 2008) 51.

63. Myrthena L. Fianza, "Indigenous Patterns of Land Ownership," *Mindanao Focus*; quoted in Abreu, "Ancestral Domain," 48.

64. Muslim, *Moro Armed Struggle*, 89–90.

65. Institue of Autonomy and Governance, "ARMM Helps: Synergy in Action," *Autonomy and Peace Review* (April–June 2012): 77–79.

66. Muslim, *Moro Armed Struggle*, 117–19. A detailed treatment of this subject can be found in Macapado A. Muslim, "The Bangsa Moro: the Highly Neglected People in the Neglected but Rich Mindanao," *Dansalan Quarterly* 12/1–4 (January–December 1992): 59ff.

67. Amina Rasul, *Broken Peace? Assessing the 1996 GRP-MNLF Final Peace Agreement* (Makati City, Philippines, 2007) 5.

68. Eddie Quitoriano and Theofeliz Marie Francisco, *Their War, Our Struggle: Stories of Children in Mindanao* (Quezon City, Philippines: Save the Children, UK, 2004) 15.

69. PCID and KAS, *Voices of Dissent: A Postscript to the MOA-AD Decision* (Mandaluyong City, Philippines: PCID and KAS, 2009) iii.

70. Glen H. Stassen, "'Yes' to Just Peacemaking: Not Just 'No' to War," *Church & Society* 96/2 (2005): 69–72.

71. William Larousse, *A Local Church Living for Dialogue: Muslim-Christian Relations in Mindanao-Sulu (Philippines) 1965-2000* (Roma: Editrice Pontificia Universita Gregoriana,

2001) 486; quoting BUF, "Statement of the BUF on the Mindanao Situation," Thirteenth Dialogue, Cagayan de Oro City, Philippines, May 2000.

72. Larousse, *A Local Church Living for Dialogue*, 485ff.

73. Hilario Gomez, *The Moro Rebellion and the Search for Peace* (Zamboanga City, Philippines: Silsilah, 2000) 229–30.

74. Michael O. Mastura, *Muslim-Filipino Experience* (Manila, Philippines: Ministry of Muslim Affairs, 1984) 147.

75. David Bronkema, David Lumsdaine, and Rodger Payne, "Foster Just and Sustainable Economic Development" in Stassen, ed., *Just Peacemaking: Ten Practices*, 120.

76. Peter Gowing, *Heritage and Horizon* (Quezon City, Philippines: New Day, 1980) 244.

77. Sebastianio D'Ambra, *Life in Dialogue: Pathways to Inter-Religious Dialogue and the Vision of the Islamo-Christian Silsilah Dialogue Movement* (Zamboanga City, Philippines: Silsilah, 1991)104–105.

78. Ibid., 105.

79. These are what Silsilah considers as the "four pillars" of the movement's spirituality. See Sebastiano D'Ambra, *Call to a Dream: Silsilah Dialogue Movement* (Zamboanga City, Philippines: Silsilah, 2008) 45–46.

80. Sebastiano D'Ambra, *Rediscovering the Mission of Dialogue and Peace in the Church in the Light of the Beatitudes* (Zamboanga City, Philippines: Silsilah, 2010) 9.

Chapter 12

Pathways to Peace
Just Peacemaking Theory and Structural Violence in Guatemala

MICHELLE TOOLEY

Just peacemaking theory provides a framework to analyze Guatemala's current and past realities and to imagine pathways toward peace. Nearly twenty years after the Peace Accords, many Guatemalans question the existence of peace and the government's refusal to apply major portions of the Peace Accords. In the shadow of recent accusations of genocide in the war crimes trial of former Head of State Efraín Ríos Montt and former Head of Military Intelligence José Mauricio Rodríguez Sanchez, the world's and Guatemala's attention has turned to the violence and impunity of the past. The testimonies and explicit statements presented by experts and survivors of massacres have called into question the impunity and lack of human rights in Guatemala, past and present. Guatemalans fear the unchecked power of governing authorities and the military, and grieve for the unrealized Peace Accords. If used as a road map, just peacemaking theory will illumine incremental steps toward peace and offer a pathway toward peace with justice, but the pathway to peace will not be complete without greater attention to structural violence.[1]

Building on the work of Johan Galtung and Latin American liberation theologians, medical anthropologist Paul Farmer's theory of structural violence clarifies barriers to peace with justice in Guatemala. In particular, Farmer understands structural violence as

> . . . one way of describing social arrangements that put individuals and populations in harm's way . . . . The arrangements are structural because they are embedded in the political and economic organization of our social world; they are violent because they cause injury to people . . . neither culture nor pure individual will is at fault; rather, historically given (and often

economically driven) processes and forces conspire to constrain individual agency.[2]

Agency is constrained by structures, systems, and what Farmer calls "hard surfaces."[3] Although often explained away as an individual's character flaws or the way that the world works, the "hard surfaces" that limit life choices are racism, sexism, political violence, and poverty. Gender, socioeconomic status, and ethnicity must be considered simultaneously, not isolated to one variable, to discern the true shape of "the political economy of brutality."[3] Woven into a group's collective identity as well as the identity imposed by the dominant group, gender, race, and class often determine access or the lack of access to social mobility, to political power, to education, to health care, or to legal standing. Farmer also emphasizes that analysis of suffering must be both "geographically broad" and "historically deep."[5] For Guatemala, "geographically broad" translates to the boundary crossings of globalization, when the young woman who dies in a factory fire is tied to the Walton family because Walmart buys clothing from the factory, or to the suffering of an indigenous community when citizens are displaced by a hydroelectric project.[6] "Historically deep" extends beyond questioning why only 12 percent of Guatemala's members of Congress are indigenous and locates the statistic in the historical context of the forced labor imposed by Spanish colonizers or the scorched-earth campaign that targeted rural Mayans in 1978. For these reasons and more, Guatemalan indigenous communities are more likely to suffer from structural violence.

To understand the complexities of applying just peacemaking theory to Guatemala, these questions arise: Is it enough to construct a present peace, or is the foundation for peace impossibly flawed because of structural violence woven into Guatemala's history through economic, political, military, and social policies and practices? Can there ever be a sustainable peace without attention to inequitable land distribution for indigenous persons? Are the strategic and political assumptions undergirding the current military actions and government initiatives sound? Are viable alternative means available to achieve justice and build peace with justice at lower cost to poor and indigenous Guatemalans and with greater probability of success? How might the application of the ten just peacemaking practices reduce structural violence and contribute to peace with justice?

Just Peacemaking Theory

From the Arab Spring to Occupy Wall Street, new practices of peacemaking have toppled dictatorships, reduced weapons and weapons trade, and given voice to new shapes of nonviolent direct action, conflict resolution, independent initiatives, and basic needs policies. In a global context where pacifism and just war theory, however valuable, prove inadequate in the struggle to reduce war and armed conflict, a new approach arose. Twenty-three scholars and practitioners worked together for five years to develop a set of ten practices supported by various theological-ethical approaches. These practices function as preventive medicine, constructive alternatives that address underlying causes of conflict and prove effective in preventing wars or reducing conflict that, without the initiative, might erupt in armed actions. In the introduction to their work, Duane Friesen, John Langan, and Glen Stassen write, "The practices of peacemaking that we are pointing to happen empirically in the real world, in the context of real threat, power struggle, and drive to security. They make power's expression in war less likely and peace more likely."[7] The authors assert that each practice has been implemented in various historical contexts, and each has demonstrated empirically for political science that it has a preventive effect.[8]

Although intended for use by both secular and religious individuals and groups, just peacemaking principles are informed by three theological convictions that correspond to three ethical imperatives: peacemaking initiatives, justice, and love and community. Each practice embodies one of the three basic imperatives. Peacemaking initiatives include the first four practices: (1) Support nonviolent direct action. (2) Take independent initiatives to reduce threat. (3) Use cooperative conflict resolution. (4) Acknowledge responsibility for conflict and injustice and seek repentance and forgiveness. Justice takes in two additional practices: (5) Advance democracy, human rights, and religious liberty. (6) Foster just and sustainable economic development. Finally, four practices embody the third imperative of love and community: (7) Work with emerging cooperative forces in the international system. (8) Strengthen the United Nations and international efforts for cooperation and human rights. (9) Reduce offensive weapons and weapons trade. (10) Encourage grassroots peacemaking groups and voluntary associations.[9]

The principles of just peacemaking theory take shape in embodied practice that Stassen says "is neither an ideal nor a rule, but a human activity that regularly takes place and that a sociologist could observe."[10] In this essay, I examine how six of the ten practices, two from each ethical imperative, are being implemented or provide the opportunity to be implemented in Guatemala.

The Peace Process

After the fall of the Berlin Wall in 1991 and the dismantling of the Cold War, activists throughout the United States dreamed of the contours of a "peace dividend," funds and social capital used for war and war-related programs that could now be redirected toward schools, jobs programs, re-educating soldiers, and repairing harms, as we constructed our own versions of turning weapons into plowshares.

Not long after US activists huddled around tables in church basements, Guatemalans in the popular movement, some in exile in the US and Mexico but most around their own versions of church basement tables, planned for peace and their own peace dividend. Their task differed from ours in the Global North in several ways. First, they were coming out of a thirty-six-year war that had rained violence on largely poor, rural, indigenous people. Guatemala's was the longest and bloodiest of Latin America's civil wars, leaving 200,000 dead or "disappeared," primarily Mayan Indians. Second, the fuel on the flame of their conflict had its roots in the Cold War with an ideology and interests that protected corporations and investments. Third, Guatemalans say that their legacy of violence began much earlier and is woven into the fabric of their country. Some Guatemalans locate the genesis of violence with the Spanish conquistadores, and others say that the violence, especially for women, began with the sacrifices of the indigenous Mayans and the later structural violence institutionalized by Spanish conquerors in collaboration with the Catholic Church.

And to make their legacy of violence even worse, Guatemalans felt isolated from the world. In spite of Ronald Reagan's geographically challenged statement that Nicaragua was only two days from Brownsville, Texas[11] (a journey that would have passed through Guatemala), the average citizen of the United States knew little about Guatemala and had no idea of the human cost of the conflict in Guatemala. Having periodically cut off much of its foreign aid, except for right-wing Christian groups and contacts with apparel factories, the United States paid little attention to this Central American country. In the meantime, in a 1984 report, America's Watch called Guatemala "a Nation of Prisoners."[12]

Guatemala's peace process, although long and arduous, lasted five years, but it was at least nominally participatory and included civil society in deliberations, if not the negotiated accords. The peace process specifically addressed injustices, and the Peace Accords resulted in concrete agreements, a return of refugees from Mexico, and a return of internally displaced persons from years of hiding. The women's sector participated in the national dialogue for peace, along with labor, youth, indigenous groups, the church, the government, guerrillas, and the military. Peace accords negotiated between the political arm of opposition groups and the government were signed and everyone celebrated. A place at the table, finally.

The 1996 Peace Accords promised agrarian reforms and indigenous access to the judicial and political systems. Guatemala's land conflicts were supposed to be resolved by providing a framework for land disputes, including the enforcement of labor laws and minimum wage, land ownership for poor *campesinos*, creating procedures for resolving land disputes, legal assistance and free translations into indigenous languages, and recognizing and promoting indigenous law.

Guatemalans doubted that the government that legislated amnesty for army officials would initiate a meaningful truth commission, so the Human Rights Office of the Archdiocese of Guatemala initiated a project, REMHI, The Recuperation of Historical Memory, sending hundreds of trained Guatemalans throughout the country with a tape recorder and questionnaires with open-ended questions. On April 24, 1998, they issued the four-volume report, *Guatemala: Nunca Mas* (*Guatemala: Never Again*). The United Nations-sponsored truth commission concluded, noting more painful historical memories. Hope grew, but then years passed with a general sense of malaise about the Peace Accords. Most administrations refused even to acknowledge the Peace Accords because their party had not been in power to sign them. We must ask what the Peace Accords mean to the women and men living in the aftermath of what the United Nations report and the current Ríos Montt war crimes trial called genocide.

Attentiveness to just peacemaking practices will ameliorate the national trauma and lessen the suffering, but they will not bring sustainable peace with justice unless structural violence is explicitly addressed.

Peacemaking Initiatives

Support Nonviolent Direct Action

The first just peacemaking practice of nonviolent direct action exists in Guatemala. In Guatemala's history, dramatic and comprehensive nonviolent direct action led to the resignation of dictator and twice-elected president Jorge Úbico. In 1944, 311 prominent citizens wrote and delivered a document that asked President Úbico to resign. At a nonviolent protest that night, crowds reiterated the demand, and the police responded with brutal beatings of protestors. The next day, women dressed in mourning gathered to pray at a church near the National Plaza. As they processed from the church, the police opened fire on the women, killing María Chincilla Recinos, a teacher. In response, Guatemala City shut down: schools closed, workers stayed in their homes, public transportation came to a halt. When opposition leaders presented President Úbico with a request for his resignation and an end to martial law, he resigned.[13]

Recently, protests have taken different forms and had mixed results. Heightened tensions over foreign mining and hydroelectric projects have led to protests, both nonviolent and violent. On May 2, 2012, in response to the murder of a community member critical of a hydroelectric plant, 200 residents of Barillas took over an army outpost, armed with machetes and guns. President Pérez Molina declared a state of siege that lasted almost one month, and he again declared a state of siege in 2013 in four towns over a mining dispute where government sources reported that local residents had taken up machetes.[14] In contrast, residents of the small town of La Puya have staged nonviolent protests for sixteen months against the Canadian mining company for an open-pit mine dug without consultation with local residents.

Another nonviolent protest occurred on October 4, 2012, when 5,000 unarmed peasants in Totonicapán built roadblocks on the Pan-American Highway to protest actions from President Pérez Molina's administration: a rise in electricity prices; proposed educational reforms that require teachers to get a five-year bachelor's degree instead of a three-year vocational degree; and constitutional changes with weaker language on indigenous rights. While the local police attempted to disperse the crowd peacefully, a convoy of eighty-nine soldiers arrived, ignored police requests to stand down, and opened fire on the crowd.[15] During the two-hour siege, the soldiers killed seven protestors, wounded thirty-four, and protestors set fire to one of the army vehicles.[16]

Although President Pérez Molina first denied the presence of the military, he later declared that he would respect the result of the investigation by the Attorney General's office and that the army would no longer be deployed at civilian protests. "The most sacred right we have, the right to live, has been violated," he said.[17] The Attorney General's office conducted a swift criminal investigation that found evidence of 100 shells, the type used only by the military. The investigation culminated in the arrests of the commanding officer and eight of the soldiers, all charged with extrajudicial executions in civilian court.

In the days following the October 4 protest, citizens of Totonicapán and indigenous organizations staged other nonviolent actions in solidarity with the protestors. Crowds of Totonicapán community members marched from the massacre site to the municipality's center to call for change, and indigenous organizations staged protests in five rural departments.

Another nonviolent gathering organized to remember the May 10 guilty verdict against the former President Rios Montt and the court ruling that overturned the sentence. On June 18, 2013, hundreds of activists, musicians, human rights defenders, religious workers, and union members joined other protestors in Nebaj for two days of demonstrations.[18] There was a candle-light vigil for those Ixil who died during the violent repression, a mock trial with a guilty verdict presented to the Ixil leaders, and a joyful parade with speeches from indigenous leaders, the women's sector, and human-rights defenders.

With little political power, indigenous social movements increasingly are responding to tensions over land tenure and the exploitation of natural resources with mass mobilizations as a viable strategy for expressing grievances and gaining media and state attention. President Pérez Molina's October 2012 decision not to deploy military forces to protests offers a glimmer of hope. Religious groups, human-rights groups, and indigenous groups must strengthen their commitments to nonviolent actions to save lives and help ensure a culture of peace.

Acknowledge Responsibility for Conflict and Injustice and Seek Repentance and Forgiveness

The question of responsibility for injustice and conflict is like the myth of Pandora's box. The story reinforces fear that the box will be opened, and, once opened, the contents will not be contained. While human-rights groups and indigenous groups yearn for acknowledgment and responsibility for conflict and injustice, perpetrators lack incentives to take responsibility for past or present grievances. In the process of repentance and forgiveness, those committed to peace ask what harm has been done and who has been harmed. Once responsibility for harm is acknowledged, acts of redress address the harm and take steps toward forgiveness and reconciliation. For the Truth and Reconciliation Commission in South Africa, truth telling was an essential ingredient for amnesty and forgiveness. For apartheid South

Africa and other situations of structural violence, Desmond Tutu maintains that without forgiveness, there really is no future.[19]

During the war, the harm was more than physical loss of property and the loss of family members. The Guatemalan government and military labeled Mayan groups as internal enemies, thereby legitimating harassment, torture, disappearances, massacres, and scorched-earth policies. Carlos Martín Beristain, coordinator of the REMHI Report, insists that all forms of violence perpetrated by the state attack Mayan collective identity and rob them of dignity, a basic human need.[20] The impact of sociopolitical trauma increases vulnerability, fractures family relations, and exacerbates psychological, emotional, and economic distress. Beristain and colleagues discovered that ". . . material losses, such as houses, crops and animals, as well as social effects, . . . continue to affect them many years on."[21]

Many persons and groups contributed to the harm and structural violence. Following Farmer's criteria of "geographically broad" and "historically deep," I analyze two main actors who contributed to the harm: the United States governing authorities and the military, and the Guatemalan governing authorities and the military. For both actors, business and government interests were intermingled. Rarely have perpetrators or intellectual authors acknowledged responsibility or asked for forgiveness, but when they have, it is noteworthy for this just peacemaking practice and for the people harmed.

The United States. The 1999 Guatemalan Truth Commission Report singled out the US Army's School of the Americas (SOA) for its counterinsurgency training that "had a significant bearing on human rights violations during the armed conflict." The REMHI Report also linked the SOA to the violence in Guatemala and named specific military officers, SOA graduates, responsible for atrocities.

Twice in Guatemala's history, the United States intervened in Guatemala through active participation in a coup d'état. First, in 1954 the Central Intelligence Agency (CIA), led by Director Allen Dulles with the support of Secretary of State John Foster Dulles, worked with dissidents from the Guatemalan Army in "Operation Success." Both Dulles brothers and other members of President Dwight Eisenhower's administration had close connections with the United Fruit Company. Historians believe that the coup to remove President Jacobo Arbenz was fueled by anti-communism and threats to the economic interests of the United Fruit Company because of land reform.[22] Then in 1963, the United States supported a second coup to prevent the return and reelection of former President Juan José Arévalo.[23]

President Clinton apologized in 1999 for United States support of right-wing governments in Guatemala that killed tens of thousands of rebels and Mayan Indians in the thirty-six-year civil war. "For the United States," Mr. Clinton said, "it is important that I state clearly that support for military forces and intelligence units which engaged in violence and widespread repression was wrong, and the United States must not repeat that mistake."[24] Clinton promised that the United States would support reconciliation efforts in Guatemala and in other post-conflict countries in Central America. President Clinton gained the respect from Guatemalans for his apology for US actions and inaction.

Guatemala. Guatemala's thirty-six-year war primarily targeted rural Mayans. Eighty-three percent were indigenous Maya, and 93 percent of these human rights violations were carried out by government forces.[25] The Guatemalan military used psychological warfare, assassination of civil society leaders, and random acts of violence like rape, kidnapping, torture, disappearances, extrajudicial killings, and massacres. The numbers are staggering: an estimated 200,000 assassinated, 440 indigenous villages destroyed, one million internally displaced, and 150,000 in United Nations refugee camps in Mexico. Indigenous boys and men were coerced into policing their own communities in civilian patrols, or they were kidnapped for military service.

The reason for the violent repression and patterns of injustice is historically embedded state racism. Indigenous peoples have been targets of structural violence since the Spaniards arrived in Guatemala in the sixteenth century. The Spaniards passed legislation that restricted Indians from participation in artisan trades and forced them to work on the Spaniards' land.[26] In the 1870s, President Justo Rufino Barrios passed legislation that exempted non-Indians from forced labor.[27] Less than fifty years later Guillermo Kuhsiek refers to the Indian as subservient, obedient, lacking intelligence, and inferior.[28]

If not acknowledged, institutionalized racism will continue to cause harm. President Clinton's apology serves as a model for Guatemalan and United States authorities. In the religious sphere, two Christian denominations offer good models for action on this just peacemaking practice. In 2012, the United Methodist Church began a process of repentance and healing with indigenous persons. They apologized to the Cheyenne and Arapaho peoples for the 1863 Sand Creek Massacre and asked for forgiveness for the deaths of over 200 persons. The American Episcopal Church denounced the Christian Doctrine of Discovery that claimed superiority and dominance over the indigenous peoples of the Western Hemisphere in the colonization period. In both instances, the denominations publicized their apologies as acts of confession and repentance, and developed programs and denominational infrastructure to educate their constituencies on harm and how to listen and learn from indigenous persons.[29]

Justice

Advance Democracy, Human Rights, and Religious Liberty

Guatemala is a constitutional democracy, but a majority of the population, the 60 percent indigenous Mayan, Xinco, and Garífuna, lack access to full participation. The Guatemalan Constitution does not endorse discrimination of ethnic groups, but the promises of the 1996 Peace Accords for Indigenous Rights have not been addressed. The constitution also guarantees religious freedom, but indigenous communities have faced discrimination for openly practicing the Mayan religion.

Indigenous Guatemalans want land reform or at least a fair process for dispute resolution; improved working conditions and wages; equal civil rights and status; and education and language instruction that acknowledges the multilingual and multicultural richness of Guatemala. Many indigenous families and communities have been displaced from their land and need assurance from the government that judicial systems will give them access to legal recourse. The location and identification of indigenous persons missing or dead since the civil war remains an open wound for indigenous Guatemalans. They want assurance that they can promote their ethnic cultures without fear and that they can participate as members of their ethnic group in local and national governance.

Indigenous peoples disproportionately lack access to essential public services, such as potable water, health care, education, electricity, sewerage, and employment. Rural Mayans suffer from among the highest levels of illiteracy and of preventable respiratory and infectious diseases in the world. Indigenous communities suffer from lower life expectancy and especially high rates of poverty, maternal mortality, and infant mortality.

Farmer reminds us that gender plays "a role in rendering individuals and groups vulnerable to extreme human suffering," and, because of gender inequality, women are violated in many ways.[30] During the war, women were active in human rights' groups, widows' groups, labor unions, and civil society. Because their husbands, fathers, and sons were killed, many women transitioned from the private sphere to the public sphere, often through motherist groups designed to locate the bodies of loved ones and to protest the impunity. Participation in the public sphere did not guarantee human dignity or equal treatment in society. In many communities in the highlands, all females over thirteen were sexually violated. Women were beaten, harassed, coerced into prostitution, and raped. Even when present with their husbands, outsiders and other family members often posed safety and health threats.

Incidents of gendered violence are much greater now than during the war. This research resonates with post-Truth and Reconciliation Commission South Africa. Nearly twenty years after the war ended, not one case has gone to court for sexual violence during the war. Often women who were raped during the war have been violated again because they now have the reputation of being easy, the "it must have been your fault" mentality that continues a cycle of victimization. Typically a young woman in Guatemala City vanishes, and her body turns up a few days later in a garbage dump or in a ditch. More than 3,000 women have been brutally murdered since 2000, and fewer than 2 percent of cases end in convictions.[31]

Although more advances are needed, particularly in indigenous rights and gender rights, some progress has been made in civil society and with the Guatemalan government. Women worked with the Legislature to pass a Femicide Law and to abolish the Rape Law, which absolves perpetrators of criminal responsibility for rape and marital rape.[32] The social network of nongovernmental advocacy groups, both feminist and nonfeminist, urban and rural, indigenous and ladina, campesino and elite, has grown exponentially. Women have named the systemic violence against women that is woven into the fabric of government and society. Activists and social scientists work with urgency and passion to encourage agency and transform women from victimized to empowered.

On indigenous rights, Guatemala ratified ILO Convention 169, the only international law for indigenous peoples. When adopted, Guatemala was one of twenty countries to have ratified the Convention, which recognizes tribal peoples' land rights and says they should be consulted prior to the approval of any projects on their lands. The court ruled that all the rights provided for in the Convention have constitutional status, which means that the state must consult with indigenous people before approving any mining and hydroelectric licenses, laws, and regulations in their territories. Unfortunately, Convention 169 has not been applied to indigenous land disputes or mining grievances. It remains the normative policy that the government proclaims, but it is not the de facto policy.

Political officers at the US Embassy in Guatemala are engaged in the kind of actions that fit well within the just peacemaking practice of advocating democracy, human rights, and religious freedom. One officer works with gender-based violence, human trafficking, and labor trafficking, and the other officer works with human rights and impunity. They report support of Guatemalan initiatives to build capacity in the judiciary and with human rights groups. From the perspective of US activists who heard United States embassy officials deny or dismiss reports of human rights abuses in the past, this may not be acknowledgment of harm, but it is right to support human rights and democracy.

Governing authorities must acknowledge the rights of ethnic groups and women, approve legislation that addresses inequalities, and share power by developing political practices and institutions that afford indigenous Guatemalans and women access. Indigenous communities must have more access to involvement in the future of their country.

Foster Just and Sustainable Economic Development

Since 1980, Guatemala has increased its rank in the United Nations Development Program's (UNDP) Human Development Index (HDI) to 133 out of 187 countries, so it now ranks as a middle-income country.[33] Especially in Guatemala City, the middle-income status is visible with clear evidence of economic growth: a new airport, a major street blocked off for shopping convenience, and a new public transportation system, the Transmetro. Over the past decade, Guatemala's economic expansion has focused on mining gold and silver and harnessing hydroelectric power. Mining and hydroelectric international investment has grown at an annual rate of 10 percent over the last five years, and foreign investment continues in the Free Trade Zone in apparel factories.

Attention to Farmer's category of geographically broad structural violence expands the national positive indicators to more focus on rural, indigenous Guatemalans. Guatemala currently ranks as the second most unequal in Latin America and the Caribbean, surpassed only by Haiti. The wealthiest 10 percent of Guatemalans earn 47.5 percent of national income, while less than 20 percent is allocated to the poorest 60 percent. Three-quarters of Guatemala's indigenous population is poor, double the proportion of non-indigenous poor.[34] Roughly one-quarter of them live in conditions of extreme poverty. Because of chronic malnutrition, 70 percent of indigenous children are of stunted height.[35] Guatemala is second worst in the hemisphere, just above Haiti, in maternal and infant mortality.

The application of this just peacemaking practice emphasizes the need for effective policies and practices to address the uneven distribution of wealth and land. Unless sustainable economic development is implemented, little progress will be made in eliminating gross disparities in economic and social rights in Guatemala.

Love and Community

Strengthen the United Nations and International Efforts for Cooperation and Human Rights

The United Nations and international human rights organizations have given visibility to the struggle for peace and indigenous concerns in Guatemala. After the 1996 Ceasefire, the United Nations Verification Mission in Guatemala (MINUGUA) served as peacekeepers, documented human rights, protected human-rights defenders, and supported capacity building and institution building. For ten years, hundreds of human-rights monitors, legal experts, indigenous specialists, and peacekeepers served in conflict zones in Guatemala, including in its remotest areas.

The United Nations continued their peace work on Guatemala when the Nobel Peace Committee chose Rigoberta Menchú Tum for the Nobel Peace Prize in 1992. The General Assembly named 1993 as the Year for the Rights of Indigenous Peoples and 1994–2003 the International Decade for the Rights of Indigenous Peoples. Menchú joined the United Nations Working Group to address injustices against indigenous people throughout the world. With the choice of Menchú for the Peace Prize and the United Nations attention to the plight of indigenous peoples, the world's attention turned to Guatemala and probably hastened the completion of the Peace Accords.

International trade can be another engine for economic growth and attention to human rights. Heavily dependent on international funding, Guatemala has signed bi-lateral and multi-lateral trade agreements with countries that ask for progress on human-rights issues in order to create a more favorable atmosphere for trade. While global trade has the potential to enhance economic growth and human rights, in the Latin American context, international trade agreements like the Central America Free Trade

Agreement (CAFTA) enriched elite business owners in free trade zones and impoverished the agricultural sector and factory workers.

Encourage Grassroots Peacemaking Groups and Voluntary Associations

Although Guatemala has made some progress on each just peacemaking practice, this practice has been particularly strong. Grassroots peacemaking groups and voluntary associations have improved the social welfare of indigenous Guatemalans, advocated for transparency in government, and increased access to civil and economic rights for marginalized and disenfranchised Guatemalans. The two organizations highlighted have enhanced human rights and built solidarity with partners in the United States.

The Protestant Center for Pastoral Studies in Central America (CEDEPCA) is an ecumenical organization and training center that provides transformative learning opportunities to persons of faith and conscience in Guatemala. Staff and volunteers develop material and implement programs that address violence and encourage analysis and social change. In recent years, their special focus on violence against women and children increased programming on alternatives to violence, sexism, and poverty.

The Guatemala Project of St. Michaels and Angels Episcopal Church in Tucson has worked for twenty years with the Communities of Population in Resistance of the Sierra (CPR-Sierra), Ixil and Quiché Maya subsistence farmers. The area where they lived, the Ixil area of northern Quiché, was one of the areas hardest hit during Guatemala's long and violent armed conflict. The long-term relationship between the coordinator of the program and the CPR-Sierra enhances community development through consultation and minimal financial support. Focusing on accompaniment and supporting health promoters in the twenty-two communities, this small project scores high on collaboration and sustaining a respectful partnership that encourages social development and well-being. Health promoters report that annual visits from project teams give them "*animo*" to continue their efforts to promote health in their communities. The Guatemala Project supports their efforts to advance women, fund women health promoters, and model women's power by collaborative work with male and female health leaders. Children's vaccination rates in the CPR-Sierra are almost 100 percent because health promoters that they support are trusted community members and organize participation.[36]

Through their voluntary associations and emphasis on peace with justice, both groups have increased peace with justice in Guatemala. In addition to program development and liberative religious education for Guatemalans and others who yearn for peace, CEDEPCA is a valuable resource for clergy and laity committed to increased justice in church and society. The Guatemala Project has provided accompaniment, encouragement, and alternative means to health care resources. In both cases, the organizations have contributed to civil discourse and increased social and civil rights. Through connections with United States and Guatemalan partners, they have decreased the isolation of poor and indigenous Guatemalans.

Conclusion

If just peacemaking practices provide a pathway to peace and away from structural violence, who will take the lead in implementing them? The agents of peace with justice for Guatemala can be governments, civil society, international entities, nongovernmental organizations, and religious groups. Farmer's work on structural violence, when integrated into just peacemaking theory, challenges Guatemala's structural violence embedded in structures and systems and offers the people of the nation an opportunity to embrace peace and to begin to dismantle injustice.

NOTES

1. See Glen Stassen, *Just Peacemaking: Transforming Initiatives for Justice and Peace* (Louisville: Westminster John Knox Press; 1992); and Glen Stassen, ed., *Just Peacemaking: Ten Practices for Abolishing War* (Cleveland: Pilgrim, 1998).

2. Paul Farmer, *Infections and Inequalities: The Modern Plagues* (Berkeley: University of California Press, 1999) 79.

3. Paul Farmer, "On Suffering and Structural Violence: A View from Below," in *Race/Ethnicity: Multidisciplinary Global Contexts*, Race and the Global Politics of Health Inequity 3/1 (Indiana University Press, Autumn, 2009) 12–13.

4. Ibid., 21.

5. Paul Farmer, *Pathologies of Power: Health, Human Rights, and the New War on the Poor* (Berkeley: University of California Press, 2004) 6–7.

6. Witness for Peace, "A People Damned: The World Bank-Funded Chixoy Hydroelectric Project and Its Devastating Impacts on the People and Economy of Guatemala" (Washington, DC: Witness for Peace, May 1996).

7. Stassen, ed., *Just Peacemaking: Transforming Initiatives*, 24.

8. Ibid., 24.

9. Glen Stassen, "Just Peacemaking: Ten Practices for Abolishing War," from the summary of the theory for the panel on Just Peacemaking Theory, American Academy of Religion, Orlando, Florida, November 1998.

10. Glen Stassen, "The Unity and Oughtness of Just Peacemaking Theory," *The Journal of the Society of Christian Ethics* 23/1 (Society of Christian Ethics, 2003).

11. Ronald Reagan, remarks at fundraiser for William Clements, 23 July 1986, http://www.reagan.utexas.edu/archives/speeches/1986/072386a.htm.

12. America's Watch Committee, "Guatemala, a Nation of Prisoners" (America's Watch: New York, 1984).

13. Michelle Tooley, *Voices of the Voiceless: Women, Justice and Human Rights in Guatemala* (Harrisonburg VA: Herald Press, 1997) 36.

14. Nic Wirtz, "Guatemala and the Siege of Santa Cruz Barillas," in *Americas Quarterly*, 25 May 2012, http://www.americasquarterly.org/node/3656.

15. Anita Isaacs and Rachel Schwartz, "Repression, Resistance, and Indigenous Rights in Guatemala," *Americas Quarterly*, Winter 2013, www.americasquarterly.org.

16. Ibid.

17. BBC News, "Guatemalan Soldiers Arrested over Totonicapán Protest Killings," 11 October 2012, www. bbc.co.uk/news/world-latin-america.

18. Robert Mercatante "Yes, There Was Genocide!: Guatemala's Ixil Vow to Keep Fighting for Justice," Americas Program of the Center for International Policy, 28 June 2013, http://www.cipamericas.org/archives/9895.

19. Desmond Tutu, *No Future without Forgiveness* (New York: Doubleday, 2000) 255.

20. Carlos Martín Beristain, *Humanitarian Aid Work: A Critical Approach* (Philadelphia: University of Pennsylvania Press, 1999; English translation, 2006) 3, 5.

21. Archbishop's Office on Human Rights, Oficina de Derechos Humanos del Arzobispado de Guatemala (ODHAG), 1998; *Guatemala Nunca Más/Guatemala: Informe Proyecto Interdiocesano de Recuperación de la Memoria Histórica* (REMHI), cited in Beristain, *Humanitarian*, 14.

22. "Ten Years of Spring and Beyond," in *The Guatemala Reader: History, Culture and Politics*, ed. Greg Grandlin, Deborah Levenson, and Elizabeth Oglesby (Durham: Duke University Press, 2011) 197–98.

23. "Denied in Full," in *Guatemala Reader*, ed. Grandlin et al., 256.

24. John M. Broder, "Clinton Offers His Apologies to Guatemala," *New York Times*, 11 March 1999.

25. Center for Justice and Accountability, "Guatemala, Silent Holocaust: The Mayan Genocide," www.cja.org.

26. Severo Martínez Peláez, "The Ladino," in *Guatemala Reader*, ed. Grandlin et al., 132.

27. Ibid.

28. Richard N. Adams, "Accustomed to Be Obedient," in *Guatemala Reader*, ed. Grandlin et al., 136.

29. The General Commission on Christian Unity and Interreligious Concerns, "Walking the Trail of Repentance & Healing with Indigenous Persons," United Methodist Church Study Guide, 2012.

30. Farmer, "Pathologies of Power," 7.

31. Julie Suarez and Marty Jordan, "Three Thousand and Counting: A Report on Violence against Women in Guatemala," Guatemala Human Rights Commission/USA, September 2007, 1.

32. "House Resolution 100: The Murders of Women in Guatemala," US House of Representatives, 1 May 2007.

33. Between 1980 and 2012, Guatemala's life expectancy at birth increased by 14.1 years, mean years of schooling increased by 1.7 years, and expected years of schooling increased by 4.7 years. Guatemala's GNI per capita increased by about 10 percent between 1980 and 2012 (United Nations Development Program, *Human Development Report 2013* [New York: UN Press, 2013] www.undp.org).

34. Center for Economic and Social Rights, "Guatemala: Visualizing Rights," fact sheet, numbers 3, 7.

35. Ibid., 2.

36. Ila Abernathy, "Millennium Development & Guatemala Project," St. Michael's Guatemala Project (Tucson: St. Michael and All Angels Episcopal Church).

Bibliography of the Works of Glen Harold Stassen

Dissertation

1965. *The Sovereignty of God in the Theological Ethics of H. Richard Niebuhr.* PhD dissertation, Duke University.

Books

1983. *Journey into Peacemaking.* Memphis TN: Brotherhood Commission of The Southern Baptist Convention.

1988. *Justice Creates Peace.* Co-written with Jürgen Moltmann. Baptist Peacemakers International Spirituality Pamphlet 13. Louisville KY: Baptist Peace Fellowship of North America.

1992. *Just Peacemaking: Transforming Initiatives for Justice and Peace.* Louisville KY: Westminster/John Knox Press.

1996. *Authentic Transformation: A New Vision of Christ and Culture.* Co-written with John Howard Yoder and Diane M. Yeager. With a previously unpublished essay by H. Richard Niebuhr. Nashville TN: Abingdon Press.

1998a. *Just Peacemaking: Ten Practices for Abolishing War.* Edited by Glen H. Stassen. Cleveland OH: Pilgrim Press.

1998b. *Capital Punishment: A Reader.* Edited by Glen H. Stassen. The Pilgrim Library of Theological Ethics. Cleveland OH: Pilgrim Press.

2001. *Just Peacemaking: Ten Practices for Abolishing War.* Edited by Glen H. Stassen. Cleveland OH: Pilgrim Press. Second edition.

2003. *Kingdom Ethics: Following Jesus in Contemporary Context.* Co-written with David P. Gushee. Downers Grove IL: InterVarsity Press.

2006. *Living the Sermon on the Mount: A Practical Hope for Grace and Deliverance.* Enduring Questions in Christian Life Series. Edited by David P. Gushee. San Francisco CA: Jossey-Bass.

2007a. *Peace Action: Past, Present, Future.* Co-edited with Lawrence S. Wittner. Foreword by Representative Barbara Lee (D-CA). New York: Paradigm Publishers.

2007b. *Authentic Faith: Bonhoeffer's Theological Ethics in Context,* by Heinz-Eduard Tödt. English edition edited by Glen Harold Stassen. Translated from the German by David Stassen. Grand Rapids MI: Eerdmans.

2008a. *Just Peacemaking: The New Paradigm for the Ethics of Peace and War.* Edited by Glen H. Stassen. Cleveland OH: Pilgrim Press. This is the third edition of the edited *Just Peacemaking* book with a new subtitle that more accurately reflects the contributors' views.

2008b. *La Etica del Reino: Siguiendo a Jesus en un Contexto Contemporáneo.* Co-written with David P. Gushee. Casa Bautista de Publicaciones. Spanish language edition of *Kingdom Ethics.*

2009. *War of the Lamb: The Ethics of Nonviolence and Peacemaking,* by John Howard Yoder. Edited by Glen Harold Stassen, Mark Thiessen Nation, and Matt Hamsher. Grand Rapids MI: Brazos Press.

2012. *A Thicker Jesus: Incarnational Discipleship in a Secular Age.* Louisville KY: Westminster John Knox Press.

Contributions to Books

1978. "Student Power to Educate the Nation: What Punishment Is Fair for War Resisters?" In *Power and Empowerment in Higher Education,* edited by D. B. Robertson. Lexington KY: University of Kentucky Press.

1980. "Critical Variables in Christian Social Ethics." In *Issues in Christian Ethics,* edited by Paul D. Simmons. Nashville TN: Broadman Press. This was a *Festschrift* for Henlee Hulix Barnette (1915–2004) by colleagues and students.

1982. "Arms Control, Disarmament, and World Peace." In *Encyclopedia of Southern Baptists,* volume 4 (Supplementary Volume). Lynn May, General Editor. Nashville TN: Broadman Press.

1983. "A Southern Baptist Theologian." In *Peacemakers,* edited by Jim Wallis. New York: Harper & Row. An autobiographical chapter.

1989. "Human Rights Are Our Baptist Heritage." In *Seek Peace and Pursue It,* edited by H. Wayne Pipkin. Memphis TN: Baptist Peace Fellowship of North America.

1990a. "Peace, Education for." In *Harper's Encyclopedia of Religious Education*, edited by Iris Cully and Kendrig Kelly. San Francisco CA: HarperCollins.

1990b. "Story and Spirituality." Co-written with James Hyde. In *Becoming Christian: Dimensions of Spiritual Formation*, edited by Bill J. Leonard. Louisville KY: Westminster/John Knox Press.

1990c. "Spirituality, Joy, and the Value of Play." Co-written with Gerald L. Keown. In *Becoming Christian: Dimensions of Spiritual Formation*, edited by Bill J. Leonard. Louisville KY: Westminster/John Knox Press.

1991a. "Capital Punishment." In *Handbook of Themes for Preaching*, edited by James W. Cox. Louisville KY: Westminster/John Knox Press.

1991b. "Peace." In *Handbook of Themes for Preaching*, edited by James W. Cox. Louisville KY: Westminster/John Knox Press.

1994. "Narrative Justice as Reiteration." In *Theology Without Foundations: Religious Practices and the Future of Theological Truth,* edited by Stanley Hauerwas, Nancey Murphy, and Mark Nation. Nashville TN: Abingdon Press. Second edition. Eugene OR: Wipf and Stock Publishers, 2006. This was a *Festschrift* for James Wm. McClendon, Jr. (1927–2000).

1995. "Shalom Initiatives: Peacemaking Practices for a New Day." In *Violence: A Christian Response,* edited by Phil Strickland and Oeita Buttorf. Fort Worth TX: Cooperative Baptist Fellowship and Texas Christian Life Commission.

1996a. "The Abbey Center for Ethics Conference to Develop a Just Peacemaking Theory." Co-written with Edward LeRoy Long, Jr., and Ronald H. Stone. *The Merton Annual.*

1996b. "Concrete Christological Norms for Transformation." In *Authentic Transformation: A New Vision of Christ and Culture*, by John Howard Yoder, D. M. Yeager, and Glen H. Stassen. Nashville TN: Abingdon Press.

1996c. "A New Vision." In *Authentic Transformation: A New Vision of Christ and Culture*, by John Howard Yoder, D. M. Yeager, and Glen H. Stassen. Nashville TN: Abingdon Press.

1998a. "Biblical Teaching on Capital Punishment." In *Capital Punishment: A Reader*, edited by Glen H. Stassen. Cleveland OH: Pilgrim Press.

1998b. "Just Peacemaking." Co-written with Duane K. Friesen. In *Transforming Violence: Linking Local and Global Peacemaking*, edited by

Robert Herr and Judy Zimmerman Herr. Scottdale PA and Waterloo ON: Herald Press.

1998c. "Take Independent Initiatives to Reduce Threat." In *Just Peacemaking: Ten Practices for Abolishing War*, edited by Glen H. Stassen.
Cleveland OH: Pilgrim Press.

1998d. "Reduce Offensive Weapons and the Weapons Trade." Co-written
with Barbara Green. In *Just Peacemaking: Ten Practices for Abolishing
War*, edited by Glen H. Stassen. Cleveland OH: Pilgrim Press.

1999a. "The Politics of Jesus in the Sermon on the Plain." In *The Wisdom
of the Cross: Essays in Honor of John Howard Yoder*, edited by Stanley
Hauerwas, Chris K. Huebner, Harry J. Huebner, and Mark
Thiessen Nation. Grand Rapids MI: Eerdmans Publishing Co.
A *Festschrift* for John Howard Yoder (1927–1997).

1999b. "Accountability in and for Forgiveness." In *Judgment Day at the
White House: A Critical Declaration Exploring Moral Issues and the
Political Use and Abuse of Religion*, edited by Gabriel J. Fackre.
Grand Rapids MI: Eerdmans Publishing Co.

2000a. "Foreword." In *Artists, Citizens, and Philosophers: Seeking the Peace
of the City: An Anabaptist Theology of Culture*, by Duane K. Friesen.
Scottdale PA: Herald Press.

2000b. "Foreword." In *Anabaptist Theology in the Face of Postmodernity:
A Proposal for the Third Millennium*, by J. Denny Weaver. Telford
PA: Pandora Press.

2000c. "Just Peacemaking: A New Paradigm for Our New World." In
*Christians and Politics Beyond the Culture Wars: An Agenda for En-
gagement*, edited by David P. Gushee. Grand Rapids MI: Baker
Book House.

2001a. "Foreword." In *Crowned with Glory & Honor: Human Rights in the
Biblical Tradition*, by Christopher D. Marshall. Telford PA: Pandora
Press.

2001b. "Baptists as Peacemakers." In *The Fragmentation of the Church and
Its Unity in Peacemaking*, edited by Jeffrey Gros and John D. Rem-
pel. Grand Rapids MI: Eerdmans Publishing Co.

2002. "Just Peacemaking." In *The Finest Robe, the Essential Vision: Reconciliation in the 21st Century*, edited by Eve S. Clayton. St. Davids
PA: Institute for Global Engagement.

2003a. "Foreword." In *Extreme Virtues: Living on the Prophetic Edge*, by
David Fillingim. Scottdale PA: Herald Press.

2003b. "Defining Violence and Nonviolence." Co-written with Michael L. Westmoreland-White. In *Teaching Peace: Nonviolence and the Liberal Arts,* edited by J. Denny Weaver and Gerald Biesecker-Mast. Lanham MD: Rowman & Littlefield Publishers, Inc.

2003c. "Jesus and Just Peacemaking Theory." In *Must Christianity Be Violent?,* edited by Kenneth R. Chase and Alan Jacobs. Grand Rapids MI: Brazos Press.

2003d. "Reinhold Niebuhr." In *The Encyclopedia of Protestantism.* Volume 3. London UK: Routledge Press.

2003e. "Peacemaking Organizations." In *The Encyclopedia of Protestantism.* Volume 3. London, UK: Routledge Press.

2003f. "War." In *The Encyclopedia of Protestantism.* Volume 4. London UK: Routledge Press.

2004. "Biblical Perspectives on the Death Penalty." Co-written with Michael L. Westmoreland-White. In *Religion and the Death Penalty: A Call for Reckoning,* edited by Erick C. Owens, John D. Carlson, and Eric P. Elshtain. Grand Rapids MI: Eerdmans.

2005. "The Ethics of War and Peacemaking." In *Toward an Evangelical Public Policy,* edited by Ronald J. Sider and Diane Knippers. Grand Rapids MI: Baker Book House.

2006a. "Jesus' Way of Transforming Initiatives and Just Peacemaking Theory." In *Transforming the Powers: Peace, Justice, and the Domination System,* edited by Ray Gingerich and Ted Grimsrud. Minneapolis MN: Fortress Press.

2006b. "The Kind of Justice Jesus Cares About." In *Transforming the Powers: Peace, Justice, and the Domination System,* edited by Ray Gingerich and Ted Grimsrud. Minneapolis MN: Fortress Press.

2007a. "The Beatitudes as Eschatological Peacemaking Virtues." In *Character Ethics and the New Testament: Moral Dimensions of Scripture,* edited by Robert L. Brawley. Louisville KY: Westminster John Knox Press.

2007b. "Real Security in the Future: International Cooperation, Human Rights, and Freedom from Weapons of Mass Destruction." Co-written with Stephen Brion-Meisels. In *Peace Action: Past, Present, and Future,* edited by Glen H. Stassen and Lawrence S. Wittner.

2007c. "War on Terrorism? A Realistic Look at Alternatives." In *Just Policing, Not War: An Alternative Response to World Violence,* edited by Gerald W. Schlabach and Drew J. Christiansen with a foreword by Jim Wallis. Collegeville MN: Liturgical Press.

2008a. "Take Independent Initiatives to Reduce Threats." In *Just Peacemaking: The New Paradigm of the Ethics of Peace and War*, edited by Glen H. Stassen. Cleveland OH: Pilgrim Press.

2008b. "Reduce Offensive Weapons and Weapons Trade." Co-written with Barbara Green. In *Just Peacemaking: The New Paradigm of the Ethics of Peace and War*, edited by Glen H. Stassen. Cleveland OH: Pilgrim Press.

2008c. "Preface." In *The Reconciliation of Classes and Races: How Religion Contributes to Politics and Law*, by Sharon M. Tan. Lewiston. NY: Edwin Mellon Press.

2009a. "Foreword." In *Peace to War: Shifting Allegiances in the Assemblies of God*. Telford PA: Cascadia Publishing Co.

2009b. "Foreword." In *Power and Practices: Engaging the Work of John Howard Yoder*, edited by Jeremy M. Bergen and Anthony G. Siegrist. Scottdale PA and Waterloo ON: Herald Press.

2010a. "Peacemaking." In *Bonhoeffer and King: Their Legacies and Import for Christian Social Thought*, edited by Willis Jenkins and Jennifer M. McBride. Minneapolis MN: Fortress Press.

2010b. "The Religious Roots of Human Rights." In *Religious Faith, Torture, and Our National Soul*, edited by David P. Gushee, Jillian Hickman Zimmer, and J. Drew Zimmer. Macon GA: Mercer University Press.

2012a. "Christian Reflection on 'Work with Emerging Cooperative Forces in the International System.'" Co-written with Matthew Hamsher. In *Interfaith Just Peacemaking: Jewish, Christian, and Muslim Perspectives on the New Paradigm of Peace and War*, edited by Susan Brooks Thistlethwaite. New York: Palgrave Macmillan Press.

2012b. "Christian Reflection on 'Reduce Offensive Weapons and the Weapons Trade.'" In *Interfaith Just Peacemaking: Jewish, Christian, and Muslim Perspectives on the New Paradigm of Peace and War*, edited by Susan Brooks Thistlethwaite. New York: Palgrave MacMillan Press.

2012c. "God's Vision for the Church—Kingdom Discipleship." In *A New Evangelical Manifesto: A Kingdom Vision for the Common Good*, edited by David P. Gushee. St. Louis MO: Chalice Press.

2013. "The Prophets' Call for Peacemaking Practices." In *Holy War in the Bible: Christian Morality and an Old Testament Problem*, edited by Heath Thomas, Jeremy Evans, and Paul Copan. Downers Grove IL: IVP Academic Books.

Articles

1962. "Anabaptist Influence in the Origin of the Particular Baptists," *Mennonite Quarterly Review* 36/4 (October 1962): 322–48.

1968. "Faith of the Radical Right and Christian Faith," *Review and Expositor* 65/3 (Summer 1968): 315–34.

1976. "Ethics and Foreign Policy," Interview with H. Wayne Pipkin, *Catalyst Cassettes* 8/2 (February 1976).

1977a. "Editorial Notes," *Journal of Religious Ethics* 5/1 (Spring 1977): 1–7.

1977b. "A Social Theory Model for Religious Social Ethics," *Journal of Religious Ethics* 5/1 (Spring 1977): 9–37.

1980. "Professional Ethicists' Testimony in Death Penalty Cases," *Annual of the Society of Christian Ethics* (1980): 125–38.

1981. "Petitioning God for Peace: How Churches Are Beginning to Pray on Memorial Day," *Sojourners* 10/4 (April 1981): 23–24.

1982. "A Theological Rationale for Peacemaking," *Review and Expositor* 79/4 (Fall 1982): 623–37.

1983. "Preparing Candidates for Baptism," *Review and Expositor* 80/2 (Spring 1983): 245–60.

1984. "Time to Confess," *Review and Expositor* 81/3 (Summer 1984): 479–83.

1985. "A New, Transformative Peacemaking Ethic," *Review and Expositor* 82/2 (Spring 1985): 257–72.

1986a. "Congress, Now Is the Time: An Open Letter on Nuclear Testing," *Christianity and Crisis* 46/9 (June 16): 1999–2000.

1986b. "Look to Congress—Carefully," *Christianity and Crisis* 46/16 (3 November 1986): 381–82.

1988. "Literature and Film in the Teaching of Ethics," *Annual of the Society of Christian Ethics* (1988): 239–43.

1989a. "What Shall We Do in a Hungry World?" *Review and Expositor* 86/3 (Summer 1989): 439–40.

1989b. "Schooling for Democracy: A Visit to East German Churches," *Christian Century* 106/39 (20–27 December 1989): 1199–1201.

1990. "A Computer-Ethical Call to Continuous Conversion," *Review and Expositor* 87/2 (Spring 1990): 195–211.

1992a. "Grace and Deliverance in the Sermon on the Mount," *Review and Expositor* 89/2 (Spring 1992): 229–44.

1992b. "Justice and Empowerment as Deliverance from Alienation and Abandonment," with Michelle Tooley and Aubrey Williams, *Review and Expositor* 89/3 (Summer 1992): 347–58.

1992c. "Just Peacemaking: Beyond 'Just War' and Pacifism," *ESA Advocate* (June 1992): 1–4.

1992d. "God's Transforming Initiative: The Sermon on the Mount's Invitation to Deliverance," *Sojourners* 21/4 (April 1992): 23–25.

1992e. "The 'Freeze Crowd' and the Peace Challenge," *Christianity and Crisis* 52/18 (Fall 1992): 402–403.

1994a. "Disciples of the Incarnation," with Michael L. Westmoreland-White and David P. Gushee, *Sojourners* 23/3 (May 1994): 26–30.

1994b. "Focus: Michael Walzer on Justice, Community, and Social Criticism," [Stassen as editor] *Journal of Religious Ethics* 22/2 (Fall 1994): 331–405.

1994c. "Michael Walzer's Situated Justice," *Journal of Religious Ethics* 22/2 (Fall 1994): 375–99.

1995a. "Challenges for Discipleship in the 21st Century," [Stassen as editor] *Review and Expositor* 92/4 (Fall 1995): 419–87.

1995b. "Transformational Faith: A Concrete Discipleship Ethic for Growing Churches," with John P. Dever, *Review and Expositor* 92/4 (Fall 1995): 471–87.

1996a. "Biblical Teaching on Capital Punishment," *Review and Expositor* 93/4 (Fall 1996): 485–96.

1996b. "New Paradigm: Just Peacemaking Theory," *Council of Societies for the Study of Religion Bulletin* 25/3–4 (September–November 1996): 27–32.

1997. "Baptist Presidents in the White House," *Baptist History and Heritage* 32/1 (January 1997): 18–27.

1998a. "Revisioning Baptist Identity by Naming Our Origin and Character Rightly," *Baptist History and Heritage* 33/2 (Spring 1998): 45–54.

1998b. "Opening Menno Simons' 'Foundation-Book' and Finding the Father of Baptist Origins Alongside the Mother—Calvinist Congregationalism," *Baptist History and Heritage* 33/3 (Summer/Fall 1999): 34–44.

1999a. "Incarnating Ethics: We're Called to Faithful Discipleship, not Credal Rigidity," *Sojourners* 28/2 (March–April 1999): 14.

1999b. "Nonviolence in Time of War," *Sojourners* 28/4 (July–August 1999): 18–21.

1999c. "Harry Truman as Baptist President," *Baptist History and Heritage* 34/3 (Summer–Fall 1999): 81–93.

2000a. "Grace as Participation in the Inbreaking of the Kingdom: Mountains of Grace Back Home," *Mennonite Quarterly Review* 74/4 (October 2000): 539–48.

2000b. "Back to Jesus' Way: How the Church Became Entangled in Death—And the Way Out," *Sojourners* 29/6 (November–December 2000): 14.

2001. "Hearts and Minds," *Christian Century* 118/31 (14 November 2001): 24–25.

2002a. "Recovering the Way of Jesus in the Sermon on the Mount," *Journal of the European Pentecostal Theological Association* 22 (2002): 103–26.

2002b. "Turning Attention to Just Peacemaking Initiatives that Prevent Terrorism," *Council of the Societies for the Study of Religion Bulletin* 31/3 (Summer 2002): 59–65.

2003a. "The Fourteen Triads of the Sermon on the Mount (Matthew 5:21–7:12)," *Journal of Biblical Literature* 122/2 (Summer 2003): 267–308.

2003b. "It Is Time to Take Jesus Back: In Celebration of the Fiftieth Anniversary of H. Richard Niebuhr's *Christ and Culture*," *Journal of the Society of Christian Ethics* 23/1 (Spring–Summer 2003): 133–43.

2003c. "The Unity, Realism, and Obligatoriness of Just Peacemaking Theory," *Journal of the Society of Christian Ethics* 23/1 (Spring–Summer 2003): 171–94.

2003d. "How Christian Is Zionism?" with Leslie C. Allen, *Church and Society* 94/1 (September–October 2003): 105–107.

2004. "Just Peacemaking as Hermeneutical Key: The Need for International Cooperation in Preventing Terrorism," *Journal of the Society of Christian Ethics* 24/2 (Fall/Winter 2004): 171–94.

2005a. "Winning the Peace," *Sojourners* 34/1 (January 2005): 18–20.

2005b. "Supporting Parents: A Pro-Lifer's Critique of Bush," *Christian Century* 122/4 (22 February 2005): 10–11.

2005c. "'Yes' to Just Peacemaking: Not Just 'No' to War," *Church and Society* 96/2 (November–December 2005): 64–81.

2006. "A Manual for Living," *Sojourners* 35/8 (August 2006): 45.

2008a. "God and Human Dignity: The Personalism, Theology, and Ethics of Martin Luther King, Jr.," *Journal of Religion* 88/3 (July 2008): 416–18.

2008b. "The Ten Commandments: Deliverance for the Vulnerable," *Perspectives in Religious Studies* 35/4 (Winter 2008): 357–71.

2009a. "What Actually Works? The Right Supports Can Reduce Abortion Rates," *Sojourners* 38/6 (June 2009): 18–20.

2009b. "How History Demonstrates That Incarnational Discipleship Is Solid Ground," *Hill Road* 12/2 (December 2009): 3–27.

2009c. "Incarnational Discipleship: Jesus and Just Peacemaking Theory," *Hill Road* 12/2 (December 2009): 35–57.

2009d. "Caring for Creation as Incarnational Discipleship," *Hill Road* 12/2 (December 2009): 61–80.

2012. "Honoring Life: How Biblical Is It to Be Pro-Life and Support the Death Penalty," with David P. Gushee and Richard D. Land, *Christianity Today* 56/2 (February 2012): 42–43.

Contributors

Rick Axtell is Professor of Religion and Campus Chaplain at Centre College, Danville, Kentucky. Previously, he was Director of Louisville United Against Hunger and a case manager with homeless men at St. Vincent DePaul. He earned MDiv and PhD degrees from the Southern Baptist Theological Seminary, where Glen Stassen supervised his dissertation, *Gandhian Development Ethics as a Constructive Response to the Modernization/Dependency Debate*.

Elizabeth M. Bounds is Associate Professor of Christian Ethics at Emory University and co-founder of the Certificate in Theological Studies at the Arrendale State Prison for Women in Georgia. Her interests include peacebuilding and conflict transformation, restorative justice and the prison system, democratic practices and civil society, feminist and liberation ethics, and transformative pedagogical practices.

David Fillingim is an award-winning author and editor whose books include *Georgia Cowboy Poets, Redneck Liberation: Country Music as Theology, Extreme Virtues: Living on the Prophetic Edge*, and *More than Precious Memories: The Rhetoric of Southern Gospel Music*. He completed his PhD in Christian Ethics under Glen Stassen in 1996. He teaches Religion and Humanities at Cape Fear Community College in Wilmington, North Carolina.

Michael Willett Newheart is Professor of New Testament Language and Literature at Howard University School of Divinity, where he has served since 1991. His books include *"My Name is Legion": The Story and Soul of the Gerasene Demoniac* (Collegeville MN: Liturgical Press, 2004); *Word and Soul: A Psychological, Literary, and Cultural Reading of the Fourth Gospel* (Collegeville MN: Liturgical Press, 2001); and *Wisdom Christology in the Fourth Gospel* (San Francisco: Mellen Research University Press, 1992). Prior to coming to Howard, he taught at a college and four seminaries in Kansas City, and he served as a missionary in Costa Rica. Michael's PhD is from the Southern Baptist Theological Seminary. He is an ordained Baptist minister and a member of the Religious Society of Friends (Quakers).

Joon-Sik Park is the E. Stanley Jones Professor of World Evangelism at Methodist Theological School in Ohio, located in Delaware, Ohio. He previously served as pastor of multicultural United Methodist congregations in Ohio and Kentucky. Glen Stassen supervised his doctoral dissertation, which was later revised and published as *Missional Ecclesiologies in Creative Tension: H. Richard Niebuhr and John H. Yoder* (Peter Lang, 2007). His publications have appeared in *International Bulletin of Missionary Research*, *International Review of Mission*, *Mennonite Quarterly Review*, and *Missiology*.

Aldrin M. Peñamora is a professor of Systematic Theology and Christian Ethics at Koinonia Theological Seminary in Davao City, Philippines. He is a consultant for Peacebuilders Community Inc., which is also based in Davao City. His dissertation from Fuller Theological Seminary is titled *The Politics of the Eucharist: A Theological Ethics of Justice, Community and Peace for the Moro-Christian Conflict in Muslim Mindanao.*

Tina Pippin is the Wallace M. Alston Chair of Bible and Religion at Agnes Scott College, a liberal arts college for wymyn, in Decatur, Georgia. As an activist educator, she teaches in the areas of biblical studies, ethics and social justice, gender and wymyn's studies, and human rights.

Laura Rector has served as a member of the adjunct faculty at Fuller Theological Seminary, a lecturer at Loyola Marymount University, and visiting instructor of Christian Ethics at the Southern Philippines Baptist Theological Seminary. She has a BA in Christian Studies from Union University, an MDiv from the Southern Baptist Theological Seminary, and is a PhD Candidate at Fuller Theological Seminary. In the past, she has taught homeless preschoolers and served in cross-cultural ministries in the United States and Asia.

Michelle Tooley is Associate Professor of Religion and Peace Studies at Berea College. Tooley earned the PhD in Christian Social Ethics from Southern Baptist Theological Seminary with graduate study at the Kroc Institute for International Peace Studies at the University of Notre Dame and at Eastern Mennonite University. Her research is on Religion, Ethics, and Society, with particular focus on peace-building, migration, and human rights.

Michael L. Westmoreland-White was formerly the Outreach Director of Every Church a Peace Church and remains heavily active in faith-based organizations working for peace with justice, especially the Baptist Peace Fellowship of North America, Christian Peacemaker Teams, and the Fellowship of Reconciliation. He teaches religion, philosophy, and ethics courses at several colleges and universities in Louisville and Southern Indiana. His doctoral dissertation, supervised by Glen Stassen, is *Incarnational Discipleship: The Ethics of Clarence Jordan, Martin Luther King, Jr., and Dorothy Day*. Westmoreland-White has published numerous articles and book chapters on human rights, the death penalty, nonviolence, and other aspects of theological ethics.

Reggie L. Williams is an Assistant Professor of Christian Ethics at McCormick Theological Seminary in Chicago. Professor Williams received his PhD in Christian Ethics at Fuller Theological Seminary, supervised by Glen Stassen. His research focuses on the intersection of Christological hermeneutics and Christian moral formation. His current book project examines the impact of the Harlem Renaissance on the theological ethics of Dietrich Bonhoeffer (forthcoming, Baylor University Press).

Tammy R. Williams is a theologian and a former divinity school professor who has taught in the areas of theology and African American church studies. Topics of her scholarly publications range from racism as social practice to Christian theologies of healing and health. Her writing interests include Ignatian spirituality for Protestants, and the intersection of the Lord's Supper with theologies of food and eating in everyday life. She is an ordained American Baptist minister. As an associate pastor in a New Jersey congregation, she is actively involved in mobilizing local churches to prevent and end gun violence.

Other available titles from SMYTH& HELWYS

#Connect
Reaching Youth Across the Digital Divide
Brian Foreman

Reaching our youth across the digital divide is a struggle for parents, ministers, and other adults who work with Generation Z— today's teenagers. *#Connect* leads readers into the technological landscape, encourages conversations with teenagers, and reminds us all to be the presence of Christ in every facet of our lives.   *978-1-57312-693-9 120 pages/pb* **$13.00**

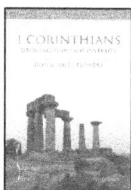

1 Corinthians (Smyth & Helwys Annual Bible Study series)
Growing through Diversity
Don & Anita Flowers

Don and Anita Flowers present this comprehensive study of 1 Corinthians, filled with scholarly insight and dealing with such varied topics as marriage and sexuality, spiritual gifts and love, and diversity and unity. The authors examine Paul's relationship with the church in Corinth as well as the culture of that city to give context to topics that can seem far removed from Christian life today.   *Teaching Guide 978-1-57312-701-1 122 pages/pb* **$14.00**
Study Guide 978-1-57312-705-9 52 pages/pb **$6.00**

Beyond the American Dream
Millard Fuller

In 1968, Millard finished the story of his journey from pauper to millionaire to home builder. His wife, Linda, occasionally would ask him about getting it published, but Millard would reply, "Not now. I'm too busy." This is that story.   *978-1-57312-563-5 272 pages/pb* **$20.00**

Blissful Affliction
The Ministry and Misery of Writing
Judson Edwards

Edwards draws from more than forty years of writing experience to explore why we use the written word to change lives and how to improve the writing craft.   *978-1-57312-594-9 144 pages/pb* **$15.00**

To order call **1-800-747-3016** or visit **www.helwys.com**

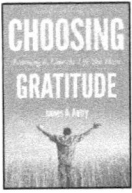

Choosing Gratitude
Learning to Love the Life You Have

James A. Autry

Autry reminds us that gratitude is a choice, a spiritual—not social—process. He suggests that if we cultivate gratitude as a way of being, we may not change the world and its ills, but we can change our response to the world. If we fill our lives with moments of gratitude, we will indeed love the life we have.   978-1-57312-614-4 144 pages/pb **$15.00**

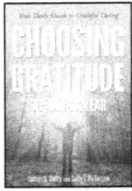

Choosing Gratitude 365 Days a Year
Your Daily Guide to Grateful Living

James A. Autry and Sally J. Pederson

Filled with quotes, poems, and the inspired voices of both Pederson and Autry, in a society consumed by fears of not having "enough"—money, possessions, security, and so on—this book suggests that if we cultivate gratitude as a way of being, we may not change the world and its ills, but we can change our response to the world.   978-1-57312-689-2 210 pages/pb **$18.00**

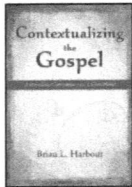

Contextualizing the Gospel
A Homiletic Commentary on 1 Corinthians

Brian L. Harbour

Harbour examines every part of Paul's letter, providing a rich resource for those who want to struggle with the difficult texts as well as the simple texts, who want to know how God's word—all of it—intersects with their lives today.   978-1-57312-589-5 240 pages/pb **$19.00**

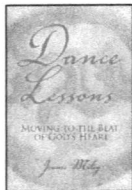

Dance Lessons
Moving to the Beat of God's Heart

Jeanie Miley

Miley shares her joys and struggles a she learns to "dance" with the Spirit of the Living God.   978-1-57312-622-9 240 pages/pb **$19.00**

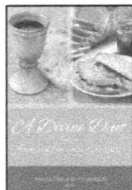

A Divine Duet
Ministry and Motherhood

Alicia Davis Porterfield, ed.

Each essay in this inspiring collection is as different as the mother-minister who wrote it, from theologians to chaplains, inner-city ministers to rural-poverty ministers, youth pastors to preachers, mothers who have adopted, birthed, and done both.

978-1-57312-676-2 146 pages/pb **$16.00**

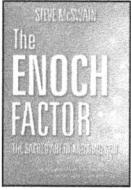

The Enoch Factor
The Sacred Art of Knowing God

Steve McSwain

The Enoch Factor is a persuasive argument for a more enlightened religious dialogue in America, one that affirms the goals of all religions—guiding followers in self-awareness, finding serenity and happiness, and discovering what the author describes as "the sacred art of knowing God." *978-1-57312-556-7 256 pages/pb* **$21.00**

Ethics as if Jesus Mattered
Essays in Honor of Glen H. Stassen

Rick Axtell, Michelle Tooley, Michael L. Westmoreland-White, eds.

Ethics as if Jesus Mattered will introduce Stassen's work to a new generation, advance dialogue and debate in Christian ethics, and inspire more faithful discipleship just as it honors one whom the contributors consider a mentor. *978-1-57312-695-3 234 pages/pb* **$18.00**

Healing Our Hurts
Coping with Difficult Emotions

Daniel Bagby

In *Healing Our Hurts*, Daniel Bagby identifies and explains all the dynamics at play in these complex emotions. Offering practical biblical insights to these feelings, he interprets faith-based responses to separate overly religious piety from true, natural human emotion. This book helps us learn how to deal with life's difficult emotions in a redemptive and responsible way. *978-1-57312-613-7 144 pages/pb* **$15.00**

Help! I Teach Youth Sunday School

Brian Foreman, Bo Prosser, and David Woody

Real-life stories are mingled with information on Youth and their culture, common myths about Sunday School, a new way of preparing the Sunday school lesson, creative teaching ideas, ways to think about growing a class, and how to reach out for new members and reach in to old members. *1-57312-427-3 128 pages/pb* **$14.0**

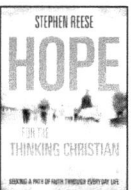

Hope for the Thinking Christian
Seeking a Path of Faith through Everyday Life

Stephen Reese

Readers who want to confront their faith more directly, to think it through and be open to God in an individual, authentic, spiritual encounter will find a resonant voice in Stephen Reese.

978-1-57312-553-6 160 pages/pb **$16.00**

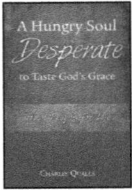

A Hungry Soul Desperate to Taste God's Grace
Honest Prayers for Life
Charles Qualls

Part of how we *see* God is determined by how we *listen* to God. There is so much noise and movement in the world that competes with images of God. This noise would drown out God's beckoning voice and distract us. Charles Qualls's newest book offers readers prayers for that journey toward the meaning and mystery of God. *978-1-57312-648-9 152 pages/pb* **$14.00**

James M. Dunn and Soul Freedom
Aaron Douglas Weaver

James Milton Dunn, over the last fifty years, has been the most aggressive Baptist proponent for religious liberty in the United States. Soul freedom—voluntary, uncoerced faith and an unfettered individual conscience before God—is the basis of his understanding of church-state separation and the historic Baptist basis of religious liberty. *978-1-57312-590-1 224 pages/pb* **$18.00**

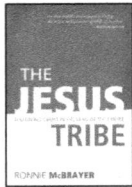

The Jesus Tribe
Following Christ in the Land of the Empire
Ronnie McBrayer

The Jesus Tribe fleshes out the implications, possibilities, contradictions, and complexities of what it means to live within the Jesus Tribe and in the shadow of the American Empire.

978-1-57312-592-5 208 pages/pb **$17.00**

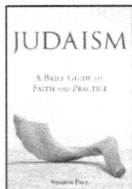

Judaism
A Brief Guide to Faith and Practice
Sharon Pace

Sharon Pace's newest book is a sensitive and comprehensive introduction to Judaism. What is it like to be born into the Jewish community? How does belief in the One God and a universal morality shape the way in which Jews see the world? How does one find meaning in life and the courage to endure suffering? How does one mark joy and forge community ties? *978-1-57312-644-1 144 pages/pb* **$16.00**

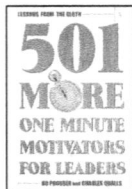

Lessons from the Cloth 2
501 More One Minute Motivators for Leaders
Bo Prosser and Charles Qualls

As the force that drives organizations to accomplishment, leadership is at a crucial point in churches, corporations, families, and almost every arena of life. In this follow-up to their first volume, Prosser and Qualls will inspire you to keep growing in your leadership career.

978-1-57312-665-6 152 pages/pb **$11.00**

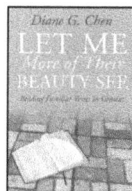

Let Me More of Their Beauty See
Reading Familiar Verses in Context
Diane G. Chen

Let Me More of Their Beauty See offers eight examples of how attention to the historical and literary settings can safeguard against taking a text out of context, bring out its transforming power in greater dimension, and help us apply Scripture appropriately in our daily lives.

978-1-57312-564-2 160 pages/pb **$17.00**

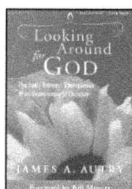

Looking Around for God
The Strangely Reverent Observations of an Unconventional Christian
James A. Autry

Looking Around for God, Autry's tenth book, is in many ways his most personal. In it he considers his unique life of faith and belief in God. Autry is a former Fortune 500 executive, author, poet, and consultant whose work has had a significant influence on leadership thinking.

978-157312-484-3 144 pages/pb **$16.00**

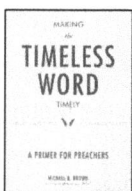

Making the Timeless Word Timely
A Primer for Preachers
Michael B. Brown

Michael Brown writes, "There is a simple formula for sermon preparation that creates messages that apply and engage whether your parish is rural or urban, young or old, rich or poor, five thousand members or fifty." The other part of the task, of course, involves being creative and insightful enough to know how to take the general formula for sermon preparation and make it particular in its impact on a specific congregation. Brown guides the reader through the formula and the skills to employ it with excellence and integrity.

978-1-57312-578-9 160 pages/pb **$16.00**

Meeting Jesus Today
For the Cautious, the Curious, and the Committed
Jeanie Miley

Meeting Jesus Today, ideal for both individual study and small groups, is intended to be used as a workbook. It is designed to move readers from studying the Scriptures and ideas within the chapters to recording their journey with the Living Christ.

978-1-57312-677-9 320 pages/pb **$19.00**

To order call **1-800-747-3016** or visit **www.helwys.com**

The Ministry Life
101 Tips for New Ministers
John Killinger

Sharing years of wisdom from more than fifty years in ministry and teaching, *The Ministry Life: 101 Tips for New Ministers* by John Killinger is filled with practical advice and wisdom for a minister's day-to-day tasks as well as advice on intellectual and spiritual habits to keep ministers of any age healthy and fulfilled. *978-1-57312-662-5 244 pages/pb* **$19.00**

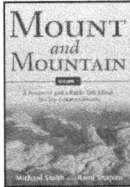

Mount and Mountain
Vol. 1: A Reverend and a Rabbi Talk About the Ten Commandments
Rami Shapiro and Michael Smith

Mount and Mountain represents the first half of an interfaith dialogue—a dialogue that neither preaches nor placates but challenges its participants to work both singly and together in the task of reinterpreting sacred texts. Mike and Rami discuss the nature of divinity, the power of faith, the beauty of myth and story, the necessity of doubt, the achievements, failings, and future of religion, and, above all, the struggle to live ethically and in harmony with the way of God. *978-1-57312-612-0 144 pages/pb* **$15.00**

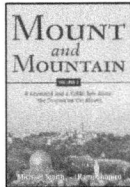

Mount and Mountain
Vol. 2: A Reverend and a Rabbi Talk About the Sermon on the Mount
Rami Shapiro and Michael Smith

This book, focused on the Sermon on the Mount, represents the second half of Mike and Rami's dialogue. In it, Mike and Rami explore the text of Jesus' sermon cooperatively, contributing perspectives drawn from their lives and religious traditions and seeking moments of illumination. *978-1-57312-654-0 254 pages/pb* **$19.00**

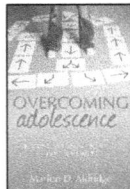

Overcoming Adolescence
Growing Beyond Childhood into Maturity
Marion D. Aldridge

In *Overcoming Adolescence*, Marion D. Aldridge poses questions for adults of all ages to consider. His challenge to readers is one he has personally worked to confront: to grow up *all the way*—mentally, physically, academically, socially, emotionally, and spiritually. The key involves not only knowing how to work through the process but also how to recognize what may be contributing to our perpetual adolescence.

978-1-57312-577-2 156 pages/pb **$17.00**

Psychic Pancakes & Communion Pizza
More Musings and Mutterings of a Church Misfit
Bert Montgomery

Psychic Pancakes & Communion Pizza is Bert Montgomery's highly anticipated follow-up to *Elvis, Willie, Jesus & Me* and contains further reflections on music, film, culture, life, and finding Jesus in the midst of it all. *978-1-57312-578-9 160 pages/pb* **$16.00**

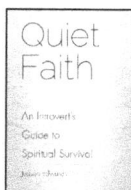

Quiet Faith
An Introvert's Guide to Spiritual Survival
Judson Edwards

In eight finely crafted chapters, Edwards looks at key issues like evangelism, interpreting the Bible, dealing with doubt, and surviving the church from the perspective of a confirmed, but sometimes reluctant, introvert. In the process, he offers some provocative insights that introverts will find helpful and reassuring. *978-1-57312-681-6 144 pages/pb* **$15.00**

Reading Ezekiel (Reading the Old Testament series)
A Literary and Theological Commentary
Marvin A. Sweeney

The book of Ezekiel points to the return of YHWH to the holy temple at the center of a reconstituted Israel and creation at large. As such, the book of Ezekiel portrays the purging of Jerusalem, the Temple, and the people, to reconstitute them as part of a new creation at the conclusion of the book. With Jerusalem, the Temple, and the people so purged, YHWH stands once again in the holy center of the created world.

978-1-57312-658-8 264 pages/pb **$22.00**

Reading Hosea–Micah
(Reading the Old Testament series)
A Literary and Theological Commentary
Terence E. Fretheim

Terence E. Fretheim explores themes of indictment, judgment, and salvation in Hosea–Micah. The indictment against the people of God especially involves issues of idolatry, as well as abuse of the poor and needy. The effects of such behaviors are often horrendous in their severity. While God is often the subject of such judgments, the consequences, like fruit, grow out of the deed itself. *978-1-57312-687-8 224 pages/pb* **$22.00**

Reading Samuel (Reading the Old Testament series)
A Literary and Theological Commentary
Johanna W. H. van Wijk-Bos

Interpreted masterfully by preeminent Old Testament scholar Johanna W. H. van Wijk-Bos, the story of Samuel touches on a vast array of subjects that make up the rich fabric of human life. The reader gains an inside look at leadership, royal intrigue, military campaigns, occult practices, and the significance of religious objects of veneration.

978-1-57312-607-6 272 pages/pb **$22.00**

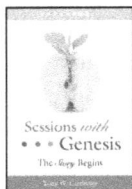

Sessions with Genesis (Session Bible Studies series)
The Story Begins
Tony W. Cartledge

Immersing us in the book of Genesis, Tony W. Cartledge examines both its major stories and the smaller cycles of hope and failure, of promise and judgment. Genesis introduces these themes of divine faithfulness and human failure in unmistakable terms, tracing Israel's beginning to the creation of the world and professing a belief that Israel's particular history had universal significance.

978-1-57312-636-6 144 pages/pb **$14.00**

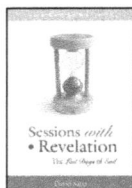

Sessions with Revelation (Session Bible Studies series)
The Final Days of Evil
David Sapp

David Sapp's careful guide through Revelation demonstrates that it is a letter of hope for believers; it is less about the last days of history than it is about the last days of evil. Without eliminating its mystery, Sapp unlocks Revelation's central truths so that its relevance becomes clear.

978-1-57312-706-6 166 pages/pb **$14.00**

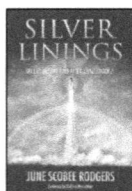

Silver Linings
My Life Before and After *Challenger 7*
June Scobee Rodgers

We know the public story of *Challenger 7*'s tragic destruction. That day, June's life took a new direction that ultimately led to the creation of the Challenger Center and to new life and new love. Her story of Christian faith and triumph over adversity will inspire readers of every age.

978-1-57312-570-3 352 pages/hc **$28.00**
978-1-57312-694-6 352 pages/pb **$18.00**

Spacious
Exploring Faith and Place
Holly Sprink

Exploring where we are and why that matters to God is an ongoing process. If we are present and attentive, God creatively and continuously widens our view of the world.   978-1-57312-649-6 156 pages/pb **$16.00**

The Teaching Church
Congregation as Mentor
Christopher M. Hamlin / Sarah Jackson Shelton

Collected in *The Teaching Church: Congregation as Mentor* are the stories of the pastors who shared how congregations have shaped, nurtured, and, sometimes, broken their resolve to be faithful servants of God.   978-1-57312-682-3 112 pages/pb **$13.00**

A Time to Laugh
Humor in the Bible
Mark E. Biddle

An extension of his well-loved seminary course on humor in the Bible, *A Time to Laugh* draws on Mark E. Biddle's command of Hebrew language and cultural subtleties to explore the ways humor was intentionally incorporated into Scripture. With characteristic liveliness, Biddle guides the reader through the stories of six biblical characters who did rather unexpected things.   978-1-57312-683-0 164 pages/pb **$14.00**

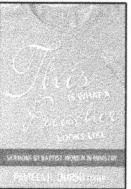

This Is What a Preacher Looks Like
Sermons by Baptist Women in Ministry
Pamela Durso, ed.

In this collection of sermons by thirty-six Baptist women, their voices are soft and loud, prophetic and pastoral, humorous and sincere. They are African American, Asian, Latina, and Caucasian. They are sisters, wives, mothers, grandmothers, aunts, and friends.

978-1-57312-554-3 144 pages/pb **$18.00**

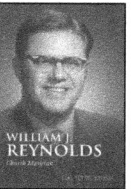

William J. Reynolds
Church Musician
David W. Music

William J. Reynolds is renowned among Baptist musicians, music ministers, song leaders, and hymnody students. In eminently readable style, David W. Music's comprehensive biography describes Reynolds's family and educational background, his career as a minister of music, denominational leader, and seminary professor.   978-1-57312-690-8 358 pages/pb **$23.00**

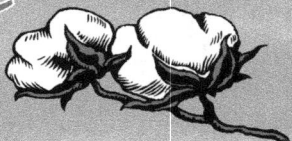

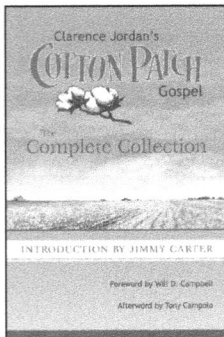

www.ingramcontent.com/pod-product-compliance
Lightning Source LLC
Chambersburg PA
CBHW062056080426
42734CB00012B/2671